School Worlds

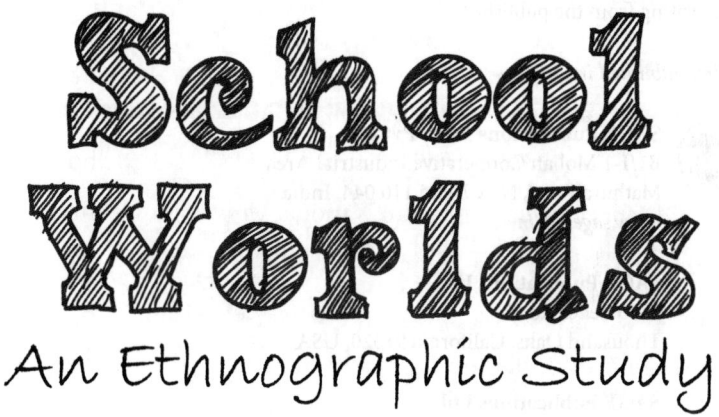

School Worlds
An Ethnographic Study

Anuradha Sharma

Sociology and Social Anthropology of
Education in South Asia

Series Editor
Meenakshi Thapan

Los Angeles | London | New Delhi
Singapore | Washington DC | Melbourne

First published in 2016 by

 SAGE Publications India Pvt Ltd
B1/I-1 Mohan Cooperative Industrial Area
Mathura Road, New Delhi 110 044, India
www.sagepub.in

SAGE Publications Inc
2455 Teller Road
Thousand Oaks, California 91320, USA

SAGE Publications Ltd
1 Oliver's Yard, 55 City Road
London EC1Y 1SP, United Kingdom

SAGE Publications Asia-Pacific Pte Ltd
3 Church Street
#10-04 Samsung Hub
Singapore 049483

Published by Vivek Mehra for SAGE Publications India Pvt Ltd, typeset in Minion Pro-Regular 11/13 pts by Zaza Eunice, Hosur, Tamil Nadu, India and printed at Chaman Enterprises, New Delhi.

Library of Congress Cataloging-in-Publication Data Available

ISBN: 978-93-515-0918-9 (HB)

SAGE Team: Supriya Das, Guneet Kaur Gulati, Shobana Paul and Rajinder Kaur

Contents

Thank you for choosing a SAGE product!
If you have any comment, observation or feedback,
I would like to personally hear from you.
Please write to me at **contactceo@sagepub.in**

Vivek Mehra, Managing Director and CEO, SAGE India.

Bulk Sales

SAGE India offers special discounts
for purchase of books in bulk.
We also make available special imprints
and excerpts from our books on demand.

For orders and enquiries, write to us at

Marketing Department
SAGE Publications India Pvt Ltd
B1/I-1, Mohan Cooperative Industrial Area
Mathura Road, Post Bag 7
New Delhi 110044, India

E-mail us at **marketing@sagepub.in**

Get to know more about SAGE

Be invited to SAGE events, get on our mailing list.
Write today to **marketing@sagepub.in**

This book is also available as an e-book.

Series Editor's Note

This series is an initiative in the field of sociology and social anthropology as research in education has been a neglected dimension of the broader disciplinary framework in India and the rest of South Asia. The aim of the series is to build and develop a focus on the sociology and social anthropology of education, taking different aspects of education into consideration for analysis. The idea is to develop perspectives that do not rely on educational misgivings, institutional features, financial outlays and state failures alone. These are only some social aspects of educational practices. There are other dimensions that envelop students, teachers, the community and society in complex ways that we need to uncover in order to provide an understanding of how education and society connect in diverse ways.

At one level, this series seeks to problematize our understanding of education, as *a process*, in the context of the making of citizens in a 'modern', changing South Asia. Education has been examined in its institutional avatar ad nauseam. Such efforts view schools, for example, as organizations that transmit and evaluate educational knowledge and provide certification based on academic achievement. The causes of inequality located in gender, caste, class and religion have perhaps been examined in this context as these shape individuals' lives in multiple and complex ways. At the same time, schools and institutions for tertiary education are spaces, *processes*, through which participants bring meaning and create worlds that hugely impact their personal and intellectual development. These remain largely unexplored. The *experience* of inequality, for example, as it is manifest within educational institutions, needs to be understood as much as the structural features of such inequality and how they impact student and familial aspirations for inclusion, educational attainment and employment.

Conflict, crises and events in everyday life are significant aspects of these processes. The ways in which youth may be both shaped by and engaged with the unfolding of crises, events and everyday life remain opaque in our understanding of how education plays an important role in the making of citizens. It is this understanding of human agency in institutional contexts that has somehow eluded scholars who seek to establish the significance of the structural and ideological frameworks within which educational processes are embedded. Once we understand that students are keen and active participants in the processes into which they are inserted, our views about education and its possible outcomes may perhaps change. It is indeed possible to examine and understand the vastly differing and multiple practices that students engage in as agents within, and outside, an institutional framework. Do they, in fact, seek to push the possibilities for making their voices heard or do they succumb to the authoritarian practices prevalent in our educational institutions? How do students seek to rise above not just the normative expectations associated with their 'roles' as students but also with asserting themselves in deeply meaningful and contextually significant ways? This means that we must pay attention to critical consciousness as it reveals itself in pedagogic encounters of different kinds and also in peer cultures and student-led organizations and movements in different parts of South Asia.

We may also see teachers as agents of both change and reproduction in education. It becomes important to identify and examine some of the processes that enable them to be pioneers and facilitators for transformative practices, rather than only being viewed as toothless agents of the state or private bodies, as they usually are, without any possibilities for bringing about change in their limited worlds. Both teachers and students are engaged participants in processes pertaining to education and the series needs to unpack the possibilities and potential for *movement* underlying the constrained and encapsulated worlds they inhabit.

This series, therefore, seeks to understand aspects of educating contemporary South Asia in different educational contexts and settings. It is important to reiterate that we need to focus on social inequalities in the context of educational processes, whether these are based on caste, class, gender and/or ethnic issues, keeping in mind an analysis of students' networks, their lives and regional variations. The homogeneity with which we seek to build an understanding of the writing of textbooks based on religious fundamentalism alone is not the point. It is equally essential to draw out other significant aspects of not only the writing of textbooks but also the aspects of their transaction and impact on children's learning. This transaction depends on teachers and students and their interaction inside classrooms. It is imperative to understand these processes by focusing on children's views and their perspectives on textbooks, and their significance in their lives. At the same time, we need to also recognize the use of language, curriculum and evaluation in educational processes that tend to define educational practice in particular ways. What are the political tools that are used to do this and how do these play out in the everyday life of institutions and of the people in them? It is imperative to understand both aspects of the organization of knowledge in particular ways: the state and its agents as well as the actors (students, teachers, administrators) at the receiving end. Evaluation and certification are other tools in the hands of those who seek to govern educational practice and become instruments through which pedagogic encounters take place within institutions.

Educational spaces are also about place and location in multiple ways, whether these are at the intersection of caste, gender and class or are about location as both territorial and imagined spaces. The sociology of education must unpack these complexities and bring out their implications in a variety of contexts. The significance of gender, caste, religion or language as defining characteristics of educational processes are germane to our understanding and need to be examined in different contexts in the region that make each experience unique and similar at the same time.

The series also seeks to foreground scholarship that uses a range of methodological tools and theoretical constructs to understand the phenomena under study. Thus, studying forms of inequality must be based on fieldwork in different contexts and not rely on statistical information alone; an analysis of textbooks must also take into account other social and cultural dimensions of schooling and students' perspectives rather than the content of the texts or political dilemmas alone. It is not necessary that the series will be concerned with only the institutional aspects of education; studies of childhood and youth are also an essential component of the proposed series. The educational outcomes for youth and their families have remained almost untouched in contemporary work on the theme in India and the region. One of the lenses through which this series aims to develop the sociology of education is through a focus on youth and aspects of their experience, both within and outside institutional spaces.

Meenakshi Thapan

Acknowledgements

This work is based on my research work involving a school in Delhi. A brief section based on this research has been published as 'Negotiating School and Gender: Peer Performatives' in Meenakshi Thapan (ed.) *Ethnographies of Schooling in Contemporary India* (2014, SAGE Publications).

I am grateful to my colleagues and friends who provided important feedback that has enriched the preparation of this book. I am immensely grateful to Professor Meenakshi Thapan for being an encouraging force in taking this work to a wider readership. Critical comments and appreciation generously provided by Professor Karuna Chanana have been of great help in addressing some of the gaps in this work.

I owe deep gratitude to the scholars who have inspired this work and all my teachers at the Delhi School of Economics, Department of Sociology. I am very obliged to the Pratyantar School for providing unrestricted access to its premises for the research. My mother and brother have extended their support in ways most kind and thoughtful. This work owes a lot to them.

Anuradha Sharma

Introduction: Negotiating Schooling Practices

This work is a study of a private co-educational secondary school in Delhi and is an attempt to understand the in-school experiences of students in the context of gender, class and religion. A significant component of social life is the experience it constitutes for the person living it. The 'experientiality' of life is possible to map and is simultaneously beyond the scope of research techniques. Research on schools has dealt with various institutions such as caste, class, religion and gender that have a role to play in constituting those schools. I will be focussing on the experiential aspect of some of these institutions as these play out for the students while they are in school. In narrowing it down to experiences of the students, I am aware that a neat categorization of experience and institutional frames is not viable. Nevertheless, I will highlight the individual meanings that are derived out of frames to bring to the fore the agential in the social. Undoubtedly, it is in this interaction between the individual and the social, in which meanings emerge. These diverse responses and understandings of what appears an institutional whole are very valuable, for it is in these minute spaces that the possibilities of change reside. These diverse experiences are a clear indicator of the complex and layered nature of social reality.

Schools are, by and large, understood to be largely structured institutions for the discipline and training that they are meant to provide to their participants. Their assessment as monolithic practitioners of these functions often obliterates their diverse, vibrant multiplicity. Schools may not hold a similar, common meaning for all the students. This understanding is significant in various ways. It therefore becomes important to focus on students as participants and makers of meaning in the process of understanding what life at school is all about.[2]

As the processes of schooling and the students' engagement with these are understood, the issue of structure and agency becomes significant. There are possibilities for the school becoming structurally imposing through a state-recommended curriculum and organizational restrictions. Structural impositions may also come in the form of certain regulations imposed by the management of the school (in case the school is managed by a private trust) or in the form of codes of conduct that schools tend to impose as righteous and justified. This work, however, looks into the agential interventions and interpretations of such structural elements of schooling by students. In this context, it becomes imperative to study the agential interpretation of the structural elements by the students. Additionally, underlining the agential improvisation of the structural elements at the level of the management and the teachers becomes significant as well. School acquires distinct meanings in the manner in which the school's goals are visualized and interpreted at managerial levels and by different teachers. Furthermore, the various ways that the school spaces allow the students to interact creates multiple versions of what the school means to them. In other words, students' experience of their schooling is not restricted merely to the curricular frames as they participate in the processes of school as a social institution.

The structural processes of schools have elements in them that carry implications for the class, gender and religious identities of its students apart from, and along with, the pedagogical and disciplining aspects of school life. The everyday practices of schools are taken as the key location where several meanings of schooling emerge. More than the stated goals and the vision of a school, the actual transmission of schooling tells us about what actually is being transmitted and how is it being responded to by students. School is meaningful for the several avenues it creates for its students, such as interacting with one's classmates, experiencing the extracurricular activities, school playground antics, being together with others and the cultures of training as well as of rebellion and resistance. Resistance to school remains a key feature of most studies on school, possibly because schools as institutions are structurally designed to teach and socialize students into appropriate codes of conduct. However, in this study, schooling is analyzed as it stands mediated by aspects of peer cultures and class experiences; religion may play different roles in the process of schooling, gender relations affect and are affected by school processes, peer relations and so on. The cultural knowledge and experience of one context may assist in overcoming the barriers in another. The meanings derived in one context may lend a new perspective to a situation in school. Just as barriers created by or in one context may hinder a novel way of learning in another.

The prominent theme of this study is, thus, to explore the multiplicity of school experiences primarily from the perspective of students. This includes the negotiations, the strategies and, before that, the meaning that these indicators hold for different students. Even as class is acknowledged as an indicator of social inequality in school contexts, I have tried to reach beyond the 'already there' implications of class denominators in a school in urban India. I try to show the everydayness of those dimensions of classed experiences in a particular context. How do these emerge, what forms do these take, how these intertwine with the other procedures of schooling and what do such encounters mean to different students? These are some of the questions I seek to answer through this work.

The space of school has been mapped through certain socially significant conceptual tropes such as class, religion and gender. The fieldwork began with a hypothesis that the empirical findings may bring out some less-emphasised aspects of these social dimensions for two reasons: first, each social reality has a distinctiveness to it which is valuable and second, young minds may have their own ways of responding to some of these categories.

In India, caste plays a significant role in everyday practices of access and denial in social life and schools are no exception

(Nambissan 2013, Velaskar 2013, Wankhede 2013). This study does not dwell on that aspect, though it is significant to note that caste relations have been re-contextualized in education to a certain extent in contemporary India (Nambissan 2013). Caste cannot be devalued as a dimension of social class identity, but its expressions have become less categorical. In the village schools attended by Dalit students, the discriminatory practices associated with purity and pollution are overtly present. Overt discrimination through separate seating and serving of food, referring to caste designations, making the Dalit students clean school premises and toilets, and making them sit at the end of the classroom or on the floor remain commonplace in rural schools. In urban schools, such blatant expressions of caste discrimination are not always apparent. The discriminatory attitudes of the educators have a more powerful social class connotation in urban schools. Caste inequality appears to have metamorphosized into class disparity. However, to assume that the transition of inequalities has been direct and essential would be to deny the complex nature of a social reality. As Amman Madan and Ghanshyam Tiwari (2012) suggest, caste, class and gender do have a role to play in sustaining inequalities, although how much and in what ways each contributes is not always easy to predict. In their study of government schools in the tribal belt of Madhya Pradesh, they show that gender seemed to play a much less stringent role in contributing to social inequality as these groups were tribal groups. There is comparatively less gender inequality amongst such groups. Madan and Tiwari also show that though caste and class could be overlapping as causes of inequality, their independent effects were more strongly visible. 'It was difficult to support the claim that class was only an expression of caste or vice versa' (Madan and Tiwari 2012: 16). An essential overlap was not present and other factors were contributing towards shaping educational inequalities. In this work, therefore, there is an attempt to bring out the less-commonly discussed dimensions of class, religion and gender as these influence and are influenced by everyday interactions.

Religion is analysed in this study as a source of beliefs and symbolic capital for the students as well as for the school practitioners, albeit in somewhat different forms. An important aspect that informs people's perspective is a belief system that intervenes in cognition, that is, it is often not recognized as a factor that influences the way people understand their social reality. Religion is relegated to the field of belief, however, it may have implications for the cognitive skills as well. A distinctive way of conceptualizing religion emerges amidst this analysis of the influences of religion on the institution of schooling. A pervasive discourse surrounding religion in the contexts of schools has been focussing on the divisive or/and exclusionary role played by it (Bakaya 2004, Benei 2009, Froerer 2007, Kumar 2000, Sundar 2004).

The validity of such discourses is not questioned; however, a need to acknowledge other equally significant perspectives is highlighted in this work. Religion provides an important thematic referential to the experience of being in this world, and its inclusion in the experience of learning is pertinent to an endeavour to understand schooling. These are some of the ways through which the multiplicity of students' experience has been highlighted with an intent to provide an alternative way of looking at schools as a social institution.

A third dimension chosen to represent school, as it is experienced by the students, is that of gender relations and gendered cultures as they appear in school practices. While not questioning the enormous stereotypical perceptions related to gender very aptly underlined by various scholars, this work attempts to gather instances of some shifts in these perceptions. Gender identity is indeed a significant aspect in the context of schooling. As a student engages with school processes, the gendered self of the student is reconstituted at various significant junctures—in a classroom during a lesson, in extracurricular activities, in peer group interactions and in imagining a goal for themselves through various selections that they make in the school. The gendered self is not contingent upon gender only; it has cross-cutting links with class, religion and region. The potential role of schools in articulating these is of interest here as is the understanding of the ways through which school processes are mediated by the gender conceptions of students.

Gendered selves in the space of school are informed by familial, class, religion, community and age-related parameters; how gender gets constructed would show variations. Within an overarching localized conception of gender characteristics, individuals also bring out their own versions of it. As McLaren points out, 'Schools perform the reproductive function...but within a cultural terrain marked by contestation and struggle' (McLaren 1986: xxv).

The construction of students' identities in different school-cultures has been an issue that has been discussed by several sociologists and educationists. School processes in themselves are not predictable in their outcomes. However, participating in these processes does leave an impact on the students. The identities that these processes generate would be dependent on the other derivatives that constitute the students' social life. The project of knowing more about the school's impact as students bring their context-specific experience to it hypothesizes that homogenization could be one of the strongest intents of schools. This happens through an imposition of order and discipline on the students, standardized uniforms, timetables, syllabi and practices that teach coordination. Yet, despite all this, homogenization may not be the outcome. The way the common practices are implemented and the fact that the common could be overcome is certainly not a part of the intended agenda. There are mediating factors and contexts that work through these structures and may bring out interesting outcomes. We may say that school is understood in its connect with the outside conditions. Identities are sensitive to the contexts in which they emerge or operate. Contextualization is very important and it can often change the image that one may have of an event.

The internalization of school culture as well as the resistance to it are also shown to emerge in various interesting ways. School processes are the structured activities that give the school its social character. Students participate in this social zone with the experiences that they bring along in terms of gender, class and religion. One of the most crucial elements that needs to be studied here is the work of agency as it emerges in this social zone. Agency refers to a will to initiate change in the structure, of which one is a part. Agency is related to the structure where it is exercised, as it is the structure that makes the need for agency to emerge; agency becomes meaningful in relation to the structure. The issue of agential action is related to the concept of identity; 'who one is' has a strong connection to 'what one does'.

Structure and Agency

Schools can be understood as sites of mediations between the inside and the outside cultures, just as these are sites of interface between the structured realities and agential responses. This mediated space is significant to the present work. Pierre Bourdieu (1990) addresses this relationship between structures and human agency in a manner where the two cannot be comprehended in isolation from each other. His concept of *habitus* elaborates on the agential possibilities as well as its limits in relation to structures. It simultaneously demonstrates that structures cannot persist on their own but are generated and sustained through agential interventions.

Structures and agency have a relationship that does not stop at opposition alone; they have a deeper association—agency acts out in relation to the structure. In surpassing, avoiding, opposing or negotiating the structure, agency is never independent of the structure; as structures exist, so agency is able to play itself out.

Structuration theory (Giddens 1984) is another such attempt that addresses the issue of agency and structure in the realm of the social. Structuration theory aims to avoid the extremes of structural or agential determinism. Language, normative order and power are the three structural categories that define social systems. School as a social system would also be constituted by these three structural forms. It is in these realms that the play of agency is to be discovered and it is around these structural categories that student identities are constituted, or to be more precise, mediated. Structures that govern the social life of individual actors are not homologous in character; the logics and dynamics of each structure may be distinct from that of others. Sewell (2005) talks about a theory of structure that takes a multiple, contingent and fractured conception of society and of structure if change has to be accounted for. Each individual has access to several such structures and the impact that particular social structural realm, say the school, is going to have is contingent upon the individual actor's access to other structural realms. It could be the structural realm of religion/belief, kinship, friendship groups, an ideology/world view, the political orientation and so on. Resources and knowledge derived from one structural realm can be applied or utilized in another; here we are primarily referring to the school. So the resources and world view available through a 'non-school' structural realm could be brought in while being in the school and that would constitute the space of agential action.

In several seminal works on schools (see Appendix I), a turn-around in the orientation towards the subject matter and definition of the subject matter is evident. There has been a shift from an objectivist study of things as they are to the representation of the subject's position and the acknowledgement of the subjects as not just active participants but also active interpreters of their worlds. It clearly marks a shift from the notions of structural imposition of dominant discourses to contested discourses; from singular determinants such as class, family, ethnicity and gender exercising influence over educational prospects to intersecting, multi-layered discursive practices.

Post-structural Understandings of Identities in Schools

Identity constitutes a key segment in this work and almost all research with a qualitative bend and an interactionist orientation has dealt with its various dimensions substantively. Any discussion of agency would have to incorporate the issues surrounding identity construction. In choosing to study the school processes as mediated by students' experiences at three levels, namely, class, gender and religion, I address the overlaps and contradictions that these three categories of identity construction will inevitably present. Within the school, the practices specific to the school regime would be scrutinized: primarily, the cultural values promoted by the school management; its interpreted versions at the hands of the teachers; peer group cultures and students' embodiment, and cultural articulation of these will also be significant.

Post-structural, discursive paradigms have provided some significant insights into the issue of identity construction in school settings especially in terms of gender and class identity. The informative principles of these paradigms could be extended to other areas of identity construction such as religious identity, as well.

Diane Reay's works on class identity (2003, 2010) are positioned between the post-modernist notion of 'identity as fractured and fragmented' and the modernist style of placing significance over the structural factors, the meta narratives. She places identity construction in a realm that recognizes the personal biography and the structural processes, and takes identity to be relational, marked by differences and exclusions. In a more recent essay, Reay (2003, 2010) brings up three dimensions that she concedes are central to assessing the identity component of class relationships in the context of schooling. I have drawn extensively on her work for my own analysis. The three dimensions that Reay identifies are temporality, that is, the presence of past in the present; relationality, that is, success and failure in the schooling context are relational, some succeed and others fail; and, spatiality, that is, geographies of schooling, classed places and spaces. Temporality manifests through the memories of the part experiences that the parents may have had in the context of education.

Identity construction from this post-structuralist paradigmatic position is contingent upon participation in discursive practices and, before that, learning the categories that exclude while they include, that is, being a boy means not being a girl. Bronwyn Davies (2004) has designed a model for a discursive location of the issue of identity along the gendered categories in the context of schools. The meanings that these categories carry are a creation of the discourses to which these categories belong. The 'storylines' are made up of these categories and their allocated meanings and it is through these that subjects create a sense of self, a personal identity or a 'sense of oneself as belonging in the world in certain ways and thus seeing the world from the perspective of one so positioned' (Davies 2004: 128). Shared discourses and shared meanings of categories produce continuities and a sense of belonging to a group. The most vibrant, in fact, the basic stream through which these discourses travel is language. It has constitutive power in it and yet can seem like a means of conveying ideas—it not just conveys, it constitutes selves, in the post-structuralist understanding of the social world. 'Images, metaphors, narrative structures, terms of address, teaching practices, can all function to position girls as marginal within educational discourse...while boys are being constituted through the same discourses as aggressively masculine...in opposition to what girls are and therefore must be' (Davies 2004: 137). Learning about the constitutive aspect of discourses is a power statement in itself as that is the first move towards unravelling the constituents of identity. Another empowering move would be having access to other forms of discourses that are non-discriminative. 'Persons as speakers acquire beliefs about themselves which do not necessarily form a unified coherent whole. They shift from one to another way of thinking about themselves as the discourse shifts and as their positions within varying storylines are taken up' (Davies and Harre 2001: 270). The constitutive reworking of one's identity is an idea that recognizes the structures but does not essentialize their impact.

Inspired by Foucauldian ([1969] 2005) notions, Judith Butler has provided certain conceptual tools for thinking anew on the issue of identity. Michel Foucault explains one of the key qualities of discourse as, '(neither related) to the primary ground of experience, nor to the *a priori* authority of knowledge; but...seek the rules of its formation in discourse itself' (Foucault [1969] 2005: 89). Discourse goes beyond language as in the spoken word, it circulates in 'speech and writing as well as visual representations, bodily movements and gestures, and social and institutional practices' (Youdell 2010: 134). Butler has presented three concepts towards laying out the constituted nature of identity: *performativity, subjectivation and intelligibility.*

Performativity: Performative are things that are said that make things happen (Austin 1962). Categories that are used to designate or differentiate people are performative designations—they create the subject that they name, they seem like descriptions but they are constitutive and they create that subjectivity through that categorization.

Looking out for gender-, class- and ethnicity-based categorizations in the discourses in school can be achieved through close, day-to-day observations of the ethnographic kind and getting to the depth of these issues through qualitative techniques such as interviewing and talking to the teachers and students. It is also suggested that rather than searching for singular categories of identity, say either gender or class or ethnicity, it would be much more fruitful to see more than one category interacting with each other as these get expressed. In actual, living contexts identities are intersecting and multiple.

Subjectivation is another conceptual tool that unravels the power of discourse as a constitutive force. It has a logic built into its working. While it constitutes the subjects; it constrains them also but does not determine them. Here possibly lies the work of human agency that it can refuse to be determined in that discursive practice which disadvantages it. It has the power to produce a subject and in that restrain the subject but this power is not absolute, in either of its workings. This leads to both subjection to power and recognition as a subject, this is the space where the subject can act.

Intelligibility is 'recognizability' of performative discourses and subjectivation discourses in the discourses where they are being presented. Unless they make sense in the institutional or contextual discourses, they may not work powerfully. This suggests that bringing in entirely different discursive practices into a certain context is not achieved smoothly. The contextual discourses resist such attempts.

Butler accords agential qualities and a political potential to the performatives. The discursive practices of a context may be resistant to new hitherto silenced or subjugated discourses, but they are not immune to it and this is the space for new meanings to emerge. For this work, the workings of such performatives in the forms that they reveal themselves are very significant and an ethnographic methodology enables glimpses of such occurrences in novel and known ways. Words, gestures, expressions and practices at the everyday level reveal the discursive details of interactions and give direction to the layer discourses within which they are taking place.

At the same time, certain everyday practices and processes in schools give form to school agendas such as disciplining, indoctrination, maintaining the status quo, reproducing social inequities of class and gender, and instilling ideological values instead of facilitating transformation. These can simultaneously be the possibilities and expressions of agential interventions by the students. Everyday life at schools takes on multiple hues within the larger framework of structural formalities and agential attempts and it is in this space of small happenings, gestures, words and activities that the larger agenda is displayed. It is also in such interfaces with the school processes that the identities of the students are not only impacted but also have implications for those processes.

Ethnography as Method and as Practice

This work is an ethnographic study of school processes. Basically, ethnographic studies of social phenomena address a methodological concern that involves the issue of objectivity/subjectivity. It redefines both and offers a repositioning of the same. The assumption that a reality exists out there and needs to be observed carefully has been questioned by the theoretical frameworks of symbolic interactionism, constructivism, modernist theory and discursive approaches (Berger and Luckmann 1966, Blumer 1969, Butler 1990, Davies 2001, 2004, Foucault [1969] 2005). The ethnographic endeavours guided by these approaches are inclined towards believing that reality is not available outside a certain subject position; it is in interactions that reality is known and expressed (to some extent). A reality can be mapped through certain themes but it is futile to look for a 'complete' reality. One can aspire to observe a 'whole' reality, that is, a social site can be observed and understood in its networks of relationships of contexts but the picture is never complete for the observer because of the limitations of interest and concern. Ethnographic studies are open-ended projects and in that sense they represent the reality that they seek to understand. In prioritizing the detailed, descriptive recording of the day-to-day interactions and practices of the chosen segment of social life, an ethnographic scheme prioritizes the complexity of the social as it involves with the subject/individual. A thematic reconstruction of those complexities involves the observer and the observed. The concept of situatedness in a cultural context comments on the dialectics of the objective and subjective in every social site. One thematic representation of a social site stands open to a revision through another thematic reconstruction as it brings along a new way of understanding the dialectics of networks.

Paul Willis (2000) has outlined some of the most central concerns that ethnographic methodology addresses. The 'lived dynamics' of 'everyday culture' (Willis 2000: 2) tend to be organized in different time frames and with different agendas or motives; their nature changes with contingent contexts and situations. This lived culture expresses itself not just in language but also through other forms of embodiment such as gestures, self-presentations and various meaning-making techniques. There are personal assumptions, materials and institutional elements through which human subjects constitute realities; the ethnographer through his/her presence obtains access to the cultural practices that are mobilized while the subjects live their lives. Primacy is given to their views, their meanings and their stories, however, the questions are the ethnographer's. At the same time, physical presence in the field should not encourage the ethnographer to feel that now they can know it 'all'. So what the subjects say is important but the form that expression takes and the expressive value of the non-verbal is often more important. Sometimes these are the opportunities where the agent/subject has possibilities of transgression of the structural order. In these cultural practices involving different uses of language, objects and actions, human agents produce/constitute and reconstitute themselves.

The shift in ethnographic practices from the liberal conception of ethnography that believed in decoding the structural text to more radical, postmodernist leanings has resulted in certain implications

for ethnographers, the methods that are employed, the social construction of realities that emerge and the different ways in which the
observed or the field is viewed. G.E. Marcus (1995) has outlined
some of those implications. Ethnographies need to be 'multi-sited'
(Marcus 1995: 83), that is, they need to study their subjects through
several modes. For once, this provides a relatively comprehensive
view of their identity in a particular context because they as individuals are being constituted by their selves in other contexts as well. At
the same time, this provides the space for a 'cultural critique'
(Marcus 1995: 69) by bringing in the other possible selves of the
subject as the other possibilities of being for that actor. These possibilities could have a bearing on their identity in the context where
they are being studied by the ethnographer. Ethnographically substantiated accounts of those other selves create conditions for possibilities which would have been dismissed as wishful thinking if not
for the documented accounts of these being active in other sites.
The 'spatiality', 'temporality' and the 'perspective' that used to be
fixed in their references and were believed to be having a reality to
them needs to be observed unobtrusively by the ethnographer in
the field, have been reworked through the more radical ethnographic orientations. These radical ethnographic practices do not
restrict the spatial to the locale of the social phenomena or to the
local frame but extend it to include other connected locales, including the spatial intervention through the electronic media.
Temporally, the shift is from the focus on historical to historical
narrative, that is, that part as created in memory and is considered a
source of identity formation. Here also the impact of the electronic
invasion is also significant.

This generation of codes and concepts is derived from the
framework provided by Glaser and Strauss (1967) and some very
significant conceptual tools by Woods (1980, 1983); for instance,
strategy, negotiation, pupil-culture, teacher-culture and perspectives in the context of school studies through an interactionist
perspective. Woods (1979) has identified three criteria that can
assist in locating the grounded concepts in situational data; these
come out in the form of themes: 'frequency of occurrence'–'effect
on people'–and 'strangeness' (Woods 1979: 269). McLaren (1986)

has presented this through the 'root paradigms'[1] that he locates in his work and are the most constant world views that he encounters as he proceeds in his ethnographic endeavour in a school.

The nature and the form of discursive practices can also help in drawing attention towards certain cultural codes present in a situation and these often have links with the larger contexts. For instance, a feature noted by some works on schools in India is that a certain brevity of words exists, be it the insufficiency of history textbooks in fully addressing the issues of religious differences (as compared to 'the vivid and dramatic' nature of memories evoked by the 'oral-lore' on these topics) (Kumar 1996: 19) or the relative lack of verbal expression of thoughts in a school, studied by Radhika Viruru (2001) in India from a post-colonial perspective. She observes that as compared to her experiences of Western schools, a lot more is communicated in this school without 'saying' much. The culture of communication was found to be distinct from western contexts; it was less verbalized, understated, silent at times and conveyed through other ways. She observes that less instructions and not too much of prompting into what the children should do, or how they should go about it, resulted in the children making choices for themselves. Viruru (2001) notices this as something distinct about schooling in the Indian context. The nature of expressiveness present in the oral lore and in the more contemporary modes of entertainment such as television and their implications on and for the nature of discourses in school is an interesting aspect to explore in the context of student's identities. This has been posed as a significant non-school context.

The ethnographic method also facilitates the study of the non-literal, figurative meanings present in the language practices; the symbolic usage and meaning of objects and artefacts, and of body expressions in a social set-up. Everyday life is characterized by linguistic accounts of all kinds where people talk about that happened, they analyze other's intentions, attitudes, responses and abilities.

The school processes themselves are repositories of various kinds of cultural codes at their most basic level. Certain practices exist in schools that have a certain basic assumption built in them. For instance, classroom teaching is meant to expose the students to a formal procedure of knowledge transmission and a certain social etiquette of listening, sitting quietly, paying attention, responding appropriately and so on; punishment regimes are meant to correct the discipline benders; uniforms, seating arrangements, punctuality and tidiness are meant to instil discipline; and extracurricular activities are meant to be the arenas for creativity, cooperation and competition (Jeffery 2005). These are the patterns through which the intended cultural impacts materialize, so these are some routes that are significant for research in schools. However, what materializes through these is not so uniform and thus, the diversity in impact needs to be looked out for. The unstructured practices that move along these routes are also important to observe as these carry significant constitutive energies. For instance, the spatial praxis of classrooms, corridors, playgrounds and stage can be significant to observe who 'fools around' in the classroom more, who answers the teacher's questions, who sits dazed, who engages in what sorts of stage performances and what sorts of students activities and behaviours goes around in the non-formal spaces of the school. All of these questions may have clues in them that could point towards forms of identity formations. Classroom activities such as starting a lesson, bringing lessons to an end, question–answer sessions, all these may be indicative of certain cultural abilities at some other level and may derive from some other cultural context. Conversation analysis can play a part in addressing these linkages (Hustler and Payne, as cited in Burgess 1985). 'Control-strategies' (Riddell 1992) employed by the teachers are also indicative of the themes that are considered significant in a setting. Riddell's work shows how the boys' potentially disruptive behaviour was controlled by the male teachers, initially through camaraderie, and then by violence. The female teachers pay attention to the boys if they seem disruptive, but if girls talk in the class the teachers let them be—the gender norms held by the teachers influence their strategies and any shift in such strategies reveal their normative orientations. No essential links can be claimed to exist but these are not happening in a vacuum either. The coping strategies employed by the students in the school context are another significant marker of the cultural resources at the disposal of the students (often derived through their non-school contexts), which they tend to bring in to cope with the conditions that schooling presents. Humour, pretence, boasting, shyness, disruptive behaviour, name-calling and exaggeration are some of the possible behaviours that are commonly observed in school contexts by students in classrooms, in lunch breaks and in free periods among the friends and foes. Peer groups constitute another significant area where identity issues are played out.

Negotiations and inculcations of the structurally directed practices are explored through observations of students' practices in classrooms, playgrounds, during their extracurricular involvements, free periods and so on. Informal interviews and conversations are supplemented by open-ended questionnaires and metaphor questions; the students are asked to respond to some questions that are open-ended and a one-word response is sought from them. The idea is to make them express the immediate association that comes to them regarding that particular issue. It is not a planned response and being a one-word response it is highly selective and, most significant of all, it highlights the key aspect of their view on the issue. Such questions are asked in relation to gender associations, peer relations, self conception, school and home. These and other responses are constantly linked to their everyday practices and expressions and their informal conversations about some of these issues. Some secondary sources are also used to collect information about the school.

An ethnography goes beyond the immediate space that is being studied through it; it goes back in time through the memory of the actors involved and takes notice of the minor 'metalinguistic' categories rather than focus on one dominant perspective. In this work, the spatiality of the school has been viewed as being constituted in several ways through codes of conduct and school regulations, and also through the ways the students define these according to their interest. The classrooms, the corridors, the auditorium, the music and dance room, the playground, the staffroom and the principal's room are the spaces in the school that constitute different meanings for students and the school authorities. The temporality of the school is extended beyond the immediate, in the vision of the school, that is, it is with a certain view of the future that the school functions in its 'today'. A memory of the other life, a life outside the school, makes its impact on what coming to the school means for the students as well as others in the school. Religion, class and gender identities of the students live in the memory of another time and another space as well. Thus, any understanding of these aspects, although it happens at a moment in time, relies much more on the way it is remembered by the actor. The pedagogical exercises and the extracurricular activities have a course to them that is meant to take the learners through several spatialities and temporalities. Perspectives, too, are not limited to a singular, dominant one but are diversified due to the two preceding factors.

Several ethnographic studies of schools have been conducted in order to read the social in everyday practices of schooling. Willis's work (1977) focuses on class culture in the students' resistance to schooling. McLaren's study (1986) explores the ritual–symbolic patterns of student states in the process of schooling and highlights the mostly resistant and sporadically accommodative nature of the students' approach to it. Among studies in the Indian context, Thapan's (1991, 2006) classic ethnography of a Krishnamurti school has explored the practices of the school to understand the manner in which a philosophical ideology is sought to be delivered through schooling and how it generates several kinds of responses, with diverse implications. Benei's (2005, 2009) study of schools in Maharashtra presents the issue of nationality, patriotism and the role that schools play in their perpetuation, and the factors that support this as well as the elements that resist it. Ethnographies of schools not only bring out the multilayered existence of the specific school studied for each ethnographic endeavour but also identify the various tangents along which schools can possibly function. This enriches our perspective on schools and schooling by challenging the prevalent curriculum-centric image of school.

Fieldwork presents a curious assortment of the known and the unknown in the field. While schools are familiar sites because of our personal experiences of schooling and through the works of scholars on schools, approaching a school as a sociological site involves seeing it to an extent sans 'preconceptions' ([Durkheim 1895] 1982). Developing a new way of looking at the school is one of the key methodological principles that has to be sustained throughout the fieldwork and even after, when the research is being documented. Research in familiar settings poses its distinct problems. In such situations familiarity can hinder a complete inspection of the site. The formulae of 'making the familiar strange' and asking questions such as 'what if this was done in some other way' (about practices in the schools that may seem very familiar, to the extent of seeming inconsequential) help in understanding school as a sociological site in a comprehensive manner. The novel links that emerged between erstwhile known social categories was another significant contribution of doing ethnography of school as a social site. The tacit rules operative in a field can be the site of the change that has come in that field as well as of the continuities; and these can be experienced through being present in the field. Tacit knowledge, 'the largely unarticulated, contextual understanding that is often manifested in nods, silences, humour and naughty nuances', is reflected in participants' actions as well as their words and in what they fail to state but, nonetheless, feel deeply and even take for granted (Altheide and Johnson 1994: 492–93). The reading of the fine print in the social presentations is one of the crucial aspects of the ethnographic endeavour.

Innovative ways of getting to know the field and privileging some tools over the others depending on the situation and specific qualities of the field is an experience in the reflexivity of doing ethnography. The focus on the performative in the field was one such device that was selected due to the nature of the field situation. Performance ethnography has emerged as a methodological orientation in field studies in recent years (Anderson 2008, Hamera 2011, Madison; Saldana cited in Leavy 2010). With its multifaceted skills, it also emerged as a key methodological format for this work as well. Performance ethnography as the name suggests is a form of doing ethnography that is present to the nuances of the embodied expressions and verbal intonations apart from the spoken word. The decision to undertake fieldwork in this particular manner was not pre-empted except for a constant reminder to remain aware of the distinctions that ethnographic research can possibly create. During fieldwork, the focus on performative aspects emerges as an effective and uninterrupted source of knowing about the field. It also justifies the presence of the ethnographer in the field. The sensory awareness and observation of the tacit in social situations grant access to the symbolic and the metaphoric in that situation.

Notes

1. A master metaphor of a cultural system.
2. A rigorous and sustained engagement with everyday life at schools was enabled through my doctoral research on a school in Delhi.

1

The Pratyantar School

About the School

The school chosen for this study is a private, co-educational school situated in an urban neighbourhood in Delhi. It has a separate wing for the underprivileged children, run in the after hours of the main school and henceforth we may refer to it as the *Pratyantar*[1] school. Pratyantar is a charitable endeavour on the part of the main school that is run by a private trust. For this study, the choice of school was not constrained by any factor since the concern was to understand the processes of a school as they are mediated by other factors; any school would provide that kind of a field for study. This school provides an interesting platform for this study as it stands at the interface between a government-run school and a private school. It aims at providing an education at par with good private schools to children who do not have the economic support to afford such schooling. Here, it needs to be mentioned that in the Indian educational scenario, the education imparted by the state-run schools and the private schools do not carry equal value. It cannot, however, be categorically presumed that differences exist in the quality of education, the discipline and the value systems promoted by these two kinds of schools. The government schools run on state-aid while the private schools are private, trust-managed ventures. Over a period of time, government-run schools broadly, have catered to lower classes while the upper and middle classes choose from a range of private schools for their children's education. Apart from other differences, one major indicator of a hiatus between these two types of schools is the medium of instruction. Private schools take pride in being English medium while the government schools primarily teach in a vernacular medium.

Pratyantar School caters to the children from economically underprivileged sections, residing in the neighbourhood and aims at providing them with a presumably better education. It is a novel attempt in a way, although, the school does not proclaim to be providing an 'alternative schooling' in a radical way. It goes a little beyond the recent drive to grant admissions to a small percentage of students from the economically weaker section (EWS) category, in the private schools. It is also a precursor to the Right to Education (RTE) Act which has made it mandatory for all private schools to reserve 25 per cent of its seats for EWS category students.[2] It dedicates a complete wing named the Pratyantar School to such students till Class 8 and promises to take them in the main school from then on. The school charges no fees from these students and then provides free textbooks, stationery, uniforms and lunch. Education is primarily imparted in the English language. The myriad ways in which these distinctions of home and school, in this case, interact with each other, with various implications for students' identities on the one hand and processes of schooling on another, need to be observed in the everyday life of the school.

The main school, as it would be addressed from now on, was established in the late 1980s and is managed by a private trust owned by a private sector company. It is an established, well-known school in that part of the city. The special wing, that is, the Pratyantar School, was started a decade later. As far as the official rationale goes, it is a philanthropic endeavour. The two schools are managed by two different principals. The main school has a very well-educated principal with a masters' degree in education. The Pratyantar School also has a well-qualified, experienced, erstwhile supervisor from the main school as its headmistress. The chairman of the school had an underprivileged childhood himself but over the years succeeded in building up a large construction company. His mother wished to do something for the upliftment of economically deprived children and that is how this wing was started. The Pratyantar School is funded by the trust. The trust obtains its resources from the main school and with some financial inputs from the private sector company managed by the chairman.

A common, general framework is apparently agreed upon at the managerial level for the Pratyantar School. The school is believed to be a facilitator, an enabler that hopes to provide the children from economically weaker sections with an access to education. The chairman extends support through ensuring sustained material inputs in the form of funds and by providing scholarships to students who need economic support for higher studies.

The principal of the main school lends his support to the Pratyantar School by extending an equal platform to its students. This intention finds expression in the words of encouragement he has for the students of Pratyantar, in his frequent visits to the school, in extending a free space to the headmistress of the Pratyantar School to administer according to her judgement, in ensuring financial backup for the wing and in his appreciation of the fact that the students are benefitting through all that the school wishes to provide them with.

The headmistress of the Pratyantar School has her distinct way of implementing the principles behind this endeavour. As a result of her efforts, the teachers' salaries are at par with those of the main school teachers. As of now, the Pratyantar School has classes till Class 8 but she wishes to extend the school till Class 10. Whenever a student displays a lack of confidence or is inattentive, they are encouraged to participate in extra-curricular activities, especially those related to performing on the stage, and she vouches by its capacity to help the child overcome his or her inhibitions or alienation. The headmistress particularly prefers people from an artistic background or from the creative arts to come as chief guests on their annual day. She is of the view that they are much more appreciative and sensitive towards the hard work and talent of their students, unlike the politicians who are often chief guests at similar events in other schools.

Apart from giving a free hand to the teachers to work, she contributes through her belief in the potential of the creative arts in enhancing the self-confidence of the students. She realizes that academic excellence may not be the strong point of every student and, in that case, honing their specific qualities needs to be ensured. Creative expressions and participation in various competitions are valued by her in this endeavour thereby bringing out the potential of each student.

It is futile to look for a singular articulation of the aim of school. It is also necessary to examine and articulate the way it plans to carry out transformations for its students and have a measurable impact of these transformations on the students. This, however, does not mean that there are no 'key definitions or structures' (Woods 1983). What is significant is how within a broad framework of aims, methods and processes of school, we must look for different contexts, situations, people's interpretations, strategies, negotiations and subcultures within these (Woods 1983). The structural, definitional understanding of the aim of setting up this school seems to be singular but its agential occurrence varies at the three levels of authority (i.e., the structural aim is interpreted in different and unique ways by the different implementers). The goal may seem to be to provide children from less privileged backgrounds access to education, but for those in authority, it stands for giving an opportunity for growth to those who face barriers. As described earlier, for the chairman, it is his way of re-scripting 'childhood', with the economic deprivation 'erased' this time, through the other children. To the principal of the main school, who has had a very long association with the main school and subsequently with the Pratyantar School as a consultant, advisor and supervisor, the Pratyantar School appears as a well-deserved opportunity for children from economically weaker sections. He believes that due to a realization of their deprivation, these students are much keener and value school much more, and this, he believes, is a sort of empowerment they have through the school. For him, just by being available to these students, schooling becomes a worthwhile activity and a sort of enhanced worthiness is achieved by those who provide such an opportunity to these students.

The headmistress looks at this school as a space where these students can be introduced to the empowering potential of creative expressions. She encourages students to participate in extra-curricular activities and competitions, academic and non-academic. She appears to be sensitive towards the contexts of the students; she believes that not all students are academically oriented and given the larger constraints of background, not everyone will pursue higher studies. For those who wish to go for further studies, school would do what it can and for the others this school endeavours to provide them with skills to realize their potential in whatever else they may want to undertake. A confidence in oneself is the greatest thing this school should try to give to its students.

The managerial definition of the school as an institution varies in small but significant ways. However, the ways in which it is interpreted by teachers and students emerge throughout this work.

The processes of the school such as the space and time management, classroom activities, intervals, lunch breaks, assembly, sports events, cultural activities, outings and so on are the other loci of observation. These have been found to be significant repositories of identity construction in the discourse of schooling and in this case there is an added complexity as school culture does not reinforce home culture or vice versa.

It is known that schools have a different agenda than home in many ways. The former have a greater onus of disciplining, teaching various skills and training to work while the latter is about other things and not so much about teaching and disciplining. In this case, there is a further division possible for many students since the school trains them to be part of the culture of another class (largely middle class) while they, in their homes, are experiencing another kind of class culture (primarily working class). How the students define this relationship between school and home cannot be presumed to be uniform. Some may not identify any disjunction while others could be aware of something of that sort; how the students negotiate these contributes towards their identity construction and are significant for this study.

Layout of the School

The Pratyantar School is situated in a quiet, middle class neigh-bourhood in the city. The school is a brick structure with greenery around and inside. It is a three-storeyed building and does not have a very colourful exterior as some of the other schools in the same neighbourhood have. For instance, there is one that has a huge arch-shaped entrance with peach and maroon coloured walls. Compared to such schools, this has sober exteriors but being a brick and stone structure it appears cool and quiet. A lot of glass windows have been fitted in the structure that makes the exterior look pleasant and gives the interiors a well-lit and open feel. The corridors are cool, airy and clean. The entrance to the Pratyantar School is just next to the main entrance and it is manned by security guards. The school functions from two floors of the building—the ground floor and the basement. Despite the extreme hot weather conditions during the summers, the school remains quite cool from inside. The basement does not seem stuffy or dark. It has good ventilation facilities. All the rooms are airy, well-lit and clean. It becomes a sig-nificant feature in the description of the school as very often schools are not considered spaces that need to be aesthetically appealing. This is a private school and for its students the other alternatives would have been a government school or a small, makeshift private school huddled in a small building. The fact that the school has been turned out aesthetically and is kept tidy is a pointer to the way the school values its students. The students' views of the school emerge in later descriptions.

'The buildings embody pedagogical principles and assump-tions about ways in which teaching and learning is organized... conceptions about what "school" as an institution is, assume visible representation in school buildings' (Gordon et al. 2000: 137–38). The corridors are decorated with paintings of historical monuments from all over India—the forts from various states in India; national monuments; cut-outs of flowers; various forms of houses people built from various states of India; festivals of India representing various religious faiths; several clay artefacts such as animal figu-rines, horses, elephants, bells, small clay pots and so on. There is an aquarium placed near the entrance inside the building in one of the corridors; it has some fishes in it of varying colours and size. The floor of the corridors and staircases is made of green, polished sandstone and some classrooms have tiled floors.

The headmistress sits in a small office on the ground floor. It is also neat and the files containing data related to the school are stacked neatly in various columns. There is a small *Ganesha*[3] idol carved out of a root of a tree placed on a side cupboard. The windows of her room have bamboo curtains and small potted plants are hung in the corridor next to her office. The staffroom is in the basement section. It has three large tables in it and several chairs arranged around those. The teachers meet here in free time and during the lunch break.

Just next to the staffroom is the music and dance room. This room has a bare floor and not much furniture except for two small tables for keeping music instruments such as harmonium, tabla and, sometimes, a cassette player. This room is abuzz with activity most of the time, either during dance or singing practices. It is decorated with large pictures of *Saraswati*,[4] the Hindu goddess of learning and arts; and of Ganesha. Students are required to come to this room without wearing their shoes; or, the music and dance teacher of the Pratyantar School insists on it since traditionally this has been the practice in various schools of dance and music in India. More of this will be discussed later in the context of students' understanding of these school processes.

At the far end of one of the corridors on the ground floor is the computer lab where about 30 computers are placed. This room is decorated with charts that carry information related to computer programs and some pictorial representations related to these. The canteen is situated between the main school and the Pratyantar School; it does not have space to sit in it. The students are supposed to buy what they want and eat it wherever they wish to be seated. The canteen however is not frequented by the students of the Pratyantar School presumably because of the cost of products and due to the fact that they are served a wholesome lunch by the school.

There is an open courtyard at the centre of the building, to be precise, at the centre of the basement; it has a seating arrangement that is designed like stairs. There are blue and red plastic chairs with iron frames, placed in the seating area that can accommodate about a hundred students. This auditorium is visible from the corridors in the first floor, providing a balcony view of the stage downstairs. There is an elevated stage which is about six feet high from the ground and is sufficiently big in terms of ground space. But it is smaller than the main school auditorium. The students from the Pratyantar School perform and participate in inter-class competitions of poetry recitation, dance, music, dramatics, elocution and so on on their school's stage and for inter-school competitions. For the competitions related to group dance they rehearse in the main school auditorium which is bigger, with a wooden floored stage, better lights and curtains. There are neat washrooms at three different locations on the first floor, maintained by uniformed service staff that includes women staff to assist young girls. There is arrangement for cool, purified water for drinking. There are five taps installed near the canteen that dispense clean water, which are within Pratyantar premises.

The wing has a playground near the entrance gate, somewhat hidden from the gate through trees and shrubs. It is a grassed ground and contains about six different sorts of swings, merry-go-rounds, see-saws and so on. These cater to the younger students and are placed in one corner of the ground; the rest of the ground is used by the other students to play, recreate or just loll around during breaks or games period.

In its spatiality, the school is several notches up in comparison to the government-run schools and round-the-corner private schools found in small nooks and corners of city neighbourhoods. It is kept clean and tidy, and water and electricity supplies are taken care of. The building's architecture makes it people friendly through its airiness, sufficient natural light, broad and well-structured staircases, polished floors and large glass windows. To this extent, the school holds a promise of a favourable environment for its students and though there is more to a school than its building, yet, a building reflects the school's values and the esteem it holds its students in.

Admissions and the Formal Curriculum

The school has around 260 students enrolled who enter at the pre-primary level and it offers education till Class 8. The school is selective while admitting students: only children from economically underprivileged families are allowed and the parents are especially interviewed to assess their commitment towards their child's education. The students of Pratyantar School come from the neighbouring low-income residential settlements. A brief profile of the students' economic background, through the occupations of the parents of about 24 students from the school's first two batches shows that about 85 per cent of the mothers are housewives. Those who are working are employed as tailors, babysitters and domestic help. Fathers are employed as drivers, electricians, vegetable sellers, paan sellers, meter readers, security guards, plumbers, workers and small shopkeepers and one works as a receptionist. Siblings of most of the students are either studying at the same school or in the nearby government schools. Besides this, the school gives preference to the girl child. Over the years the proportion of girl students in the school has gradually increased.[5]

The teachers of the school belong to middle-class families. Out of the 15 teachers, 13 are women and two are men. The women are the working members in families where others also have well placed, well-paying jobs. The spouses of the married teachers work as doctors, engineers, computer engineers, businessmen and other professionals, some working in multinational companies. The male teachers are the sole working members of their family and hence there is a class distinction between the staff members. Staffroom conversations are about various issues. Sometimes domestic issues are being discussed: the temperament of the family members and the behaviours of the spouses. Discussions about travels, mostly within India, sometimes abroad, experiences from pilgrimages and shopping notes are exchanged. Impending birthdays and anniversaries of the fellow staffs are also discussed. The students' idiosyncrasies and attitudes are talked about. Issues related to health, everyday chores, school activities, assignments to be prepared and corrected are also discussed by the teachers in their leisure time during the school hours.

The school is affiliated to the Central Board of Secondary Education (CBSE). The medium of instruction in both the schools is English. This school follows the same syllabus as the main school. The curriculum is decided by the main school teachers and the Pratyantar School also teaches the same. The subjects taught are English, Hindi, Sanskrit, mathematics, social studies, EVS., the sciences, general knowledge, music, art and craft, and computers. Classes 7 and 8 have an additional subject 'life skills education'. For Class 7, the syllabus reads as follows—environment, accepting challenges in life, negative thoughts and fears, and exploring the inner self. For Class 8, the life skills education syllabus includes 'civic sense: a virtue', etiquettes, traffic rules and our heritage (dances of India, monuments, temples, festivals meanings of symbols such as *aum*, *Srichakra*, *Shivalinga*, *Swastika*, Cross, Cauldron of fire and any other). This particular subject is not taught separately; it is incorporated within the other classes.

The main school remains closed on Saturdays and Sundays but Pratyantar School opens for half day on Saturdays also so that the students benefit from an additional schooling day. Students have about 40 periods per week. A look at their timetables shows that from Class 6 onwards the number of periods allotted for dance, art and games reduces while those for computer, science and Sanskrit (added later for Class 6 and onwards) go up. Each period is of 35 minutes duration. The school begins at 1:15 PM and goes on till 5:30 PM. There is a lunch break at 3:30 PM. There are 15 teachers in all in the Pratyantar School, two of whom are male. One is for music and the other for Hindi and Sanskrit.

Other Activities in the School

The school organizes visits to museums, parks, the zoo and the planetarium every year. Buses from the main school ferry the Pratyantar School students on such outings. Class teachers and some other teachers from the school accompany the students.

Over the course of the year, various inter-house activities are also organized such as an English elocution, a Hindi elocution, a general knowledge quiz, music and dance competitions and craft and art competitions. The Pratyantar School, like the main school, has four houses. Students are divided into groups that are named after persons from history or mythology and colours are used in some as a nomenclature guide. The practice of having 'houses' like these primarily draws inspiration from Christian missionary schools, especially urban schools. As Nita Kumar (2000) notices in her study of some schools in Banaras,[6] St. Jones School had houses named after national heroes such as Gandhi, Nehru, Tagore; somewhere else it was Carmel, Fatima and Lourdes; in a Ramakrishna mission school it is Vivekananda and Netaji Subhash Chandra Bose. Students often do not know why the houses have been named thus. At Pratyantar, the names of the houses are after four mythological figures from Hindu mythology; they are young boys who have been known for their exemplary qualities: 'Dhruv' has the motto which reads 'devoted endeavour'; 'Eklavya' is associated with 'perseverance is the key to success' ; 'Prahlad' is described through 'fortune favours the brave' and 'Shravan' has the motto 'service before self'. There are stories that describe these qualities of each of these characters. Girl characters are conspicuous by their absence although it is a co-educational school.

Another routine followed in the Pratyantar School is the lunch break where lunch is provided to the students by the school. This was not a part of the school project initially. The teachers involved with the early batches noticed that some of the students were lethargic as often they were in school on an empty stomach. It was then that the school decided to make the provision for a free meal. The lunch is served at 3:30 PM in the classrooms. The students wait in their seats while the canteen staff provides lunch in paper plates and paper cups. Twice a week the students are served milk and on other days there is either a fruit or a sweet that accompanies the main dish. Vegetarian food is served comprising rice and lentils, rice and kadhi,[7] and rice and chick peas. Occasionally they are served kachori[8] with a vegetable curry, a vegetable burger with milk and similar other dishes. The menu of the lunch is set for a fortnight and then changed after that for another fortnight. The teacher in charge of this segment has to check the quality of the food an hour before it is served. Once or twice, after tasting the food, she was overheard telling the canteen staff to keep the food as less spicy as possible or to prepare a certain sweet better the next time. After the meal, the students dispose of the paper plates. In the junior classes, the school service staff assists the children in disposal and wipes their desks for them once the meal is over.

What emerges is the way in which the school takes care of the students. They are served in their seats, the food is fresh and hygienically served, there is no chaos and no one goes hungry during school time. The students are in the habit of washing hands before their meal and say a little prayer of thanks for the meal and for everything else too. The prayer is said in English and is ritually different from the way the students have their meals at home (unless they have inculcated the value of saying a prayer at their home as well). What do the students think of this culture of washing hands before the meal, spreading a handkerchief on the lap or on the desk during the lunch; saying a prayer before the meal; eating quietly without spilling over the food; disposing off the dirty plates; washing hands thereafter? Do they value it? Do they find it imposed? These are some questions of interest to this work.

Working Definitions of Some of the Focus Terms

School Process: School as a social institution has a set of beliefs, norms, aims and a framework of agenda on the basis of which it carves out a context for itself. School processes involve practices and beliefs that constitute the functioning of school. It can be seen through several vantage points and would appear somewhat different from each, but as I call this a working definition so that we can put the initial framework, the starting point to be that of its organizers and the larger scheme of social context from where it derives its validity.

School processes would have to be understood through the temporality and spatiality of the schools as the perspectives are embodied through these tangents. The temporality and the spatiality of schools have a distinctive character than that of home, neighbourhood and other social arenas that matter to students. This is commonly considered a place where learning is meant to take place and the processes are geared towards this broad concept. Apart from this, disciplining students is another concern that schools are supposed to be involved in. The official discourse of most schools is replete with certain key terms—knowledge/learning, disciplining, imparting values and training for vocations. School processes are distinct ways of organizing time, defining spaces, using language and gestures, applying certain codes of conduct and expecting consent from its students as well as the teachers.

It would not be wise to take the point of distinctiveness of school as a sociocultural space too far because of the links it has with the larger socio-economic environment. Yet, in its specific ways of addressing the socio-economic-cultural parameters of the social set-up of which it is a part, it stands on its own ground especially due to its distinct set of practices and procedures, of its ways of doing things. Schools as social sites have a distinct sort of apparatus, activities and discourses that set the stage for the identities of those involved with it, to take on an array of forms. Classrooms, classroom interactions, playground activities, extra-curricular activities, lunch breaks, free periods, cultural events, admissions, farewells, punishments and rewards, and textbooks are instances of those apparatus and activities that make up school processes.

School as a social site shares a boundary, albeit a porous one, with the other social sites. The research question that is central to this work is how certain social constituents of identity, especially class, gender and religion, influence and are influenced by the processes of a specific social site called school.

Class identity remains a significant link in this scheme of things. Social class as a concept would be taken in its most simple sense, as a position in the economy depending on the nature of occupation of the parents of the students (Riddell 1992). The class-axis of this analysis is addressed in a distinct or uncommon way as the school being studied for this research project is basically a segment of a private school (not a government or government aided one) which provides school education to children from economically disadvantaged families. In this school these children have all the facilities of a private school which, due to their economic barriers, they would otherwise not be able to obtain. The school is distinct from home, in this case, on the tangent of class also. What school processes mean to this class of students and to their parents, how the school conducts its processes as directed towards these students in terms of their class background, and the teacher's and the management's attitudes are significant aspects of this study.

Gender would be taken as the social construction of sex distinction. The ways in which it is constituted in the expressions of boys and girls; the teachers' gender codes within the school context for the students; the way gendered selves are constructed through non-school contexts, especially family and popular media (television programs), are observed through this research.

Religion is chosen as the third angle in this axis of school processes and students' experiences, as it is a significant source for the construction of identity and meaning-making. The world view that one's religious affiliation provides or as one perceives it to be is very significant in influencing how one constitutes oneself. A usual course of action would have been to select a school with an overt alignment with a particular religion. On the contrary, I examine a 'mono-ethnic' (Connolly 2003) set-up, which does not officially associate itself with any particular religious leaning.

The ethnographic panoramic view of the school brings out the structural, formal aspects of school as a social entity in its complexity. It authenticates some of the claims made about the school and at the same time pronounces some unstated facts as well. In all, such an approach promises to render the social reality of the institution under study open to scrutiny.

Notes

1. Pratyantar is a pseudonym to protect the identity of the school.
2. For details about the Right to Education Act, see http://righttoeducation.in/ (accessed on 27 January 2016).
3. Ganesha is one of the most revered deities from the pantheon of Hinduism, who is known to bestow intelligence and is believed to be a destroyer of hurdles in any venture. He is the elephant headed deity who is worshipped at the commencement of significant tasks and ritualistic worship.
4. Saraswati is a goddess in the Hindu pantheon who is associated with learning, arts and knowledge. She is depicted as holding a musical instrument in her hands (a *veena*: a long strumming instrument).
5. At present, Class 8 has only 30 per cent girl students, Class 7 has 40 per cent and the lower sections have nearly 50 per cent girl students.
6. A city in Uttar Pradesh.
7. A curd based curry.
8. A deep fried stuffed bread.

2

School Practices: Benevolence and Discipline

The already complex interactive field of the school and schooling gets further complicated by the ideological perspective, if any, of the school. The ideology may not have been clearly verbalized or expressed formally at times but undercurrents of some functional principles do exist more often than not. Benevolence and discipline emerge as parallel discourses of the Pratyantar School's agenda. Schools do portray a dominant vision that they ascribe to— an ideology, a disciplined life, a value structure, an orientation— that guides its everyday processes but there are sub-structures at work along with the prominent structure. These sub-structures are created through the staff's interpretation of the reigning vision of the school; the mechanisms chosen at various managerial levels to project that one vision may lead to minor variations from the vision. At the structural and processual levels, the school's project is also not monolithic despite a prevailing dominant vision. The students too, on their part, actively appropriate, that is, choose or refuse to comply with the school's agenda. Ethnographic details bring out such formally unstated, yet operative principles that add to the agenda of schooling.

Benevolence has several dimensions to it which lend a complexity to its meanings and implications. Its multiple meanings appear to be relevant for analysing the place of benevolence in Pratyantar. Various dimensions of benevolence emerge in the behaviours of school members as individuals. They sometimes find expressions in the attitudes of a social class towards other classes. A particular understanding of benevolence may influence the aim of the school as an educational institute and, at the same time, another meaning of it could have implications for its social prestige as well. The source of this benevolence is not always the same. Different individuals and groups could be resourcing it from their personal ethical–moral repertoires. These are the reflections on benevolence from the point of view of the giver. The benefactor may similarly have myriad responses in receiving it.

Benevolence as Extending Help

Benevolence could mean extending assistance or help to someone who may not have requested it but needs it. It often has a hierarchical undertone to it whereby the giver occupies a higher position while the receiver is in a relatively disadvantaged position.

Pratyantar School's official discourse presents this dimension of benevolence as its key goal. It is a charitable school, managed and run by the trust of a private school in Delhi. It promises to provide quality education to those students from the neighbouring residential areas who cannot afford to avail of such schooling due to financial constraints. The three key functionaries associated with the school at the managerial level are the chairman of the trust and the principal and headmistress of the school. While the chairman supports the school financially, he also prioritizes the opportunity that the school provides to the students of this school. The management of the school situates it in the larger discourse of a debate about providing private-school quality education to children from the social class who cannot afford it due to monetary constraints. The principal and the chairman facilitate the material support needed in this by bearing the cost of education and providing free uniforms, textbooks, stationery and meals to the students. The commonly reiterated discourse of the school is one of providing opportunity to the students to become educated, confident people who can then explore various avenues of a better life for themselves.

While the chairman extends *benevolence as help* by extending financial support for the structural expenses of Pratyantar School, the principal does so through voicing the concerns of the school to the chairman from time to time and also through his words of encouragement for the teachers and the students of the school. The headmistress has her own way of extending this *help*. She encourages and actively supports the teaching of art, music, dance and drama to the students. In her view, the creative arts have great potential to enrich human beings. She understands these to be a valuable gift for her students who are from marginalized backgrounds. School provides lunch to its students to facilitate sustaining them through the duration of the school.

Benevolence as Fair Play

Benevolence is a leveller of inequalities in a way and thus fair treatment to the recipient/s is significant to its meaning. Pratyantar School tries to be fair to its students by extending curricular, spatial and cultural facilities to them, which are beyond their means. The medium of instruction at Pratyantar is English, which is considered an indicator of 'good' quality education in India. The teachers take classes regularly and students are periodically evaluated for their academic exercises. Handwritten homework sheets with questions and exercises to do are photocopied and evenly distributed to the students before every vacation. The academic assessment of the students is undertaken seriously. Teachers discuss students' performance in exams with the parents at biannually held parent–teacher meetings. Pratyantar School teaches students till Class 8 and, beyond that, the students are transferred to the main school which is a senior secondary school. The co-curricular activities in the form of art and craft, music and dance encourage the students to explore their potential substantially.

Benevolence as Trust and Reliability

Trust and reliability are the less-apparent dimensions of benevolence. In order for a culture of benevolence to operate, trust in the reliability of the provider, by the receiver, is essential. The students of Pratyantar School have this trust in their school. Their reliance on this school emerges convincingly in their responses to a set of anonymous questionnaires. They share their opinion of their school through some direct and indirect questions. They appreciate the facility that this school is for them. They reiterate that in comparison with several other state-run schools, their school is committed towards providing 'good' education to them. Most of their younger siblings are enrolled in Pratyantar which shows their trust in the school. Older siblings and in some cases, other siblings are enrolled in state run schools. At the parent–teacher meetings, the parents discuss the shortcomings of their wards with their class teachers. The teachers highlight the poor academic performances of students and the parents take note of these rather than defending their wards.

Apart from this relationship of trust with the 'outsiders', Pratyantar as an institution attempts to foster bonds of trust among the teachers as well as between them and the office bearers. The principal leaves the design of running the school at the everyday level to the discretion of the headmistress. The headmistress believes in treating the teachers with respect. One of the teachers shares his experiences from his engagements at previous schools where despite the hard work put in by them the principals were rude to them, were suspicious of the integrity of the teachers and employed odd mechanisms of surveillance. He states that Pratyantar's headmistress is strict, but she never demeans her teachers. The headmistress trusts her teachers here, unlike at some schools that have a bias against the teachers. Even on the days when the headmistress is away on leave, the classes are held regularly. The practice of celebrating birth anniversaries of the fellow teachers has also been initiated by her, which is well liked by the teachers.

Dual Paradigm of Benevolence: Hierarchy and Egalitarianism

Gloria Vivenza (1995) traces the roots of the concept of benevolence to ancient economic thought and finds it to be characterised
by a dual paradigm comprising of hierarchy as well as egalitarian-
ism. The class profiles of the students and the teachers presented
here assists, to some extent, in situating the dilemma that the
teachers come across in the course of their efforts as teachers. The
school expects the teachers to carry out the process of educating its students in the most up-to-the-mark manner by keeping
records of the students' assessments, attendance, holding regular
parent–teacher meetings, assignments, extracurricular activities,
cultural events and so on. And in the midst of all this effort there
exists a certain wariness on the issue of familial support in education, home atmosphere of the students and the kinds of homes
they have to go back to, which do not have the support system to
sustain the learning-conducive atmosphere. Teachers as well as the
management have this concern which sometimes dejects them and
sometimes propels them to work even harder.

Teachers' articulations of this difference in the backgrounds of
the students and the school's efforts can be seen in various contexts in the school. One such articulation is present in the resource
book brought out by the collaborative efforts of the main school
teachers and the Pratyantar School teachers. A teacher who is one
of the earliest teachers of the Pratyantar School and comes from an
upper-middle-class family, writes in the resource book, 'everyone
deserves a good start in life and getting good education sets you on
the right path'. In her everyday interactions with the students she
associates the schooling with the only chance that these students
have to move on the path towards success. In her discourse, the
students are taken towards an experience of the class that they
aspire for. She tries communicating in English as much as possible
so that her students get used to this language. However, when she
is confronted by the students' barriers in certain areas she worries
about the impact that the schooling can have after all the effort.
This is a common dilemma that the teachers and management of

the Pratyantar School come across despite their orientations and practices that aim at shortening the gap between the students' home background and their school experience.

A senior teacher at Pratyantar School, who teaches in the main school as well, puts forth her views in the resource book. She writes, 'for this child (the economically weak) there is neither any play-material nor any encouragement (at home)…if they get stimulating environment at least at the school, they can perhaps attain healthy growth and development'. Here also the home is not seen as generating much scope for development and growth of the child due to material and cultural deprivation. School, perhaps, is the only possibility these students have of having a better life. The home environment is not seen as too promising in this perspective too. A teacher from the main school who teaches only the main school students but comes across the economically weaker section students also rues about how, the medium of instruction being English, many parents of the EWS students are not able to understand the instructions given by the teachers in the diary and find it difficult to communicate with the teachers. She finds it to be a major problem not just for the students and their parents but also for the school. The teacher from the main school, who probably comes in contact with parents from middle-class backgrounds—who are familiar with English and share similar classed experiences—does not see not much possibility in this interaction between public school, English medium culture and economically underprivileged, low income, semi-literate home culture.

Some of the teachers from the Pratyantar School differ in their opinion on this gap. A young teacher, who is sensitive to the barriers poverty can place and has been involved in charitable activities as a member of a young peoples' informal group working in slums, insists that with some extra effort by the school the students can overcome the barriers they face due to deprivation at home. She quotes an instance when a Class 2 student was facing challenges at home, her parents were not literate and were economically weak, and she was lagging behind in her class. With remedial work and some extra effort (put in by the teacher) she stood first in the class in her later exams. This teacher's resolve is to 'celebrate individual differences and find a median somewhere'. In her everyday interactions with the students she is friendly with her students and communicates with them as learners, and does not bring the class context in between though she is aware of its presence. Another teacher from the Pratyantar School, who has been with the school since its inception and was earlier at the main school, explains the role of the teacher in the context of the Pratyantar School. She writes, 'a teacher's work is not just restricted to eloquence and ability to explain the subject matter but also involves lively cooperation and thoughtful understanding...a teacher has to solve various behavioural and social problems in the classroom before he/she can actually start teaching'. She too, like the earlier teacher, reiterates about the work that a teacher needs to put in to educate the students. Teachers and the school have better cultural resources to support the students who may not have the privilege of materially and culturally supportive homes.

The dilemma whether or not schooling makes a different does not matter as far as the students from the underprivileged class are concerned, but it remains in the minds of most of the teaches of the Pratyantar school. In their practices, they work towards making schooling effective but once in a while the students' background surfaces as an odd point in the programme of schooling. The class background of the students is often understood by their teachers to be a strong reason behind their reverential attitude towards the school and the teachers. Ironically, the lack of good manners and indiscipline is also attributed by the teachers to these students' poor class status. This paradoxical perception of their students' class background by the teachers complicates their pedagogical exercises.

Benevolence and Reciprocity: Gratitude of Students

An acknowledgement of indebtedness by the receiver is a form of expressing gratitude towards the provider of benevolence. I draw this dimension of benevolence from Vivenza's work (1995). Students of Pratyantar are grateful to the school for all the opportunities it provides them. As they reflect on the significance of their current school in their lives, the students perceive the relationship between their school and their homes and attempt to comprehend it. In their everyday practices, students of the Pratyantar School do not refer much to their class identity. In fact, they dissociate themselves with the conditions which, ironically, have been significant in bringing them to this school. They have internalized the school's agenda of being a facilitator in downplaying their material disadvantages. They distance themselves from the government school students on the basis of their affiliation to this school. The students downplay what they are, in relation to what they aspire to be. More than coming *from* a home, they highlight their coming *to* a school. The school is seen as promising, for the future possibilities it can open up. Students associate the school with 'good education'; 'study and play and enjoyment and freedom'; 'provides facilities that we need' and a rare remark like this one, 'an opportunity for poor students like us'.

By and large, the students of the Pratyantar School are believed to be reverential, obedient and grateful towards the teachers and the school. The teachers, the headmistress and the Principal of the main school often state that they get much more satisfaction by educating these students. Obedience is seen as a virtue because it is associated with a sort of surrender to the teacher. It is seen as the opposite of arrogance, which has been associated with the main school's students' attitudes. The students from the main school have access to greater cultural capital apart from the material support that enables them to access knowledge from sources other than the school teachers. They have access to private tutors, internet, magazines and literature and have parents and siblings who are educated and can assist as well as guide them in learning. For them, teachers are *one* of the several sources of knowledge. However, to the Pratyantar School students, the cultural capital is not directly in synchrony with the school ethos; the material support and the guidance of parents is also comparatively less than what the main school students have. For the Pratyantar students, the teacher is one of the *core* resources of knowledge that can assist them in getting educated.

While the teachers find themselves to be special in teaching these children, (from the Pratyantar) for the sense of significance it brings to them as teachers, they often find themselves facing a situation over which they think they do not have much control, that is, their home environment which is in discontinuation with the practices of the school.

Patronizing Benevolence?

It is in the actual process of interactions that some of the significant issues get illustrated. A lesson in Class 7 on civics is going on. The issue of equality is being discussed. While explaining the concept of social class disparity, the teacher uses the example of this school and explains how poor students get equal opportunity through such schools. There were several occasions when, while encouraging students to do well and study hard, this allusion to the class identity of the students has been made in relation to the school's benevolent presence in their lives. The students are told, '[Y]ou have got this opportunity, make full use of it', 'If you do not do well for yourself then what is the point of all this effort?'.

In this particular classroom interaction, the response of the students is surprising. They too respond as though poor is an adjective that applies to someone else. It is very uncommon for students to identify themselves as poor though the school is organized to address this very aspect of their social identity. It has been observed in a study by Kathleen Lynch and Anne Lodge (2002) that only four percent students in a class acknowledged that social class is an issue and a problem; most of them denied the existence of any such problem or differences. 'Working class identity is in several respects a negative identity (Reay 1998, Skeggs 1997); it is increasingly one which can only be named or claimed indirectly' (Lynch and Lodge 2002: 55).[1] It is an instance of a partial acceptance of the teachers' definition of the situation. The teacher tries to underline the benevolence of the school; the students acknowledge it but, at the same time, resist being relegated to an inferior position in this discourse. The agenda of benevolence is not entirely accepted by the students. The teacher, in this instance, highlights the students' status as beneficiaries of kindness. This covertly tends to remind them of their disadvantageous class status as well. Accepting the latter is usually hard and hence they accept the argument as a third person account. This situation reflects the constant to and fro that goes on in the school over the social class issue. The school stands as a benevolent provider but is not sure whether to claim that status for itself, because in doing so the benefactors are placed in an inferior position while the school proposes to enhance their self-confidence through schooling. Expressions of 'benevolence can be unwelcome because it is or seems patronizing, or misdirected, or mistimed, or ulterior' (Chappell 2014: 88). Extending charity can be a sensitive exercise as the generosity of the provider can weigh heavy on the receiver if the dignity of the human being who receives it is not respected by the provider. Acts of benevolence follow a recognition and awareness of someone's neediness, however, the act is meant to bridge the gap. A subtle acknowledgement of the inequity in this relationship of beneficiary–benefactor is already present. Benevolent behaviour can acquire a wide range of meanings merely in the ways that this subtle understanding is handled. Students of Pratyantar School are no exceptions to this discourse of 'help' that their school extends to them. They are aware of this unequal relationship between them as a social class and their school. In some situations, the gap glares in their face, often through a patronizing remark of a teacher, and sometimes just the reality of it becomes apparent.

What is important to note is that the students are not always weighed down by this realization. There are individuals who do not harp on the 'benevolence' of the school. Their own notions of self-worth assist them in strategizing their everyday existence in the school.

The element of deprivation is not the core theme of their responses in an open-ended questionnaire that they fill. There emerge certain contradictions in what their teachers say about them and what the students think and express themselves to be. For instance, almost all the students describe their homes in positive adjectives 'peaceful', 'restful', 'sweet', 'heaven', 'happy', 'beautiful' and so on. Some less common adjectives are 'familiar', 'important', 'religious' and 'small'. Their teachers are concerned about the homes of these students having fewer facilities, less space, not being 'education-conducive' and so on. Most students however do *not* see their home as primarily a space of disadvantage. In response to another redirected question the students stated that they enjoy their vacations very much, which means that school is significant but home, is an equally interesting space to be in. Many mention their parents' names when asked to give the names of people who inspire them. The school personnel are hopeful of a materially, socially improved future for their students as they have observed marked changes in the behaviour and attitudes of these students during the schooling. They are believed to be confident and self-assured, though not arrogant.

This attitude squarely addresses the students about the social class primarily with an intention to make them utilize the opportunity this school presents. However, in this context, pedagogy takes a backseat and the teachers' anxiety about the outcome of such efforts overtakes their professional role. In situations where the teachers take the class issue to be a barrier in learning, two kinds of students' responses emerge. The teacher, if she recognizes the barrier and shows that it can be overcome, becomes a facilitator. If she recognizes the barrier and her practice constantly reminds her and the students of the barrier, she sometimes, perhaps unknowingly, reinforces the barriers.

This 'being' or identity does not just find expression through the gestures but gets generated through these gestures. The school processes aim at generating gestures that constitute their students as per the school's vision and it is through a negotiation of these gestures that agential space emerges amidst the structural frames. Actions of everyday existence are not abstract and meaningless but are expressions and declarations of certain ways of being. 'Domination is not simply reproduced but is constantly being "worked up"' (McLaren 1986: xii). Such activities often have a tendency to order, control and subdue the experiences that the students bring with them to the school. As mentioned earlier, the school provides lunch to all students. This ritual is also a site where the school's discipline and benevolence are practiced. It is also the site where students display some internalization and some negotiations with the school's norms.

Benevolence, Self-interest and Prestige

'The virtue which was considered to prompt the beneficial attitude is ambition, love of glory, care for one's own reputation rather than (or together with) benevolence' (Vivenza 1995: 204). One cannot help but wonder what the facilitator intends to achieve through the acts of benevolence. The manifest intention could be assisting the vulnerable, but a latent desire to be renowned as a benevolent person could not entirely be absent. The self-interest of the receiver in acts of benevolence is readily apparent, however, that of the giver is also present though not always so overtly. The self-interest of the giver need not always lie in gaining prestige or favours from a larger social community; it may as well be the in the gratification of being worthy, a do-gooder and just a very basic happiness, a sense of fulfilment that one derives through 'giving'.

To the principal of the main school, who has had a very long association with the main school and subsequently with the Pratyantar School as a consultant, advisor and supervisor, the Pratyantar School appears as a much deserved opportunity that the children from economically weaker sections should get. He believes that due to a realization of their deprivation, these students are much more keen students and value school much more, and this, he believes, is a sort of empowerment they have through the school. For him, just by being available to these students the schooling becomes a worthwhile activity; a sort of enhanced worthiness is achieved by those who provide such an opportunity to these students.

The official discourse about the significance of operating this school for the marginalized children largely rotates around the key term 'facilitation', however the tax benefits that running such a unit brings under Income Tax provisions is a self-interest for the giver that follows on its own. I have not had the chance to enquire about the underpinnings of *dana*[2] in this venture as the usual recourse of the school has been to project a secular, progressive image. Elsewhere in this book, I have discussed the implications of invisible religion present in the space and everyday discourse of Pratyantar School. It remains a conjecture whether some linkages with the concept of 'dana' could be present in the prevailing theme of benevolence by school.

The Other Discourse: Discipline

Several factors central to the structures of schools make discipline imperative. Primarily, the large number of students that the schools need to manage makes it essential. A submission to rules, basically rules about what is to be learnt and the manner of that learning, can be broadly defined as discipline (Hamm 1989). Discipline in schools does not always operate only beneath this broad canopy. It acquires multiple and complex meanings due to values considered relevant at individual, institutional, cultural and other levels.

The school's ideology plays a very significant role in defining the meaning of discipline for the institution. However, parallel ideologies operative in the institution may have an impact on the framework of discipline chosen by the school's officials/managers.

A persistent insistence on maintaining an order in the school is at work. However, extremes of any kind are avoided; if the school is not lax on the issue of discipline, it is not punishment oriented either. Persuasion into the discourse of discipline is preferred and force is applied but in moderation. Incidentally, most of the teachers know the names of most of the students with whom they have interacted and even the headmistress recognizes many by their names. Such face-to-face familiarity, in this small-sized school contributes and facilitates disciplining through part force and part persuasion. The discourse of benevolence too acts as a force that elicits orderly behaviour. It sometimes comes out in the rebukes of the teachers when the students misbehave. This is the larger background of the practices of pedagogy at work in Pratyantar School.

Teachers work with an awareness of disciplining of students as a vital operative discourse. Different teachers bring in their individual perspective regarding the ways in which pedagogy has to be weaved in with this concern. Teacher attitudes play a significant role in the practice of schooling in Pratyantar School even if there is some formal delineation of the meaning of discipline for this particular school. Teachers have to work with a working under-standing of it and each recreates it in their agential interpretation of these concerns. Each individual teacher's definition of the situ-ation of disciplining is likely to be influenced by their deep-rooted beliefs about relationships, a general outlook on life—its fairness and unjustness, power-dimensions, rights and wrongs—and most of all, who do they perceive themselves in their role of a teacher. Morrow (1967) observes in his study of schools in Britain that nor-mative connotations of middle-class values are pervasive in the attitudes of most of the school teachers. Even those who have a lower class background are initiated into middle-class normative practices through teacher-training programmes.

Seeking to Undo the Faults

An attempt to rectify the student's 'faulty' practices (read lower class dispositions), Pratyantar School is often found socializing its stu-dents in 'right' mannerisms. The teachers at Pratyantar visualize a set of 'problems' that mar their students. Most of them hold the social circumstances of the students responsible for the problems they have. The teachers and the headmistress keep tutoring the students about good conduct, hygiene and hard work. Use of foul language by stu-dents, mostly when they are fighting, is reported to the headmistress, who makes efforts towards making them quit this habit.

The school also provides lunch to students and that emerges as another site where inculcation of good manners and awareness of hygiene is ensured. Washing hands before meals, offering prayers of gratitude to God and practicing table etiquettes are some of the ways through which Pratyantar School teachers try to undo the rogue training that the students are believed to be mired in.

Studiousness is extolled as a virtue by the teachers at Pratyantar. As observed at PTMs of school, the recurring lament of the teachers is about students not being hard working and studious enough. Watching television programmes and playing with neighbourhood friends for long hours are seen as habits that students find difficult to break away from. By voicing these concerns the teachers hope to change attitudes of their students. A social class connotation shadows this concern to a large extent.

Patterns of Disciplining

Each teacher's outlook on life and perhaps their own experiences at school as students combine to create a perspective on the meaning of discipline and ways of implementing it. I have discussed typologies of teachers, based on their pedagogic styles, elsewhere in this book. If we look for a broader vision of the teachers as well as the officials of Pratyantar School towards discipline, two key factors emerge. First, this school is not punishment-oriented in implementing disciplinary measures for errant students. Second, the discourse of disciplining is influenced, to a great extent, by the parallel discourse of benevolence. A general consensus prevails in this matter so that educators at Pratyantar consider it to be their duty and right to inculcate good values in their students. Some often-heard comments and phrases from teachers highlight the 'social' pattern as compared to intellectual, aesthetic, moral patterns, and so on (see Morrow 1967). 'Social' pattern focuses upon self-control, consideration for others, obedience, hygiene, respect to elders, and so on. The key operative principles of benevolence and discipline at Pratyantar function within the encompassing paradigm of benevolence.

Notes

1. This is contrary to Willis's (1977) study which shows that working class identity is valued and celebrated in his school.
2. The concept of *dana* in Hinduism has several connotations. It is a practice of giving a gift, sometimes material and sometimes non-material, that has multiple socio-ritual meanings. In its simplest form, it means giving away something in charity. This giving, however, is supposed to bring merit to the giver since the receiver is not capable of returning the favour.

3

Classroom Interactions: Pedagogical Pluralities

Pedagogical interactions in the school between the students and the teachers are marked by varied perceptions that have implications for the way learning and schooling is then perceived by both. This chapter focuses on the varied perceptions of learning that different teachers and students have and through which the school practices acquire multiple meanings. It focuses on the classroom interactions between the students and the teachers and deciphers the ways in which the overtly pedagogical interactions are about so much more.

In some classroom situations discipline is given more importance than teaching. The teacher's authority is accentuated in such interactions while education becomes a secondary concern. In a class for Hindi language, the teacher discusses a poem about the value of freedom, from their textbook. As the class is about to end, a student cheekily remarks 'Shall we start a new topic now sir?' The boy is made to stand for the rest of the period. The teacher had repeated the lesson for a flawless presentation before the observer, showing an anxiety for order and discipline. Subsequent minor disruptions in the classroom order were mildly rebuked but the major sarcasm hurled at teacher's discretion was not tolerated. During the lesson when someone talks or jokes about something, they are reprimanded mildly by their teacher. The poem analysis goes on. The teacher's definition of the situation gives premium to the orderly representation of the teaching process with a disregard for the students' perspective. The lacklustre attention in this case points towards students' readings of this absence of integrity. These students have been attentive in his other classes where he taught with integrity.

Another instance is of a Hindi teacher interacting with Class 8 students. She is order-oriented and maintains discipline in her class through warnings, scolding and occasional hitting. Discipline takes priority in her classes as well. A boy is scolded for not sitting in the front seat as asked by her in the last class. She allows students to express themselves during the lesson and does not scold too frequently, but is otherwise known to be very strict and oriented towards maintaining order.

The day's lesson is on the difference between writing a letter and a SMS on a mobile phone.

| One girl: | The letters can be really expressive, detailed and can be saved for the future. |
| A boy: | SMS is brief and can reach out quickly. What you say on a telephone can be forgotten but what you write in an SMS can be saved. |

The students talk about the possibility of saving the content through 'fax' also.

As the discussion goes on, the students are asked to note down the points they might have missed in their answers. A boy and a girl are asked to read aloud their answers as theirs' are considered very lucid and expressive. The students are asked to decide on writing a brief or a long answer. They chorus back that they will write a long answer which can be shortened later. The teacher identifies some students who have poor spelling skills and asks them to be more careful. A girl moves to her friends' desk to talk about something and the teacher reprimands her for doing so. The teacher in this instance is quick to discipline the erring students, especially those found to be hindering the lessons. She has earned the reputation among the students of being hard on them, but the students understand that discussions related to lessons do not invoke severe responses from her and anything else that is found to be out of order is met with some punishment. The students know their limits with her. Both 'coercion' and 'incorporation' (Denscombe 1985: 63) are at work in this classroom and teaching relies on the constant presence of the chastising element.

An overt emphasis on either the benevolence agenda of the school or discipline 'at all costs' elicits responses from the students which tend to deter the school's agenda instead of promoting it. In some other classroom situations, disciplining and benevolence are interpreted in a different manner by the teachers. In Class 1, the teacher engages with her students in a congenial, equal and friendly manner. No particular lesson is being taken but the students are to finish an assignment given to them earlier. One student who has not brought his exercise book is asked the reason for not bringing it to the class. His excuse is that his mother kept it somewhere and forgot. At this, others exclaim that they never forget theirs' ever. The child is excused. The teacher sets a target of a count till twenty to finish the work given. The students request it to be extended till 'thirty'. The class quietens suddenly and the students start working quickly to finish in time. They keep submitting their class work notebooks as they finish their work. One student is asked whether he has finished his work and he very confidently raises his brows, keeps his notebook on the teacher's desk and comes back to his seat. Some students start counting faster than the teacher herself. Those who have finished their work are either engaged in paper craft, or reading a picture book or discussing some issue. One child keeps exclaiming how some of the students have yet not completed their work. One student reminds the teacher of the coming count, while he himself is not finished with his work. The students feel free to express and explore various aspects of learning and being responsible. It is lunch break after this and they are out in small groups for washing their hands; are asked to make sure their classmates got their lunch and then are asked to spread handkerchiefs beneath their plates.

There is a certain freedom that the students enjoy in interacting with most of their teachers. This allows them to come up with queries and gives space for self-expression which often suffers in classroom situation where teachers are concerned about the discipline and keeping the class quiet. This freedom to express becomes even more significant in this school as its students come from a class background which is hierarchically weaker than that of the teachers. In a math lesson in Class 8, the students are working on a problem and there is a minor debate about how the sum should be solved. The math teacher is relatively much friendlier with the students than some other teachers. She seldom scolds and is sensitive towards their idiosyncrasies. She asks them if they are done with the problem; some need more time which she allows. Students move around in the classroom once in a while, discussing the problem,   but are not scolded. They are excited about their work. Finally, all wait for the teacher to announce the result so they can know if they are right. She solves the problem on the blackboard, explaining each step; the students are describing the steps along with her, and they are alert, 'with her'. At one point she stops and asks for a step to be explained and there is some confusion. At this, a boy runs with his notebook to the teacher and shows her his way of solving that step. He is brimming with confidence, the teacher approves of his point and the session moves on.

This same class has their science lesson with her in the next period. In both the episodes, what is most palpable is an eagerness to respond and to participate in the discussion. Students speak in clear loud voices. One girl's response to a question is more textbookish; she is encouraged to express her point in simpler words. Another girl is not able to respond to the question posed to her but she is not reprimanded for this. The teacher explains the point to her and the other students also contribute to the lesson through eager participation.

An eagerness to learn is a common pattern that emerges during classroom observations. Avenues to express themselves in these settings are also appreciated by the students; in responding to the teacher's questions, in asking her for clarifications regarding the confusions they have, in speaking to their desk-mates or desk neighbours during the lessons or discussions. Another common behaviour pattern is students moving in the classroom to ask someone about some work and going to a friend's desk for some help once in a while. They are not petrified of their teachers. They read the normative expectations each teacher has of them and work accordingly. They read the underlying implications of each teacher's pedagogy and act accordingly. In some instances they offer resistance to teacher's definition of the situation.

On being asked about their experience of teaching the students of the Pratyantar School as compared to the students from the main school or other public schools, a common reply that the teachers give, during different conversations, is that these students are keen on learning and that they value what they get here much more. Another common understanding among the teachers is that the family backgrounds and the environment at home and in the neighbourhood often becomes a hurdle in their learning career. Back home, they have neighbourhood mates who are not much into studying; they have difficult material circumstances and many have to help at home; there are only one or two small rooms their homes; they too watch television if someone else is watching television. Many teachers are aware of these conditions and maintain that for these very reasons the students are eager to learn and acknowledge their school. Yet, at the same time, some of the students are not able to fulfil what the school expects of them as learners. This remains an underlying theme with the teachers, however, each teacher reads into this theme according to their perspective and attitude.

As Jeffrey comments on the experience of schooling 'clearly children are not being exposed to a coherent set of values but to diverse values that may well also be contradictory' (2005: 30). The experience of being schooled emerges as a multifaceted exercise due to the several collective and personal agendas that are at work in the school. Bourdieu and Passeron (1990) comment on the interplay between schools as systems and class as a social category. They recognize school as systems whose 'predispositions are central to the retranslation and relaying of the primary determinisms linked to social origin, especially social class' (1990: 88). In this school, the predispositions and the central metaphors are of discipline and benevolence. What emerges in these instances and perspectives is that the metaphors shift from teacher to teacher;

while it is 'disciplining' in one, it is 'unquestioned authority' in another and 'involved educator' in yet another. The experience of the school for the students is not determined entirely by a single denominator or key denominators as laid out in the structural intention of the school, but is disseminated in a more localized, context specific manner.

Forms of Knowing

I now examine classroom interactions between the teachers and the students in the context of the transmission of textual content and the teacher as the source of that knowledge. Students' responses to these contexts indicate a non-textual axis of knowledge or knowing that is used by the students. The cultural resources that the students bring in the classroom are varied, while the teacher is bound by the limits of the text and set patterns of transmission of the texts. This aspect of classroom interactions lends a complexity to school experience that needs to be looked into for its implications for agential action by the students.

Textual Contexts

It is the teacher who is privileged in the power equation between the teacher and the students on many accounts such as knowledge, age, authority and sanctity of the teacher, and in this case social class as well. As Woods points out, a teacher has law, authority and tradition on her side but students have strength in numbers and access to cultural forces replete with strategies of defence and offence (Woods 1983: 31). During classroom interactions, the teacher is the authoritative voice on the texts and the texts are an authority in school education, but it is observed that students bring in their understanding of the texts through their sources of knowing from the extra-textual contexts as well. These negotiations by the students on the one hand show the spaces the students create for themselves in the classroom interactions; on the other hand these show how the teacher's authority is influenced by such negotiations by the students. These negotiations are not just related to the content of the textual information but also to the norms of its transmission in classroom settings. The students are applying their knowledge through cultural sources as well to interpret the texts and wherever those sources are missing or lacking, the students look to the teachers or employ strategies to deal with the situation.

Extra-textual Sources of Knowing

Textual knowledge represents the structural framework within which school education is largely imparted. While texts are meant to present knowledge in its logically systematized forms and these open up new perspectives for the learners, these may also be limiting in their impact. These texts cannot decipher the contextual dynamics of the classrooms where these are being disseminated, although the teacher's mediation plays an important role here. The focus here is how, within the frame of the texts and with the mediation of the teacher, there still exists a space where students draw on their extra-textual sources of knowing. This further becomes a commentary on the classed experiences as well as on the child as a learner in the school context.

Class 1 is being taught a lesson on 'Family' as part of their English course. The teacher is explaining family composition and terminology for the family members. The family is introduced as Sanya's family. The text is a subtle attempt to place the girl child in the forefront and a Muslim family is being represented as an example of family. There are five members in Sanya's family. Once the class has finished discussing the members of Sanya's family in relation to each other, the teacher asks the students (as part of the exercise at the end of the chapter) to draw the pictures of their own family members. Queries of very practical nature begin to pour in. The pictures of family in the book are somewhat different from their knowledge of what family is, and the students address this distinction.

One boy: We are a family of twenty people but now we are only nineteen as my grandmother is no more.

This shows, for him family does not mean the nuclear or a small family of five; family back home means the extended family as well. The members who have left now are to be considered a family or not is another issue that needs to be addressed before the picture can be drawn.

> Another boy: We have thirty one people in our family.

No student poses it as a problem that the book shows a family of five or four but we have bigger families. They are not shy of having a structure of family that is distinct from what the teacher presents to be the norm from the text.

> One girl: If we do not have certain members in the family, do we have to draw their pictures?
>
> Another girl: Does the grandmother has to be shown wearing spectacles?

The teacher responds to each of these queries.

The students decipher a distinction between the text on family and their own family and understand the practical logic that constitutes their families. In Class 1, the students have certain notions about who they are, the presence and absence of certain members in their family and the associations it brings; their dilemma about should one draw a picture perfect family or portray what really is; and the courage to find out what would be appropriate or a certain pride in having large extended families.

In the principal's room, a senior teacher recounts an incident related to a junior class. She says, 'I asked them if you have a small neat house on the one hand and a large dirty one on the other, which one will you take? A student replied "'the big one"'. She says' I redirected the question, drawing attention to the element of hygiene involved in the query, "The big one is dirty." He replied, "I will take the big one even then because one can always clean it up"'. The teacher has the textual context in mind where the lesson is related to cleanliness, but the student reads it from another aspect and focuses on the practical benefits.

There is another instance similar to this when a child is asked to solve a puzzle where on the one end of the maze is a flower and on the other end there is a butterfly. The teacher asks the child to chart the path of the butterfly to reach the flower. The student replies 'the butterfly will fly off to the flower'. The puzzle was about the textual logic of problem solving where hurdles have to be avoided and a path charted to reach the goal. The student here too, privileged the practical logic over the logic of the problem solving puzzle.

In Class 1, the teacher is telling the students about the importance of drinking water everyday: 'One should have six to eight glasses of water every day.' One student asks 'What if someone drinks more than eight?' The teacher explains 'this is an approximate number'. Another boy informs everyone, 'My father says, drink one glass every hour.' The textual explanations bring out the students prior knowledge about the issues being discussed. They often bring these out in the classroom interactions with their teachers. The text is not always privileged by the students, as these incidents show. It is not easy to know how far the textual knowledge is ingrained in the minds of the students; that it is interrogated by knowledge from other sources, is visible in these instances.

Class 2 is being taught a chapter on 'my food'; the teacher asks them to name some of the milk products they can think of. 'Butter', 'ghee', 'curd'—the class and the teacher are moving together in finding out these names. Then one girl replies, loud and clear, '*lassi* too' and adds, 'I love to have *lassi* (buttermilk)' with a grin on her face. This latter part of the answer to the teacher's query is extra-textual in its source and also associated with the experience of fun. Teachers encourage the extra-textual sourcing of knowledge but do not allow too much diversion into the emotions associated with it. As in this case, the teacher replies, 'Yes, buttermilk is one and what else?' She obliterates the emotional expression that is associated by the student with the response. The extra-textual knowing is allowed, but the moment the teacher feels that it poses a threat to the discipline in the class, it is downplayed.

What must be added here is that the textbooks used in the school are pictorially rich and have exercises in them that encourage creative responses and thinking in the students. Teachers, on their part, follow the text and direct their students towards responding to the topics being discussed through reflections on the real life. And yet, if the discipline in the class is at threat due to this recall of the extra-textual, it is tamed down. The agency of the teacher plays an important role in such scenarios. The texts encourage interactive studying and the students can draw from other sources of knowing; the structural logic of school teaching values discipline because the school has to engage with groups of students all present in the same space.

Within these possibilities and constraints, the teacher's agency matters when it comes to encouraging the extra-textual sourcing of knowledge by the students. The students are found to be self expressive in classroom contexts but are much more so with the teachers who go beyond the normative boundaries of classroom control. Students are much more involved with their lessons when this extra-textual sourcing is encouraged as they are able to associate what is being taught with the life they experience and live. As observed in Class 3, a lesson on the city of Mumbai is in progress. The names of the important ports in the city are being read aloud; next comes the reference to the language spoken in Mumbai. The teacher asks the class, Does anyone speak *Marathi* here?' One boy responded, 'Yes ma'am, I speak, but at home'. She says, 'Ok, that is good, please sit down'. The discussion comes to Bollywood. The book says Bollywood is to India what Hollywood is to America.

The teacher:	All of you watch movies?
Students:	Yes, ma'am. (smiling)
Teacher:	Those are made in Mumbai.
One boy:	Big stars live in Mumbai.
Another:	My brother works in Mumbai.
Teacher:	In a film studio?
The boy:	Yes ma'am.

The class is listening to this all with complete attentiveness. The other segment is on the popular food of Mumbai. '*Bhelpuri, pav bhaji*', the students added, '*panipuri*'. They are explaining to each other, 'Don't you know what panipuri is—it is like our *gol gappa*', 'Ma'am he does not even know what panipuri is'. The teacher finds this to be signs of disruption of the classroom discipline. She scolds one boy who is discussing panipuri's nuances with the fellow who sits behind him. The teacher makes him stand and asks to name the foods popular in Mumbai. He mumbles, 'pav bhaji and bhel'. Suddenly the cheer related to the salacious dishes being discussed in the context of 'studies' is gone and as he answers the question the teacher mellows down.

If the teacher allows allusions to the extra-textual then it is legitimate, but the moment students seem to be going into a casual, celebratory mode due to this the teacher stops them. This is the prioritizing of the teacher's and school's definition of what learning means and how should it be accomplished; the students' version is considered less significant. However, for the students the extra-textual knowledge is a significant source of negotiating the text. When these fail to assist, the students either fiddle with protective strategies or they wait and listen to what teacher tells them. For instance, in this same lesson *shrikhand* (sweetened yoghurt) is being talked about.

Teacher: Have you tasted *shrikhand*?

Students: (no one had).

Teacher: Ask your mom to give you shrikhand.

The students just listen to her with no response. Similarly, at one point she asks them to name the major airport in Delhi. Again no one knows. She repeats 'the major airport?' Here, the class repeats back 'the major airport'. She asks, 'Yes, the name?' They repeat 'major'.

The teacher finds the students to be unresponsive and difficult to teach because of their kind of backgrounds. Alluding to their class identity, the teacher finds the students' level of extra-textual know-how to be somewhat deficient; however, the observation shows that the students are using several extra-textual contexts and falter only when a certain context is unavailable to them. Wherever they have access to a link in the real world with the text that they are being taught, they quickly associate with it. The teacher fails to locate the technique used by the students, looks only at the unsuccessful episodes and reiterates that much more effort is required to teach these students as compared to her own children at home.

The students are taken on an outing to the planetarium. Class 2 students report back to their teacher, 'Those things seemed like crackers on *Diwali*'. That's how they make sense of it all initially; the teacher explains to them what it actually was. They however, had created their own understanding of what they have seen.

One day, Class 7 is being observed while they are having their Sanskrit lesson with their teacher; the students are asked to translate Hindi sentences into Sanskrit. The teacher writes the correct responses on the board. One particular boy occupying the last bench in one of the rows sits uninterested in all that is going on; he sits straight and does not disturb the others. Once this class is over, another teacher enters the room and asks for the ventilators to be opened. Now this student is suddenly alert and active and is standing in the front, instructing the others on how to go about it. Classroom contexts can be seen as unappealing and not very significant by the students in the absence of an immediate association with some meaning that makes sense to them. Contradicting the teacher, being dull during the class and becoming active in other contexts are pointers towards how, in the absence of meaning that appeals to the students, classroom interactions can prove to be insignificant to the students and challenging for the teachers. Students sometimes find it difficult to memorize the poems but can deliver songs from popular films with flawless precision. The skill is certainly not missing but unless the interaction is meaningful the contexts are not remembered. The use of extra-textual sources of knowing makes texts meaningful; students of all ages employ these to negotiate texts. When class experiences fail to provide extra-textual contexts to learning in classrooms, the students employ other strategies to give it some meaning.

English Language: Coping Strategies

In schools in India, the medium of instruction is one axis through which the schools are distinguished from one other. The distinction witnesses a culturally privileged place for English medium schools which are primarily private endeavours as compared to the vernacular medium, state-run public schools. 'English thus remains a class factor in Indian society...the reproduction of this...divide is firmly secured through the dual educational system, with government schools using Hindi' (Waldrop 2004: 204). The socio-economic background and world view of the parents determines the choice of school. English medium public school management claims that even if somehow a few students from the less privileged backgrounds manage to get admission to these schools they face many obstacles in terms of what school can potentially provide to its students from upper middle-class homes. Language is a problem in classroom comprehension; parents and school may have communication problems and the school's value system could prove to be very different from the child's value system. That same school would appreciate parent support for the upper middle-class students but would expect the child from the underprivileged background to delink from his home associations as much as possible.

Social class, in the Indian context, correlates with the medium of instruction in schools in a way that shows a link with a kind of value system that gets transmitted through these. This reflects not just in everyday activities in schools but also in the textbooks. Most non-elite school students have access to the NCERT books usually. English language textbooks focus on the issue of unity and diversity, a narrowly defined nationalist agenda, rather than on the pedagogic exercise of mastering the language. There is a quiz-like structure to the lessons where the focus is on arriving at the correct answer and not so much on understanding the contexts or getting educated in the creative expression of ideas. English teaching in non-elite schools that are vernacular in medium remains a poor exercise in terms of leaning a new language and its structures as the predominant cultural values are different from elite English medium schools

(Advani 2009). Class, in India, has a strong language component. The vernacular has other ways of expressing its discourses. The vernacular medium, very often, is not only a shift in the medium of expression but is a different value system altogether. Language is not just a means of communication; it carries a cultural content in it because it has a cultural location to it. This cultural space that a language creates has significance for the categories it deals with. Class, religion, value systems, all these are correlated with the language. The language with its cultural location can create different images of a similar sounding concept. In India, the medium of instruction of the school is not comprehended as merely a matter of language but correlates with the social class of the students that attend that school. The divide is not just between the private English medium schools and the government-run Hindi/vernacular medium schools but within the English medium based schools as well; one is the category of those schools where the students belong to a home culture where English is spoken and another is the category of those where the students are the first generation of English learners. Both are formally called English medium schools, but the latter aspires to be what the former is already. This cultural divide which manifests itself in the medium of instruction at the school has a class aspect to it and the issues surrounding language, in this context, in India, have deeper meanings.

English is the medium of education in this school and this points towards an agenda that the school has for its students. It aims to provide education at par with the main school. The students communicate in English during the lessons as far as they can, though there is no pressure on them to use it in interaction with the teachers or among the classmates. The teachers take lessons in English but often use Hindi to make a point clearer or to make them understand a concept or an issue. Sometimes some teacher explains to me why they have to use this mode of bilingualism, '[T]his is how we have to carry out the lessons…to make them understand…since their (English) language is not too good'; 'We have to use Hindi intermittently'.

The students, in another context, state that in a list of contributions that their school has made to their lives, proficiency in English language remains the last and the least. Students say that they get a good education but they feel that English is not a priority of the school. The school on its part arranges for texts in the English medium and the whole curriculum is in the English medium. The teachers primarily instruct in English and yet, at the end, proficiency in English suffers. In the Indian context, the English language has come to be associated with a certain social class. Parents try hard to send their children to schools that can make them proficient in English, even if it means paying fees which are not easily within their means. Low income group families who can send their children to schools but cannot afford high fees settle for government schools where English is not the core medium of instruction. In urban areas as well as in provincial towns, there is a clear preference for English medium education.

While the Pratyantar school promises a certain future by making its medium of instruction English, the teachers perceive a roadblock in this which they often attribute to the class background of the students. The students express themselves as placed much more favourably as compared to the 'government schools' but they too identify a certain lack in this sector of being educated. All the students are first generation English learners and share a peculiar relationship with this language. They want to be proficient in it but also have barriers. The school's instructional mode and textbooks promise its availability for them and they are proud of this but they sometimes realize that they have not yet mastered the language. When the interactions with the teachers go smoothly in English and the teacher encourages them to communicate in English, they are reassured of their connection with the language. However, if the process of learning this language faces problems such as the inability of the students to pronounce words correctly since they are not habitual listeners of the language, or when they cannot spell certain words or when they fail to express themselves coherently in English, then the students employ other strategies to place this lack in a meaningful context.

Several teachers not only teach the students in English but also communicate with them outside classroom contexts in English so that the students improve their language skills. Class 5 is having their social science lesson on the British *Raj*. The teacher of this class is also their class teacher. She always speaks to her students in English and is never found stating the presence of barriers in these students' capacity to learn English. She is a young teacher and is very serious about her work. The pace and atmosphere of this lesson is very different. The students not only communicate in English but are also quick in their responses to the teacher's questions. They not only carefully provide answers but are also particular about the pronunciation. Students asked counter questions relating to something they learnt earlier. To a question the students reply, 'The cape of no hope'. At this, one student asks 'Ma'am where is Copenhagen?' She replies and associates it with the environment issues as well. Meanings of terms, explained in English and sometimes in Hindi, synonyms of words, events and meanings of terms associated with those events are often discussed in this class with this teacher. She asks the meaning of 'monopoly'. One boy replies 'That's a game'; the teacher says, 'No I am not talking about that'; some other student explains the meaning correctly. If the teacher decides that the students do not have a handicap in learning the language, then the students too display a greater efficiency. The point is not so much about blaming the teacher for what the students perceive themselves to be; rather, it is much more about how the 'definition of the situation' leaves a clear impact on the self-conception, both for the teachers as well as for the students. The definition of the situation is surely not the only factor that determines the course of an event but it is a strong pointer towards the perception and intention of the actors involved in the event. Significantly, different outcomes emerge due to different actors' perceptions and intentions.

When the students find the language to be eluding them in some way, they employ strategies to give another meaning to the situation. They use their knowledge of their first language, Hindi, to cope with this lack. Often students will fill my questionnaires in a mix of Hindi and English words or as one student asks, 'Can we write the Hindi words in English (alphabets)?'[1]

In Pratyantar school, the teachers try to instruct and communicate with the students in English but most of them have this underlying perception that the students here cannot be expected to be very proficient in this language beyond a point. Some teachers give in easily and some try a little harder, but the students are not yet very easy with the language. During the visit to the planetarium, the students are asked by the planetarium projectionist to choose the language in which they want to see the show, they are asked to raise their hands for Hindi and then those who wanted it in English were to raise their hands. Except for the senior most batch, that is, Class 8, most show a preference for Hindi. The teachers are in a debate about the language of the commentary during the show. Most of them are in favour of Hindi for now, since the complex information that they are about to receive will be lost on them if it is in English. The teacher who is taking this lesson with the students in the Class 8 is keen to allow the commentary be in English. Her argument is that if they have to study this lesson in class in English then why do it in Hindi here. Some of the Hindi terms, the special terminology on astronomy, she says, can be equally difficult to understand. Finally, the show runs in English.

This incident brings out a dilemma that first generation English learners often face. Students aspire to be proficient in the English language for the status, prestige and career prospects it promises in contemporary India. Teachers in this school make regular pedagogic efforts in this direction by teaching these students in English with assistance in the form of explaining in Hindi (their first language). The students are well aware of some of the factors that may be working against them and undoubtedly use forms of resistance to counter these factors. They either resort to or insist on using the language in as many ways as possible for instance by watching television programs that use English and by using it more frequently in the interactions with the teachers; some insist on using English as the medium of response to questions or write-ups even when the option to express themselves in Hindi is available. Another common practice among the students, when encountering the issue of English proficiency, is to bring in humour or a stylized usage of the language.

Some of them use words such as 'outstanding', 'mind blowing', and a simple sentence or phrase in an over stylized accent, for example, 'What are you doing mister' 'excuse me', 'behave yourself', 'stupid', 'great' and so on. The use of phrases and adjectives from English is easier to implement as the rest of the sentence is in Hindi. Stylized utterance is a form of excess that is used to deal with a constraint in the student's experience. English language has come to represent a cultural capital that separates the classes in India. They are not entirely resigned to the situation they find themselves in and try to overcome the constraint.

Norms of Classroom Interaction

The normative behaviour expected by teachers in classroom interactions represents the larger agenda of the school as an institution. I focus on the presence of the teacher in the classroom and the students' responses to the classroom behavioural norms expected of them. Negotiations of these norms by the students reflects on their assessments of the teachers while, conventionally, the teachers assess the students.

There are three basic norms that are widely accepted to be fundamental in directing the classroom interactions between a teacher and the students. These are: to respect the teacher, which involves greeting the teachers when one of them enters the classroom, following the instructions and believing that the teacher knows better. The second is: maintaining a certain decorum in the classroom, which includes sitting quietly, sitting straight, making no noise, not laughing, not talking and answering one at a time, and asking for the teacher's permission before answering a question. The third is: maintaining a certain formal distance between oneself and the teacher. Being too informal or surpassing the teacher's command is also not expected in an ideal classroom context as the school sees it.

Students in Pratyantar school adhere to most of these norms, most of the time. Any teacher entering a class at any point of time is greeted collectively by the whole class. They stand and sing

'Good afternoon ma'am'. Teachers' instructions are obeyed. There are spaces within this discourse where the students negotiate these norms that have implications for the students' understanding of their teachers.

About respecting the teachers, students conform to this norm of greeting the teachers and obeying them but there are teachers who are favourites of the students. With these, the students go beyond respect and are simultaneously reverential and expressive in relation to them. The students' behaviour in certain classes and their preference or liking for certain subjects has got a lot to do with their perception of the teacher who takes that subject. Class 8 students are asked about their favourite subject. A girl initially replies, 'We like all the subjects'; subscribing to the norms of classroom behaviour. A little more prompting leads some boys to say in unison, 'science'; the girls add, 'We like math too'. On being asked about the languages and social science, they kept silent. The teacher's assessment by the students plays an important role in distinguishing the regular teachers from the favourites. There us a similar liking for the class teacher who takes their social science classes as well. The computer teacher is also one of the favourites. During one of her classes the students show great enthusiasm about work. She does not demand too much discipline in her class but enquires about their assignments. She declares that they are going to the computer lab today' the class jumps with joy as though they are to go for a picnic! The lab is well lit and has about thirty computers. Each student occupies a seat before a computer and chooses the topic of their presentation. They are asked to prepare a presentation with an instruction that it should not need the click of the mouse to move, that is, it should be that good. Their teacher says that the younger batches are more favourably placed than the older classes as the new lot gets to start from Class 3 onwards. The science and math teacher of Class 8 is also liked a lot for her friendly disposition towards the students and her concern for the well-being of the students, both academically and emotionally.

Teachers in Pratyantar school can be placed in three broad categories depending on their attitudes towards students that are reflected in their implementation of classroom norms. The students' behaviour changes in response to teachers in different categories. There are *discipline-oriented teachers* who raise their voice, reprimand often and are feared by the students. These teachers feel a strong need for discipline-inducing pedagogy and rely on punishment-driven control mechanisms. Students assess these to be the teachers who must be appeased by obedience and the students restrain themselves in their presence.

There is another category comprising *old fashioned discipline inducers* who exercise authority with benevolence, that is, these types often scold and raise voices, but for the sake of the unobstructed learning and training. These teachers focus much more on making the students learn what they are supposed to but except for this there is not much faith in the power of punishment. They are more concerned about being thorough in the traditional way and the students focus on learning in their classes.

There is a third category, *involved-pedagogues,* who believe in complete engagement with the students when the process of teaching and learning is on. Their most powerful pedagogical tool is complete engrossment. The last category is the one which complains the least about disciplinary issues. The students are too busy learning in their classes to be bothered about the behavioural norms related to class discipline. Students participate in these classes with interest and teachers do not fear a breakdown of discipline.

These three categories represent three versions of the way school's twin agenda of discipline and benevolence have come to be represented in the teachers' attitudes and persons. These are ideal-type categories; while teachers who fit in one of these three are identifiable, at a particular point of time a teacher could be sharing the attributes of more than one ideal-type category.

Classroom interaction norms, especially the one that expects students to respect the teacher, undergo negotiation by the students depending on the category the teacher represents to them. Students make the distribution subtly; more than criticizing those whom they do not appreciate, they display their liking for certain teachers more freely. The negotiation by the students is not a direct challenge to the school's norms but is nevertheless a creation of their own space and choice within it.

The students negotiate their position as having knowledge, apart from the one learnt from the teacher, through different ways. Class 1 is being taught a lesson in English when the teacher instructs them to repeat after the key reader in a chorus. This exercise is usually carried out in younger classes to make the students familiar with what they are reading. It is supposed to keep the students alert and involved. The students chorus back with full energy. One boy plugs his ears with his fingers as he too shouts along. The boy is commenting, through his gesture, that this noise is a nuisance. He also knows that this is unavoidable as the teacher thinks this is a good idea that the whole class recite together. He plugs his ears, part obedience and part negotiation.

During a poster-making exercise in Class 8, a student enquires from his teacher, 'I am asking for a donation for an ear operation. Is it ok?' The teacher: 'Why for an ear, make it for an eye or something'. She means that an ear operation does not sound urgent enough. The student however decides to keep his idea as final, saying, 'But a ear can also require an operation'. The teacher relents.

The other norm followed in the school is that of having a noise-free and well-disciplined classroom. Though there is an apparent logic to this norm, there is another dimension associated with this norm, as suggested by Denscombe (1985: 148), 'classrooms are not normally riotous settings (as) quiet is peaceful (and is) productive for learning (while noise) is a sign of poor classroom control'. So, noise-free classrooms signify an 'ideal' setting for learning and a suitably obedient behaviour towards the authority of the teacher. Noise and disorder is taken as the contempt of the teacher; obedience becomes a virtue held high by schools in general. Apart from this, sitting still, not making noise, not talking during the lessons and answering one at a time after the teacher has permitted are some other practices that are a part of classroom norms.

In practice, the students obey these normative dictates but subvert these sometimes through another sort of logic. For instance, answering one at a time after the teacher permits is a norm that is supposed to exist for the clarity in communication but the teachers may use it to select their favourites to answer a question. It is a double-edged exercise; it proposes better learning but has a prospective bias in it. The students subvert this norm. They raise their hands to answer a question but before the teacher selects someone two or three students will say the answer aloud; they do it to prove themselves before anyone else gets the chance. Sometimes students, in their eagerness to answer, start walking towards the teacher's seat from their desk, to draw her attention. This may not seem like a very desirable state as far as discipline is concerned, but it is an indicator of several traits in the students. It indicates their involvement with their lessons, it shows an alignment with the larger goals of learning and participation, it suggests competitiveness among the students and it shows that the students value their classroom interactions with the teacher. It raises the decibel levels but is not unruly behaviour. Within the space of the classroom, in the presence of the teacher, walking over to a friend or classmates' desk on some pretence, asking them for a pencil or some book or other small things is quite common among the students, unless a class is moving at a very serious pace. Teachers admonish them for this but it goes on intermittently. These movements are frequent if it is a craft activity or class work. Moving around, with some purpose though, during the presence of a teacher is a statement of negotiation. Students do not move around during proper lessons but do so when the exercises from the texts are being done. They assert their independence in the course of the learning. It is not a defiance of teacher's authority as students do not do this when the teacher is addressing them during the lesson; however, this movement signifies a mature breach of the norm. When students think it is not significant, they take liberties with it.

Another favourite movement in the course of the lessons is leaning back against the chair. This is a privilege enjoyed by the students who occupy the back row, as they have a wall for support and free space to move the chair to and fro. However, this is not a typical back benchers' behaviour. Some of the serious students, who give good answers and are considered intelligent, do this as well. Classroom norms require students to sit still and be attentive in the class, but such a restriction on movement is not appreciated by young students who are new to such regimentation. Any excuse that legitimizes any break from this norm is seen as liberation from the restriction. It is not deviance but defiance of the absolute authority of the teacher. The teachers restrict such actions but only when these tend to disrupt the lesson in any way.

Circling a teacher's desk during classroom activity or reaching out to a teacher to show some good work or for seeking some advice or clarification is a negotiation of the rule of a respectful distance maintained from a teacher. In students' language it means the accessibility of a particular teacher. Two boys are seen moving towards the staffroom with their charts with them. On being asked where they are rushing to, they reply 'To the staffroom to show our charts to our teacher'. The staffroom seems empty but the students know their teacher is there. They exclaim pointing to the corner where their teacher is sitting reading something 'There, you see our invisible teacher'. She is a favourite and is very slender, thus this remark. The craft teacher is surrounded by the students the moment she asks them to show the things she had asked them to bring for their upcoming craft exercise. The very strict teachers never allow this sort of access; they teach sincerely but do not go beyond a certain limit of informality.

Defying the teachers' authority upfront is not easy and can have repercussions for the student; however, at times students want to express their discontent. One way of doing this is muttering under their breath. Class 1 students are returned their notebooks of their previous day's work. One boy is heard muttering to himself, 'I got neither a 'good' nor a 'very good', everyone got something or the other, some a star, some, 'very good' I got nothing.... I did my work properly, drew the pictures, coloured them and yet nothing for me'. He keeps muttering sitting on his seat but does not come up to the teacher. He judges the teacher's sense of fairness in this muttering. He points to the absence of good sense in his teacher, all sitting on his bench, but does not say this to the teacher. Negotiations of a teacher's authority in the classroom are carried out by the students after reading the situation. They venture to defy the norms of classroom interaction only when their actions are not likely to offend the teacher. They restrain themselves if it comes to that. However, the negotiations of authority are valuable to the students and so they keep looking for spaces for its practice.

Students experience school not just in and through the classes, but also through the other locations within the school. There are areas other than the classroom that constitute the school. Corridors, classrooms in the absence of the teachers, classrooms during the lunch break, codes of hygiene that the school imposes/ expects, behavioural expectations from the students once they are in the school all these are non-classroom contexts where the ethos of the school, is expressed. Gregory Bateson 'has defined ethos as the expression of a culturally standardized system of organization of the instincts and emotions of the individuals' (Reed-Danahay 2005: 107) while Bourdieu and Passeron (1990) have used the term disposition for the same and have showed that dispositions are socially produced. 'Habitus was described by Bourdieu in terms of dispositions, which are feelings, thoughts, tastes and bodily postures' (Reed-Danahay 2005: 107). School habitus is vis-ible in the practices of the social agents that interact in the social space of the school.[2]

Discipline: Recurring Reminders and Internalizations

The need to discipline the students has been one of the prime agendas of schools in general. How schools attain this goal differs from context to context. Whether they do it by sheer force, pun-ishment or through inculcating a reverential attitude through ideology or through daily drills and habit-formation exercises is a matter of the school's discretion. In Pratyantar school, the inculca-tion of values such as reverence and obedience towards the school, the teachers and education is aimed through the practice of regular training rather than through the rule of the stick or adherence to a certain ideology.

The students are asked to move in a queue when the whole class has to shift to some other location in the school such as going for games, or to the auditorium or the music and dance room, or for an outing. They are asked to remain quiet when moving through the corridors and are encouraged to be busy with some-thing or the other when free rather than to make noise. They are not allowed to loiter aimlessly in the corridors and are taught to be polite and well behaved while interacting with the teachers as well as with each other. Discipline is valued and implemented though students are not subdued too much for the sake of the discipline.

The school is certain of making an impact on the personality of its students. The class position of the students is associated with the various dimensions of inculcating discipline. These students are considered to be ideal recipients of an education in discipline as it is believed that they have no other source that can teach them this. Simultaneously, these students are praised for their obedience when compared to the students from the main school, who are considered less reverential towards the school. Alternately, the students of Pratyantar school are considered difficult to train in discipline because of their unsupportive backgrounds. It is against this backdrop of issues related to discipline that the school practices its agenda.

The persistent but not oppressive disciplining is observed in the relationship between the headmistress and the teaching staff as well. Not many restrictions are imposed on the teachers but a laxity in terms of orderliness and time management is also not accepted. The school appears to steer clear of extremes of one kind or the other. The teachers are accountable for their work but there is no overt supervision over them as to how they take the lessons or when do they do the correction work. The teachers report to the headmistress about the progress and proceedings regarding their classes, but they were not dictated the models of work. In this sense the working definition of discipline in *Pratyantar* school applies largely to all the members of the institution. How far do the students internalize the value of discipline and whether they negotiate it, is observable in their everyday practices in the space of the school.

I now focus on instances of *internalization* of the school's agenda of inculcating discipline. Class 4 is being monitored by a girl monitor and everyone is doing their work. Some are drawing pictures, some are reading and a few are talking softly to each other. Work and leisure are going hand in hand and one sees a disciplined class. Another day, the Class 8 class teacher and I are together moving towards her class when we notice that the door of the room is shut and apparently there is no teacher in the class. She says 'Let's see them quietly from the window; they must be into some mischief'. The students are having conversations, laughing a bit and are within the prescribed limits of expected behaviour. The teacher is pleasantly surprised and pleased as this is her class.

Class 6 students are being given assignment sheets for their holidays. The teacher asks them to keep these with care. One boy exclaims, 'I have already kept those in a folder'. It was a plastic folder of yellow colour. At this the teacher remarks 'Look at that, how smart'. Another boy says, 'I have even started working on my holidays' homework'. Good, neat handwriting, completed assignments, good diagrams and pictures in the notebooks are all qualities in the students' work which are appreciated by the teachers. The students, most of them, understand that the school appreciates these qualities and hence they exhibit these with pride. Whenever I peep into the notebook of any of the students, at least 10 to 15 students hurriedly gather around to show the same work in their respective notebooks. This is shown with great earnestness—the diagrams of biological organisms, parts of body, the monuments, any 'star', 'good' or 'excellent' they've got, handwriting, neatness and so on. Some will come up and show how poor their handwriting is to elicit a reassurance that it is quite readable nevertheless. Class 7 has learnt to make ships out of cupboard. A sample piece is on display in their class. An inquiry about the same leads them to bring all the other 'ships' from the craft room. There is a mini parade of the exhibits and the students carefully take those back to the room. Valuing the school work, following the instructions regarding what is worth display, the manner in which the display is managed without chaos all point to the internalization of the school's goal of disciplining, the students.

Running errands for teachers when asked for is also a practice observed in the school. It is not that the teachers make them do their personal work, but when teachers need assistance for some activity related to school work, the students' help is asked for and they oblige. This assistance is seen as its own reward and students feel privileged to be given the opportunity to assist the teacher.

They are not asked to clean up places or fetch things from the market or carry the load of the teacher, as happens very frequently in some provincial schools and government schools where the teachers' authority is exaggerated though class and caste identifications. Teachers in Pratyantar School are disciplined enough to not practice such abuse of authority. A student's selection for running errands for the teacher signifies an approval from the teacher, an acceptance as a good, ideal student. Being deputed by the teacher to carry out a task is seen as an approval by the teacher, of the student's value internalization.

In another instance, the internalization extends beyond mere deputation; the student completely takes over the role of the teacher for a while. A very young girl from the preparatory section, or prep as it is known, portrays the role of a disciplinarian to the core. She is asked impromptu by a teacher to keep her classmates in control. She is a little girl who has joined school in the youngest group of students. The moment she is asked to supervise her class, a transformation takes place. This is a five year old girl. She states loud and clear and very sternly. 'All of you, finger on your lips...I say finger on your lips'. (She gives this instruction in English). She now bears a no-nonsense expression. She pulls out one boy and asks him to go and sit away from the group. When the students see such valour, they start complaining about their peers who are talking, laughing or teasing. She is called out from one corner, then another and then another. She enters the centre of the group, warns them to behave and gets very irritated.

She comes complaining to the teacher, 'You please ask them to stop complaining so much, I can see everything within a very short time (She means that let them not underestimate her disciplining capacity). After a while small sounds of slapping are heard; at this, she is called back by the teacher and is asked not to hit her classmates. Then she resumes her work and now only shows her straightened palm to them (a threat of a slap). 'I can see all of you, so don't think I do not know', she says. She is controlling girls and boys bigger in size than her.

After a point of time all are asked to keep finger on their lips, a posture that reminds the students that talking is not allowed;

very soon there are finger on the lips and gradually the fingers rest on the chin, there are fingers on the lower lip, there are fingers in the mouth, finger almost on the verge of entering the nostril, fingers everywhere except on the lips. Students talk despite the finger on the lips. The disciplinarian too joins in by keeping a finger on her lips to maintain the decorum.

The internalization of the norm of discipline has happened at a very young age in the character of a student. The words and technique through which the disciplining is achieved is very school-induced as she has already not learnt this at home. She is suddenly treating her class fellows as subordinates and behaves in an authoritarian manner. The students treat her like that for some time and gradually the impact wears off. In other instances of students monitoring the class in the absence of the teacher, the monitors assert a sense of distance between the students and themselves. In senior classes, the monitors sometimes indulge in mischief but they remain strict and vigilant, by and large.

School habits get formulated through the recurring reminders of what is right in the space of the school. Students are reminded of maintaining good hygiene and are asked to wash hands before lunch. Having a good and neat handwriting is appreciated and the ones who write in bad hand are constantly reminded of the need to improve. Noisy classrooms are approached by a passing-by teacher or the headmistress; the mere appearance of a teacher in the room is effective enough to restore the quiet. Constant reminders of moving in queues, not being allowed to loiter in the school corridors or playground, being under the supervision of some teacher when a certain subject teacher is absent are all the ways in which the students are made to internalize the body postures and dispositions that the school thinks are appropriate for students. The students have internalized these dispositions and body postures to a large extent and it is displayed in their everyday behaviour. A student who has least regard for these dispositions is either talked about during the informal talks among the students or is complained about to the teacher. In displaying these traits the students have internalized the school habits, they are being obedient. They are acknowledging the school's pattern of socialization and are in the process of internalizing a class culture also. It is also a predominantly urban culture.

The fact that this school tries to live up to its thematic promise of benevolence also, makes these experiences by not being overtly dominating or invasive. However, there is presumably a culture that these students bring along from their homes and it is possible that it may not be in sync with the school habits. This is not to say that at home they do not have a context of good behaviour or hygiene or hard work but the way in which these aspects are prioritized there, could be very different from the way they are at the school.

Resistance to Disciplining Processes

While the students exhibit some integration with the school habitus, there exist equally palpable points of *negotiation* by the students. The negotiations are not too subversive in the Pratyantar School, though the expressions vary.

Defiance need not mean deviance. These negotiations are not an expression of the denial of what the school stands for in its totality but are a way of rejecting some aspects, redefining and then internalizing them. The students are numerically a larger group than the teachers and hence the forms of negotiations are also varied. The negotiations are responses to the class distinction and to the authoritarian disciplining. The students value the benevolent tutoring the school provides because it promises a better future for them but the controls it then imposes on their dispositions and body is resisted by the students. It is significant to know what all is resisted.

'From an official standpoint any negotiation of 'rules' is problematic; it may mean (or be) translated as deviance or anarchy or meaninglessness but these are meaningful and linked to school processes' (Woods 1983: 14). School rituals of domination and control 'function to discipline, administer and limit the activities that students bring with them to school…and student resistance is rooted in the need to dignify and affirm those experiences that make up their lives outside of school' (McLaren 1986: xii).

A school's use of spaces within it, inculcates certain discipline whereby the school wishes to control its students according to its vision. When school acts through its spaces, it is called 'spatial praxis'(Gordon et al. 2000). It is habitual, that is, it recurs and seems almost like one's second nature and yet this is also that space where domination or control is negotiated, recreated or even overlooked as part of identity negotiation. A school's spaces are extremely regulated and the areas under surveillance—staffrooms, the principal's office, classrooms, corridors, playgrounds, canteen, washrooms, activity rooms, library, laboratories, school transport, school stage—are spaces that are meant to give a certain sense of being to the students (as well as to the school authorities) as to what that particular school is about. Absence of any of these bracketed spaces means a lot to their life as a student. The areas in school that are open and accessible, and the meanings students draw from access to these physical spaces, reflect on the school's ideology. It is a reflection of the school's plan for students and also the vision of the school management.

During the observation of Class 1, a boy is seen returning to the classroom, he had gone out to have water. He comes running towards the door and just outside the door he collapses then, on his own, he jumps up and runs towards his seat. It is a bit shocking to see such an act but his bench mate informs wryly 'He keeps pretending to 'fall' all the time, he sometimes falls with his chair, sometimes presents to slip and fall'. The 'actor' acknowledges the truth of the comment with a smile. In the school, the classroom is set and staged by the school; where and how one will sit is prescribed and there is punishment or displeasure of authorities on breaking the norms. However, this student reads in all this, a possibility of having control over one's own body in the act of falling, whenever, wherever in whichever manner, and that it is not going to be treated like a breach of the norm of school's control on the body of the student. This act, and through similar antics, the Class 1 boy is creating his personal code of conduct in the space of the school.

Any moment free of the disciplining gaze of the teachers is welcome. The students are to conduct their movement in the corridors also. However students are often seen doing a little jig on their way to the water tank or washroom, half-skating on the smooth floor of the corridors, humming, walking with a bounce, talking to the fellow walking along and asking for permission to go out and bring back the fellow who has been away for too long. As Gordon puts it, 'if running is forbidden, to run becomes a way of displaying defiance' (Gordon et al. 2000: 152). The students have to make a queue to move from one room to another but the senior classes usually avoid making a straight, neat queue. They always make a semi-structured line that is often interspersed with groups of twos and threes walking along. One day a boy of Class 7 is scolded badly by their male teacher. They are to make a line to go out for the games class and the teacher repeatedly instructs them to get into the line and that boy murmurs, 'Sir, get into the line'. The teacher hears this and thus the chastising. Making fun of the authority-exercising agents is one of the ways of neutralizing the power imbalance. The absence of the teachers in the vicinity often, though not always, leads to a very uncannily common behaviour among the students. They then indulge in a favourite pastime, pushing, shoving and hitting each other.

It is not meant to hurt and is not malicious but it is a celebration of the disorder. This jolly banter appears a complete subversion of all that is not allowed in the space of the classroom. Girls participate in this hooliganism with equal zest, which indicates a non- stereotypical self-image and is a sign of the sense of complete freedom they experience in the presence of their male peers.

Movements, 'bodily comportment' (Gordon et al. 2000: 148), that is, how the bodies are to be placed in the space of the school is regimented. Students may not always conform to the school's notion of its spaces and the meanings it associates with the processes that materialize there. A compliance with the rules related to the mannerisms prescribed by the school, such as the movement through the corridors along the classrooms should be noiseless and non-disruptive; coming punctually to the school; walking in queues; no running in the corridors; no moving around in the classroom; talking to the teacher in prescribed controlled manner; these prescriptive behaviours are ways through which the school imposes its authority over the student's demeanour in the school. It elicits a certain identity-construction among the students and, often, this is the space where agency tries to create a space of its own. Disobedience in these matters by a student may seem like deviant behaviour to authorities but very often these could be signs of another code of conduct taking precedence. It is a form of identity-assertion that obtains its strength from some other institutional set-up—it could be the family, the peer group, religion, neighbourhood, class, gender, media—as these too 'educate' a person in their own ways. Defiance need not always be deviant as in it may not intend to disrupt the order just for the sake of it. The defiance could be an assertion of an alternate way of being and may come up when a student feels that some significant aspect of his identity is being compromised. This can be a potential source of knowing about the identity portrayal through the school processes and identity assertion through avoiding those school processes or by refusing to abide by those parameters of identity construction.

Even after years of being trained to be disciplined the students continue to look for ways of subverting it even if for a while. The teachers see this as a breach of norm, disrespect for the institutional codes and a failure in socialization both by the teachers and the students. The teachers look at it as some sort of deviance that must be curbed while the students look at it as defiance that must be exercised once in a while. These cathartic sessions of going berserk sometimes make the discipline bearable to the students. More than a class based response, it is a resistance to the culture of the grown-ups—the adults. Classroom codes are subverted by shouting out the answers instead of raising a hand to take permission, showing a lack of interest in the proceedings, leaning back in the chair while responding, day-dreaming, working in almost slow-motion, doing some other work in the classroom and so on. These too are not mere acts of resistance to work but to the kind of image that this work seeks to create for the students. The resistance to work and codes of conduct is a mute assertion of some other image that the student has of him/herself. There is not a sustained uniformity to such behaviour also. The attitude of students is influenced by the teacher's perspectives that are reflected in their classroom interactions and in informal interactions as well. Diverse contexts such as the ones mentioned above play a role in the channelizing of the school's agenda in directions that are not always predictable. It is a response of the younger members of the school, reclaiming the child's space in a disciplinary framework. Constraints on the body and movements in the regimented space of the school are set aside for a while through such excesses. Excess in one location is a sign of constraint that is experienced in the same or some other sphere.

Dwelling on the formal pedagogical normative parameters of schooling highlights some of the common mainstream patterns of expectations of schools in general. There appears to be some logic to these expectations from the students. However, its actual implications are not that straightforward. In intersecting with the sets of meanings that each unit of action carries, the school space becomes a playground for the game of strategies and negotiations, reiterations, resistances and reformulations. In this chapter, the social class and its concomitant aspects have been seen in relation to the normative prescriptions of schooling. Students, as representing the 'other' class and as representing the 'other', the one who must learn, perceive these efforts in ways that are not entirely predictable. This space of intersections is relevant for a worthwhile comprehension of schooling practices.

Notes

1. I distributed questionnaires to approximately 150 students seeking answers to a range of questions about their peer relations, views on religion, self, family and school.
2. For detailed information on habitus please see Reed-Danahay (2005: 54 ff).

4

Beliefs in/of a Secular School

If schooling is about developing perspectives about one's identity, about the world and the other, then students learn about this in another sphere as well. Cultural perceptions are also learned—some in school, several of those before schooling begins, outside the school. Religion finds a place in this broad field of culture. Sally Anderson (2011) studies the presence of religion in faith based schools and notes that 'what is interesting about religion does not take place in school' (Stafford as cited in Anderson 2011: 154). It is a significant space in school where religion appears in its myriad forms especially when the school is formally 'secular'. Philip Reiff maintains that 'religion is operative in all cultural realms' (Reiff as cited in Zondervan 2005: 157). This way of reading the presence of religion in various social contexts is especially a comment on the status of religion in a secularized world. The presence of religion and belief systems derived therein, are searched for in the subtexts of schooling practices and also in the minds of students. In this chapter, the cultural experiences associated with schooling are examined in some depth. Schools have a contested relationship with religion with the issue of secularization at the helm and are required to state their position in relation to religious education. They are either religious or secular schools and what is being examined here is the presence of religion in the school through three locations: through the cultural socialization that students have imbibed even before they come to school; through the repertoire of religious symbolism that the school relies on for representational purposes; and through the cultural and mythical logic that pervades the extra-curricular aesthetics in the school and that derives from a religious source. The students' experiences of religion will be explored in these contexts.

I make an attempt to draw out some of the less researched ways of associating schools with religion. The students' conceptualizations of 'God' are explored for the meaning these constitute for them. Religion and its occurrences in schooling have three links for our purposes, one of which lays outside the immediate influence of the school, that is, the 'God' conceptualizations cultivated prior to being in school. The other two are in the school yet not in the curriculum but in the outside, that is, in the extra-curricular. Though religion is present through the religious rituals and other practices in non-secular schools, the meaningful presence of religion is not associated with the space of the school by the students. Here, a 'secular' school is examined to look for the presence of religion in its space despite its declared secular status. The premise is that 'invisible religion' (a concept developed by Thomas Luckmann) continues to permeate the social realm despite attempts at secularization, and that religion lives in the 'cultural memory' despite attempts to erase the specific markings of religion as a cult or a set of rituals (Assmann 2006: 32). There are multiple ways in which religion becomes meaningful for its practitioners and it is through this perspective that the school's and the students' engagement with religion needs to be explored.

What Religion Means Socially

Religious identity has predominantly been discussed in India in the context of identity as visualized through difference. Simply put, it is a sense of identity which defines itself clearly as not-this, not-that with a hint of hostility towards the other. Identities based on religion in India have passed through a contested terrain as well. The historical memory of conflicts and mistrust between such identities has occupied substantial space in the everyday public domain. Religious identity has been problematized in social science debates as well wherein it is seen as one of the most sanguine sources of conflicts and hostilities (see Benei 2009, Froerer 2007, Kumar 2000, Sundar 2004). There are factual reasons for such conflict and it is not always imaginary. At the same time, this is not the only way in which religious identity may be studied.

There may be several other equally vital possibilities for situating meanings of religion in the context of identity. First of all it may be the source of an identity as visualized through otherness. 'As Nietzsche pointed out, this logic of difference, in which the other is defined by its negativity, can only give rise to a politics of resentment… The alternative is to begin to construct a theory of otherness which is not essentialist.' (Gilroy as cited in Grossberg 1996: 97) Religion in the public domain has not always been problematic. The *difference* from other religions need not be the basis of defining one's own faith. Acceptance of one's religion as one of several others is possible, without making it any less relevant. In this work, I explore spaces in public discourse that represent such a 'neutral' stance towards other religions.

Along with this, religion has to be acknowledged for its quintessential quality as 'a way of knowing', as opposed to the commonsensical, and scientific and artistic forms of knowledge. A religious way of thinking transcends the realities of everyday life to wider realms to rectify and complete the puzzling loose ends of this world. Its defining concern may not necessarily be about taking action upon those wider realities but acceptance, or faith, in them.

> It differs from the scientific perspective in that it questions the realities of everyday life not out of institutionalized truths. And it differs from art in that instead of effecting a disengagement from the whole question of actuality…it deepens the concern with fact and seeks to create an aura of utter actuality. It is this sense of the 'really real' upon which the religious perspective rests. (Geertz [1973] 1993: 112)

The cultural space of religion is thus about correcting and completing what is not there and what is missing. It is about acceptance of the truths that religion portrays and amidst all rationalities of science, realities of class and factuality of life, this space believes in that wider reality which is categorized as myth but is believed to be as true as can be. As a well-known Polish philosopher has put it, 'a real participation in myth assumes its approval in the so called cognitive order, that is, assumes a kind of intellectual trust. (Kolakowski 1989: 119)' The significance of myth in the resolution of the crisis of the real life is due to its principle of resolving the problem by its internal logic. Its resolution at one level, though mythical, assures its ability to be resolved to some extent.

Even as a form of knowledge, religion operates at two levels: invisible religion, that is, the symbolic universes in general and visible religion, that is, the religious cosmos in particular is a distinction presented by Thomas Luckmann (1967: 32) Issues of secularization, loss of significance, marginalization and divisive nature of religion pertain to the 'visible religion'. The invisible religion and its formations must also be recognized as making religion significant. 'Invisible' religion permeates life in the form of everyday ethics, wisdom, cultural symbols, aesthetics, artistic expressions and so on. 'The analysis of religion in its cultural dimension focuses on…historically transmitted pattern of meanings embodied in symbols, a system of inherited conceptions expressed in symbolic forms by means of which men communicate, perpetuate and develop their knowledge about and attitudes toward life' (Geertz 1993: 89). Some of our perspectives on life, morality, beauty and propriety are informed by the repertoire of knowledge available to us through religion. It may however not always display its connection to its source and hence may not appear as overtly 'religious' to us. Whenever the question of significance of religion in social life arises, this dimension of religion ought to be accorded equal worth for a holistic assessment of its meaning.

In this work, the idea of 'God' is used as a key query through which students express themselves about the meanings that religion holds for them. The idea is to see whether or not students talk about religion in terms of *difference* or in terms of *otherness*. How do students as children conceptualize the 'God' concept? The next set of enquiry subsequently explores some religious inspirations directing the cultural values that the school is inculcating in students.

Meaning of Religion: Concept of God and Agency of Child/Student

I explore the students' notions of religion asking them about their conceptualizations of God. The reason for choosing the concept of God as the key idea in this enquiry about religion is that it represents the focal point of the overarching set of concepts central to religion. The imagination of a world view, with all its human ideals which is the aim of theology, finds its ultimate personification in the image of God. In conceptualizing God as eternal, transcendental and absolute, the distinctiveness of religious thought and perception is given a form. 'God is a highest conception, not to be explained in terms of other things, but explainable only by exploring more and more profoundly the conception itself' (Kierkegaard in Kaufman 1981: 21). The 'set-apart' quality of the sacred that defines religion according to Durkheim (1912), in his *The Elementary Forms of Religious Life,* is the one that finds expression in the concept of God in almost all religions. Kaufman describes the concept of God as encompassing all the dimensions and experiences of this world and yet not entirely of it. The extraordinary, transcendental, omnipresent being that God is portrayed as in almost all world religions is a depiction of the qualities associated with the realm of religion. This mystical dimension that is linked to an image of God actually constitutes an essential quality that is central to the beliefs and practices in religion. The simultaneity of being in this world, and yet not of it, of being nowhere and yet everywhere are the contradictions that find unique cognitive resolutions in the realm of religion, as well as in the concept of the 'supernatural being/s', the highest conceptualization of which is the idea of a God.

It is in this context that the students' association with religion and the idea of God emerges in this study. This contextualization takes into account notions of God, humans and world views, focussing not on the conflicts or politics of faith but on the significance of faith itself. Questions about belief in God, significance of God, qualities of God and other concomitant cognitive, ethical issues form the core of enquiry from the students. These questions have been answered by the students themselves and their responses range from a very mundane necessity to have a God in one's life to some of the most basic issues of life being associated with 'one's' God. The questions students are asked are related to the conceptualization of God in their thoughts.

Before I proceed to present the outcome of these dialogues with students in relation to religion and God, I wish to remark on the altered state allocated to that the subject as well as the object of this discourse. A common note is the attempt to diffuse conventional patterns of thinking about religion *and* about children. Just as religion is being assessed as a system of cognition and belief, responses from the students on these issues are being seen as responses by 'children'. The agency of the child emerges in the responses of the students. The idea is to comprehend the students' perspectives on the questions of this form of knowledge and also simultaneously, acknowledge the agency of the student as a child as well. Just as the students are being seen as children, notions of childhood are infused with unconventional associations with philosophical insights, morality and spirituality. Some of the recent works on children and religion try to understand children's perspectives on religious beliefs and practices as relevant for their identities and meaningful in their everyday social contexts (Anderson 2011, Boyatzis 2011, Christensen 2010, 2011, Ridgely 2011). A taken for granted, simplistic, childish stature of children's thought patterns are questioned and reframed to accord a broader ground for their complexities to reveal themselves. The voice of the child-student is given priority through non-restrictive ethnographic techniques.

Sources of this knowledge for all the students are their parents, grandparents and some also recollect reading some book or stories about God. The school does not emerge as the source of this knowledge at all. It appears that the school emerges as one of those modern, secular public schools that do not adhere to any religious ideology. At the same time, the responses of the students point towards a 'well-educated' state when they are asked to discuss God through very closely placed queries. They are asked at least three questions that seem similar to each other and yet the responses to each of the three indicate a variety which displays a certain grounding in faith.

The responses of girl students and boy students did not display any particular distinction that needs to be mentioned here.

All the students responded in affirmative when asked whether or not they believe in God. Out of the hundred odd students interviewed, only three stated that they do not believe in god. One girl out of these three said so because she was a follower of Buddhism but she nevertheless talked of faith in the path shown by the Buddha. She insisted on walking on the path shown to her and clearly placed herself away from the concept of existence of a God. The other two students who denied believing in God however did not stop from commenting on what God is supposed to mean to people. On being asked as to what God does, one of the students very categorically stated 'Doesn't do anything'. This resonates with Eck's view, 'Even those who are uncomfortable with the term God, who quarrel with God, or who reject God, have an idea and an image of God' (Eck 1993: 47). This observation by Eck reiterates the centrality of the idea of God to conceptions of religion. In the popular imaginary, the concept of God is widely known and recognized. Even in its denial, the familiarity of the notion finds an initial acknowledgement. This has been the reason for me to select the concept of God as the preliminary indicator in enquiring about matters of faith.

The responses to the query 'Why do you believe in God?' came out in some deep philosophical formulations which were somewhat unexpected in comparison to their otherwise childlike behaviour in other contexts. There were responses such as 'If we remember him only then he will remember us, if we forget, he will also forget us'; 'He is the only one who listens to our thoughts and watches everything that happens to us'; 'Because we have god in ourselves'; 'If you believe in devil you have to believe in God too, because demons are killed by God'; 'Because I am a theist and think God to be the best'; 'Because whatever is happening and will happen has been written by God'; and 'There is nothing called God, I believe in good karma'. The students come up with very interesting, varied responses to a basic question about God. This shows that though what they 'know' about the qualities associated with God, they have internalized the concept in a very individualized, personalized manner. The students did not take a lot of time to respond and that depicts their familiarity with some dense issues related to human behaviour.

At the same time, the philosophical comments that emerged in their responses so readily is a very significant assertion of their wisdom. 'In many religious traditions…people speak of the Divine as both ultimate and personal, beyond and yet within, transcendent and yet near' (Eck 1993: 47). While God is someone 'who created the world', he/she is also someone who 'gave us brain so that we may study'. Similarly another student responds, 'Some people ask where is God—God is in our heart' and adds 'parents are our Gods'. Another one said, 'God is like our mother and father'. God is also spoken about in terms of being there in good times and in bad times: 'Sometimes I get what I want, sometimes I don't'; 'Watches us in good and in bad'. There is an oxymoronic way in which God is spoken about and from being the creator of the world he/she is also seen as somebody who fulfils the mundane wishes also such as 'helps us pass the exam because God can do many things'. The quality to be transcendental and omnipresent is one of the most centric states associated with Godhood and the students are able to translate that into acts that are closer to their own lives. The most predominant metaphors used by the students for God are of God as protector, God as somebody who helps people out of all sorts of troubles and God as creator of the world. A powerful benevolent God is recurrent in the discourse on God by the students: a God who fulfils the wishes of his/her followers.

Despite such beliefs in the cherished qualities of their God, they manage to maintain a functional distance between the realm of belief and 'reality'. The impact of this belief in the existence of a benevolent God is not overtly observable in the daily interactions of the students but shows up once in a while. However, it remains one of the sources of how they contextualize the world around them and how they visualize themselves in it. It is an 'education' that they have not received as a lesson to be memorized for an exam in a near future but an experience that they have internalized from home and parents which they have accepted as a truth forever. Religious mythologies and philosophical assumptions about non-historical essences such as the nature of humanity, the essence of law and transcendental values come under the same category (Kolakowski 1989: 95). These conceptions about God in the minds of the students address some of the queries common to all human beings about what makes things work in nature and in human beings. That these questions have not disappeared even after we have science to 'explain' these phenomena to us is a matter of contemplation. The students study sciences, geography and social sciences which answer many of these questions but how is it that the students never say in their classes or in their notebooks that God has created this earth, us and everything else and that it is who 'provides' all things. And yet when they are asked about God, they attribute all these powers and qualities to God. They are never perplexed by the two zones of knowledge while recognizing both to be important in their own ways. In their minds, science does not easily displace religion and religion never questions the validity of science.

The religion is not experienced as an individual, by an individual, as his own way of knowing; it is collective, and yet 'each individual's biographical narrative (is not) simply a microcosm of the grand narrative of some "official" religion (more so in modern societies)' (McGuire 2008: 12). These students are not responding to my questions in terms of some goals of religion or in terms of the difference from other religions or in terms of essential religious rituals and dogma. When they talk of their immediate concerns about protection, care, jobs, education, good knowledge, health, happy families and so on, it is an expression of a certain agential freedom that they have, although within the institutional framework of religion in its socially structured version. Historian Robert Orsi (2005) brings in the concept of 'lived religion' where religious creativity and its lived experience are considered not an aberration but a norm.

Institutionalized rituals are given prominence by a larger number of students when it was asked what one should do for God or rather what they do for God. Here, the route to God's grace was believed to be largely the one prescribed in their religion. The students refer to ritual reading of the holy books, and offering prayers and performing prescribed rituals. This is where the structure of religion seemed predominant although this predominance was again not absolute. Some very strongly replaced rituals by belief—'Believe in God with a true heart'; 'Remember God'; 'good deeds'; 'help the poor'; 'Have feelings for God'—and some went on to question the capacity of mere humans to 'do' something for God. They said, 'It is not possible, it is God who does everything for us'; 'Whatever I do will be less' and so on. And when they were asked as to who is God, a large number of students provided conventional answers with the various popular names, but there were improvisations which pointed towards a felt need to precisely define who their God is to themselves—it went beyond the nomenclature. One stated 'His name is "real friend"'; some said, 'Parents are my God'; some stated 'Children are God'; some were more eclectic, 'Different people know God by different names—Hindus call him Bhagwan, Muslims, Allah'. 'All Gods are same and I believe in all'; 'Gods of all religions are mine but my favourite is... "Bhimrao Ambedkar"'. Once again, the wide range of personalized nomenclature depicts the familiarity that the students have with several dimensions of Godhood. These also point towards the ways in which the young minds weave these dimensions into the complexities of their lives to the extent of blurring the distinction between humans and God. The response of one of the students who refers to Ambedkar as her God indicates that she is clearly asserting her identity as a Dalit.[1]

Some students gave brief replies to explain: 'Miracles have happened in my life because of God'; another insisted 'There is delay but not denial'; 'Om^2 includes all Gods'; 'God has many names, not one'; 'God is one'; 'We used to get scared at home when alone so when we remembered God at that time'; 'Since I was a child I have been believing in....' These variations in the expositions on the concept of God tells us that while one inherits the working concept of God from the religious traditions that one belongs to (Eck 1993) and while 'plausibility structures' (Berger 1967: 21) are given, very soon 'it becomes more than a concept and we experience God for ourselves...we need to acknowledge our own responsibility for the image of God that we are content to believe in' (Eck 1993: 48). There is an indication of choice here, an appropriation of God in the way the individual experiences the presence of God in his/her life context and the meaning this holds for them. A recent work addresses this aspect where 'children's own perspectives on spirituality, religious beliefs and religious practices are positioned as central to their social identities, everyday lives and social relationships' (Christensen 2011: ix). Ridgely suggests that 'children sort through the networks of support in their lives to find meaningful ways to express their religious beliefs' (Christensen 2011: 13), 'for many children classification as Protestant, Hindu, Buddhist or Catholic might be the least salient part of their identity. Instead the key element of their faiths may be a focus on coping within suffering, practicing yoga, or working for peace' (Ridgely 2011: 14). These observations made by researchers on children in schools around the world and the responses from the students of Pratyantar indicate the analytical capabilities of children to traverse between the visible, institutional religion and the invisible religion. While they are well-versed in the outer, institutional manifestations of religion, they are wise enough to delink their concerns from it if it does not address their immediate concerns. They instead move to its subtler, more meaningful symbolic manifestations.

In a final query in this link, when the students were asked to respond to the issue of non-believers or what they consider the implications of not believing in a God, about half of the students stated that that would lead to bad outcomes: 'God will not help us'; 'No work (would) get done successfully'; 'It is an insult to God'; 'There will be difficulties in life'; fears of losses, illness, failures, punishment, vulnerable state, ignorance, loneliness, no *jannat* (heaven) and so on. A smaller section of students denied any possibility of such a backlash if one does not believe in God. While some simply stated that nothing will happen (i.e., nothing troublesome), some gave reasons why it is so and, corresponding to such views, a slightly larger group of students provided more personalized versions of what leads to and what are the consequences, if any, of the attitude of not believing in God. A student responded, 'You cannot believe in anyone (then)'; a certain archetype of trust is associated with the notion of God here and this statement clarifies that if God cannot be believed in then how can one keep faith in a world which is not perfect. There were other explanations offered for not believing in God: 'Not all are alike. Some believe. Some don't, it does not matter, the one who has faith will believe'; 'Nothing (bad) will happen because it is each person's will whether he wants to believe or not; but those who do not believe, one should not talk ill about those'; 'Nothing, because he (God) does not say that you have to believe in me, he is not against anyone'; 'Even though we may not believe in God, nevertheless he stays with us'; 'Nothing, these are all superstitions that if you do not believe something bad will happen to you'; 'God doesn't ask that you believe in me—he loves everyone alike on this earth'; 'Nothing, but if we indulge in bad deeds then very soon we get its repercussions'; 'God doesn't mind if you do not want to believe in him, it is up to humans who they want to believe in'; 'Atheists do not believe (in God), God doesn't do anything (bad) if someone doesn't believe'; 'One's inner belief may break because God is that source which consoles'; 'Nothing, its each person's viewpoint'.

These are some of the key responses to the issue of belief in God. These put the onus of believing or not-believing on the individual. Each statement carries its logic as to why somebody not believing in God is not the concern of the God but the choice of the individual. While larger number of students clearly align with the view that not believing is like inviting trouble, but even that has not been explained as something necessitated by an institutionalized version of religion. Several stated that for your own good, have faith. Their ability to go beyond the institutional versions of religion through their own cognitive skills of comprehension validates the view that students as children possess identities that cannot be simply limited to conventional presumptions of a student-state and childhood. They are not parroting the institutional tenets of religion but are able to interpret the larger logic and finer nuances of belief and faith. As it emerges from their responses to the issues of God, religion and belief, they convey a sense of knowing a way of life in its practical totality. By totality, it is meant that they had answers to all aspects of that reality; it is available to them and this sense of complete availability provides an assurance. It reminds one of the 'sanctity-state' (Mclaren 1986) where in another context students who are rebellious in their street-corner state are much more settled in this state. It is the space where they experience a presence of something magnanimous and which functions in accordance with its unique set of rules. Though it was associated with subservience and it possibly does inculcate that value at one level, yet the students were most at peace here because despite embodying power the persona of God promises more than it threatens, for most of them. This is one framework through which the students draw their cultural values; though it is one of the several frameworks that they draw from.

Margins of Religion and Schooling

While those schools with a declared affiliation to some or the other religion have logos, mottos and vision statements clearly associated with their respective religious backgrounds and have a school calendar keeping some space for religious activities to be held at regular intervals, there are schools which do not have any affiliation with any particular religion and yet the logo, motto and vision statements are borrowed from religion, mostly Hinduism, and the language used is Sanskrit. If one does not know the background of the school it will be really difficult to tell from their logos and mottos which category a particular school belongs to. The religious and the non-affiliated schools both have logos and mottos that, for example, depict light, book, sunrays, lotus (the logos) and only in some of the logos of religious schools an iconography specific to that particular religion was present. The mottos talk about higher principles of life, knowledge, serving others and hard work.

What emerges is a certain intermingling of the religious and the cultural where religious schools pick up the cultural values that stand for knowledge in their religious cosmic imaginary to represent themselves. While it is beyond the scope of this study to comment on these schools in any depth, what is significant is that even a cursory glance at the representations of these schools through their websites tells us something important. The schools with a declared affiliation to some religion or the other have logos, mottos and vision statements clearly associated with their respective religious backgrounds and have a school calendar keeping some space for religious activities to be held at regular intervals. 'Secular' schools also often end up borrowing cultural idioms from a religious repertoire, though they do not intend to highlight the sacral per se but focus on only the cultural. 'An activity is religious when it is seen as symbolic of some transcendent truths' (Geertz 1993: 98). When it comes to the vision statements, the religious schools are clearly putting forth their agenda of promoting their religious philosophies and ways of life. There are references made to 'Omnipresent', 'God', 'Holy *Gurus*', *Allah* and also to certain practices of engagement with the sacred according to the religious doctrines, such as regular reading and recitation of religious texts, and formal religious prayers and ceremonies which the students are supposed to attend regularly. All religious schools state a parallel aim of socializing their students in the way of life of their religions; they also talk about training them to be part of a modern world. This, in brief, is how religious schools present themselves to the world.

What is interesting is that except for some schools who try as much as possible to abstain from any reference to the 'holy' in any way, many other non-religious schools are using metaphors of religion in presenting their agenda. For instance, use of terms such as sacred, liberation, devotion, realization of the supreme, service and faith, and use of Sanskrit terms that have religious-neutral as well as religious-specific connotations—words such as *gyanam* (knowledge; knowledge of the holy) and *sewa* (service to others; service in relation to the holy). There is mention of spiritual and moral upliftment, Indian cultural values, rich culture of India, core value system and so on. These references to values are not meant to convey modern principles but traditional principles drawn from the past.

As also noted by A. Gupta (2006) in a study of teaching practices in India in the context of post colonialism,

> A review of randomly selected mission statements and brochures of private schools in New Delhi revealed that the articulation of the institutions' educational goals and school philosophies was couched in the language of the philosophical texts indigenous to India as well as in the language of western progressive early childhood education.... Many of the schools also have names and school mottos that reflect Sanskrit words and phrases taken from Hindu scriptures and philosophy. (2006: 3–4)

The schools do not devalue the modern in any way but these are chosen widely by several schools for representational purposes and for statement of intent.

The everyday discourse of Pratyantar sometimes draws from the cultural repertoire of religion. Religion is not formally existent in Pratyantar, that is, it is not present in the larger physical structure of the space of school, it is not in the curriculum and pictures of Gods, goddesses or divine personas are not on display, as noted in RSS.-affiliated schools, Christian schools and *Madrasas*, but religious metaphors, similes and wisdom often keep showing up in the everyday running of the school. The use of the cultural repertoire of religion is not so much to propagate differences but to draw the moral values and ethical inspirations from it. The predominant discourse of theo-cultural values is the one drawn from Hinduism. As Veronique Benei observes,

> [J]ust as in a predominantly Christian nation-state the majority culture is informed by Christian ethics, rituals and rhetoric—regardless of all multiculturalists assertions, policies or even lip service conveniently paid to these conceptions of citizenship—in India, the dominant cultural idiom is that of Hinduism, regardless of the definitional issues involved. (Benei 2009: 263)

The dominant ideology of Hinduism pervades the popular culture in most of India. Despite a stated commitment to secularism, classical aesthetics, gestures, vocabulary and pervasive cultural tones are largely derived from a Hindu repertoire.

There is a very fine line of distinction between perceiving religion as a final truth, an essentialist notion of it, and religion as yet another way of perceiving reality, one of the several perspectives available to human beings for comprehending their world. Though there are several institutions/educational institutions that clearly state the urgency to promote and propagate 'their' religious ideology, there are many others which do not subscribe to this agenda and still value religion as a source of a broadening of horizons. It is not easy to place an institution in one of these two categories but the distinction is significant in terms of what religion stands for in different hands. The distinction between religion as a cultural resource, as *invisible religion* and religion as an exclusive, excluding identity, as the conception of a specific cosmological construct is significant to understand. An exclusive, excluding identification places the highest value on exaggerating the distinction with an intention to separate and stratify. It is not easy to draw a line between these two conceptions when the religion is being actually practiced. Formally, institutions such as schools declare their stand regarding what relationship they as an institution promise to hold vis-à-vis religion, but in actual practice it is not easy to carry out such promises. The first and foremost reason often seen to be behind this muddle is that religion does constitute a significant source of values, ethics, symbols and meanings; languages are full of words that have roots in the religious imaginary; key cultural concepts have been drawn from the religion of a people. To disengage from them is not only difficult but also futile after a while because it is overwhelmingly present. Although keeping religion out of matters of public spaces where people from more than one religious affiliation interact is one way of dealing with religion as an exclusive, excluding identity so that the presence of other religion and its insignia may seem imposing or even a threat, but this is not easy to implement. Here, we will not be discussing the spaces where this secular option is totally rejected but spaces where it has been adopted and yet religion remains present in those spaces. What are the ways in which it marks its presence and what are the implications for the schools where it so remains? Is it possible that religion and secular agenda be present in a common space? This contradictory nature of the social realities is very important to understand as most of the time there is a tendency to exaggerate some conceptual truths as the only operative principle existent. Acknowledging the complexity of social phenomena and the simultaneity of several diverse principles influencing social reality is important in order to have a comprehensive view of the social phenomena being analysed.

The students of Pratyantar learnt about their religion from their homes. The school declares itself to be a private, progressive school. In this frame where students have knowledge of their religion from home, family and where school abstains from taking up the agenda of religious coaching, whether religion is indeed present or not is the question we need to explore. This debate has been alive in European countries as well where increasingly people from diverse religious adherences are becoming a part of the socio-economic fabric of these countries. Cristiana Ottaviano (2010) traces the problematic in the context of state schools in Italy. In 2003, a Muslim parent petitioned to have the crucifix removed from his son's classroom in a school of Ofena. There was a roaring response in the media about the use of this symbol 'that goes beyond its religious significance, where it stands for common values and not least, as a symbol of national identity'…(the then education minister is quoted) 'the crucifix is an inalienable symbol that is bound to our history, to our traditions and to our national identity' (2010: 198). 'The then Chairman of the Culture Commission…suggested a campaign for the crucifix in schools on the ground that Christianity is not a religion like others because it is founded in freedom and, unlike Islam, does not demand before all else total adherence to its own precepts' (2010: 199).

When the Muslim parent wants the crucifix be removed from the classroom in which his son studies, he is looking at the insignia of a religion which is not his. This is religious identity as *difference*. Similarly, when the officials state that Christianity is not a religion like others, they too are talking about religion as *difference*. For situations like this, where the presence of the other religion's symbols is seen as a threat to one's own religious identity, secularism was thought to be the only way out, that is, one should not bring in religion in any form to spaces in the public domain. The problem arises when religious symbols are understood, by the believers to not just be representatives of their religion but also their culture, tradition and national pride. Religious symbols are theo-cultural: part religion, part culture. It is difficult to assess when the schools intend to promote a set of cultural values in the form of religion and when the schools could be promoting certain religious values in the form of culture.

Asking to keep religion out of such public domains is not futile but is not really foolproof either. An alternative was suggested by a Catholic jurist, Arturo Carlo Jemolo, in 1978 when he wrote:

> ([R]eligion) in schools must be not indoctrination, not seek to provide certainties, but must explain that in human experience there features this element known as religion, that there have been periods in which culture and art have been manifestly religious and that almost all peoples have their foundation in a religion. (Ottaviano 2010: 200)

A non-believer educationalist, Raffaele Laporta, is quoted saying that schools must address issues related to the meaning of life and an alternative to secularism (anti-clerics) is 'secularity' (individual freedom to know the holy). Secularity is explained as a possibility of being open to religious, spiritual quest and experience the holy in whichever form an individual finds most agreeable or suitable (Ottaviano 2010). It is being suggested that the cultural aspect of religion should be acknowledged and the exclusive, excluding part of it should be corrected to avoid clashes. The logic of religion as culture and culture as being religious too is not as problematic as the practical intention and dexterity that is required to implement it, non-antagonistically. The actual living out of this issue is what is most significant because several studies of schools in relation to religion show that the actual practice is much more multifarious than the stated goal of relationship between schools and religion.

School Space and Religion

Although the formal curriculum of the school does not adhere to any religious teaching, like numerous other secular public schools, yet religion as a cultural system is present in all social spaces through agents, through a world view, some cultural dialect of its own and memory in the agents. In this school, religion is discussed in the space of the 'extra-curricular'. Music and dance classes constitute an important contribution towards this endeavour.

It is a diverse terrain that we are exploring in a way, ranging from the religious experience through the concept of God to creative art forms to popular culture. Identities also have several projections to them. Just as religion as a social reality operates at several levels, similarly, identities also are multifaceted. These different aspects of a social reality may have clear connections with each other and may just coexist alongside one another. 'Many group identities are available to individuals…narratives change in response to different social contexts…. Such changes prompt a dynamic, fluid, re-crystallization of individual identity through a readjustment in which a person forefronts certain group identities while de-emphasizing others' (Gottschalk 2001: 106). In other words, individuals draw from various sources of identification. Their position at a certain point of time, in a given social situation does not rely only on the resources and boundaries particular to that social situation but traverses several other cultural contexts to create a satisfactory identity at that point of time.

Performatives of Religion in Schools

The problematic that emerges through this exploration is, What does it mean to have references to religion made in the context of schools? Does the presence of religious iconography and allusions to religious terminology mean the same thing in all schools or does it vary with each context? Is the presence of religious discourses in schools decipherable in an essentialist sense or is there a possibility of performativeness to it? By performatives it is meant a possibility that individuals may interpret these religious discourses in their particular specific ways. The meanings, significance and expressions related to the religious discourse are not uniform and there is diversity present in the performance.

Sanjay Srivastava's (1998) description and analysis of the morning assembly in Doon School touches upon this issue.

> In its form, the assembly has the potential of being interpreted as either a Hindu or a Christian ritual. The time of prayer is announced by the ringing of bells, the 'worshippers' are gathered in an enclosed space, and signing and music accompany the enactment of the ritual. However, it is through the performance—the ringing of the school bell, the single file entry into the hall, the geometrical organization of space occupied by the students within it—that an ambiguity is introduced in the symbols of meaning which animate the assembly. In other words, taken individ-ually, the elements which constitute the morning ritual of assembly at Doon School may lend themselves to specific religious interpretations; however, it is their combination—a combination of contrasts—that gives birth to an altered context, that of secularism. (1998)

However, he refers to an absence of any Islamic prayer in the prayer book for assembly at Doon School and thus a certain kind of 'sec-ular' is at work (1998: 94). Another element which is associated with, religion apart from the assembly (which the school formally acknowledges as a representation of the religious outlook of the school), is food (this however the school does not associate with religious meaning). Srivastava states that in the Indian context food has come to connote religious significance and it seems the school consciously avoids assembly before breakfast because that is a Hindu practice. The noise and melee before the assembly reminds of a Hindu 'pre-worship activity' and is soon converted into an Islamic and Christian practice of silence as the beginning of the worship. This and other references made earlier constitute 'the process of the performance of the ritual' (1998).

While the Doon school denies the presence of any religious markings present in its space, the school's crest is a 'long stemmed oil lamp' which is evocative of the Hindu rituals of worship. The 'site' of the school as marked on a map refers to 'sites of signifi-cance' belonging to the tradition of Hindu community. The motto too was proposed to be in Sanskrit and to go with the icon of the lamp. This, Srivastava says, is being done in a school that considers itself secular and there is a clear absence of consciousness about the *Hinduness* of these symbols of school. Very often Indian values and Hindu values are used as interchangeable concepts in schools. The students are not present to this religious significance of various symbols pervasive in the school space, at least they do not verbalize it, but over the years this leads to a certain way of associating secular within the Hindu context.

The symbolic references provided by a religion are too entangled and engaged with the cultural representations to be explained unilaterally or to be erased through the intent of secularization. Religion is much too complex to be seen only in relation to sermons, icons or religious symbols. Religious philosophy, belief, norms and perspectives pervade the way of life of a people. 'This much is clear: no simple linear narrative or causal explanation, least of all logic of progressive demythologization, disenchantment and secularization is capable of assigning clear, univocal designation to any "concept" of religion' (Vries 2008: 2). When religion is politically kept out of a public space for the sake of a faith-neutral atmosphere, its obtuse cultural representations may often persist and the people engaged in the exercise of presenting a secularized space may be absent to these presences. There are various ways in which religion is represented in the everyday discourse and practices of schools, and possibly with various sets of meanings associated with such representations.

The actors at school engaging with metaphors of religion may not be, always, consciously using them as belongings of a particular religion; they could very well be taking these to be 'values' that make good human beings or a very matter of fact way of speaking or behaving. In such circumstances, the impact of such practices is difficult to predict but its possibilities can be searched for.

References to Religion in Pratyantar School

While students of Pratyantar School have their own perceptions of God and the meanings of religion which have been with them prior to their joining the school, there are certain contexts within the school where religion surfaces in different forms.

To begin with the motto of our school, there is an allusion to 'light' like several other schools in India. Here it must be pointed out that 'light' is not a metaphor associated with Hinduism alone and other religions too have this as a key metaphor associated with the divine. Several schools across religious affiliations of diverse kinds have 'light' or 'illumination' as a key iconic presentation in their school logos. The school logo in this case shows only rays of illumination that reminds one of the sun in an abstract form, so although the representation remains with the commonly used trope of illumination associated with knowledge, it does not seem to represent any religious ideology. What needs to be reiterated is that this has come to be representative of many schools across religious affiliations so though at times 'cultural' representation are not free of religious particularities, sometimes they cut across religious particularities and then it points towards the symbolic character of ideas associated with religions which make them an easy source of being abdicated for representational purposes.

The resource book of the school has contributions from teachers from both the schools and if references to religion are located they are primarily of three kinds. The preface by the principal (main school) refers to teaching as a sacred and noble profession, capable of transforming individuals. In the *first* reference, the profession is being associated with the sacred, and the transformative potential of the sacred is the reference point: transformation that would help the students in facing the challenges in the future and ensure an all-round development of the students. In his other speeches and addresses to the students on various occasions, the principal motivates the students to be 'excellent citizens-excelling not only materially but also in every other sphere through humane and kindly deeds'. In the school magazine, the principal is referring to 'education with value system' and quoted a well-known quote said to be associated with Ignatius Loyola the founder of the Jesuit order, who was later elevated to sainthood, '[G]ive me a child for seven years and afterwards, let God or the devil take the child, they cannot change the child'. These comments in addresses to students by their principal show a frequent reference to the realm of religion for its metaphorically expressive concepts but references to any particular religion are not apparent. The teaching profession is represented through a capacity similar to sacred and even greater than sacred when it is said let 'God' or 'devil' take the child once it has been educated by the educators.

The *second* location is an article-cum-poem by a teacher from the main school, senior section, where she talks of faith having the capacity to move mountains. There is a picture of an angel, a guardian angel.

> Success is failure turned inside out,
>
> the silver lining of the clouds of doubt,
>
> And you can never tell how close you are,
>
> It may be near when it seems so far....
>
> trust in your hopes,
>
> never trust in your hurts.

This reference to the religion is in the inspirational poem (the poet is unknown) which is frequently used by motivational coaches and in the context in which that poem is placed. The figure of the guardian angel is also specific to Christian theology and popular conceptions of Christianity but the context in which it is being talked about remains the key concern. In this as well as in the earlier instances, the ideas that are being promoted are about the value of a good education, importance of steadfastness under difficult circumstances. Religious iconography or terms are used to accentuate the impact of what is being conveyed.

The *third* location is an article by the music and dance teacher from the Pratyantar School. It is not a direct association with some apparent religious representation that this article refers to but associates music with 'fundamental experience of education', 'touch(ing) the deepest chords of human hearts' 'musical harmony allures the celestial influences and changes affections, intentions, gestures, notions, actions and dispositions'. The reference to some form of sacred in the article by the music and dance teacher of the special school, represents a way of talking about these arts as having deep sanctity as well as a transformative potential, and this time the sacred is alluded to in the context of the mundane and, to a certain extent, the lowly profane attitudes of the people in schools. She refers to teachers being unimaginative and school authorities being concerned with the regular presentation of some sort of cultural program in school but, she laments, these problems and the examination driven educational system leave no space for imaginative, creative, interesting endeavours. She associates music with therapeutic capacities, transcendental potential and transformative calibre. She suggests that exposure to such forms of arts not only helps the students learn new forms of expression and articulation but also make them understand that multiple viable alternatives exist to resolve any issue.

Allusions to immersion, transcendence, transformation and alternatives are derived from the religiosity of cultural forms, a common pre-modern way of relating to the cultural art forms, in India.

> Unlike some traditions that have considered music as a secular or profane art, the relationship between music and the sacred in Hinduism holds no ambiguity. Encompassing a broad spectrum from the chanting of ancient Vedic priests to the melodic *bhajans (songs praising the divine)* of modern day devotees, Hindu religious chants and music are firmly rooted in theological principles of sacred sound found throughout the vedic and Hindu Scriptures and associated with spiritual power and ecstasy from the earliest times. (Beck 2006: 113)

A sense of transcending the mundane is recurrent in most accounts of the ancient forms of arts. Music, dance, sculpture-art, architecture and drama are all understood to be sources of moving beyond the human condition and reaching out to approach the divine.

'Musicological treatises such as *"Sangita-Ratnakara"* discussed *Nada-Brahman* (musical sounds and non-linguistic sounds heard in deep yogic meditation) as the foundation of musical sound' (Beck 2006: 114).

> [I]f the music is both understood as *Nada-Brahman* (musical sounds and non-linguistic sounds heard in deep yogic meditation) and performed

properly in the spirit of *Bhakti* (i.e., devotion), then the musician and the listener are said to gain momentum for eventual release and the association of God in both this life and the next. (Beck 2006: 126)

This is the context from which the music teacher expresses her belief in the sanctity and potential of music. Her engagement with the craft of music and dance under this thematic background makes her make allusions to the sacred while she discusses it in the context of schooling of a comparatively secular kind. Music and dance lessons are part of the timetable which makes space for other subjects too which are not discussed as 'sacred' by their teachers, but the school resource book does not exclude her article for referring to the subjects (music and dance) as closer to sacred. What is notable is that sacred is not connected to any specific ideology by the teacher but a link nevertheless exists.

Performatives of Religion in Pratyantar School

Religious iconography is minimal in the school space. There is one small idol of Ganesha (a Hindu God) placed in one corner of headmistress' room. It is carved on a wooden plank and she explains its artistic specialty that it has been carved out with great effort as this wood is of a certain kind. The headmistress choses not to refer to the religious significance of the deity, although in choosing to keep an artistic figure of Ganesha and not some other artefact the significance of its religious meaning is existent.

The second and the only other location in the school where religious iconography is present is the music and dance room that has a big poster of Goddess Saraswati. The goddess Saraswati holds a veena (a musical instrument) and a book in her hands. She is the goddess of music and learning in Hindu pantheon. Students are supposed to venerate her for a successful career.

The poster's presence codifies the context of music and dance in this space; however what forms it takes will emerge in the actual teaching–learning process and the content of what is taught and what is learnt. The presence of the icon on the wall of this room declares the association that music and dance have with the sacred.

The school also sanctions the presence, if only in this context. What the students make of it is another matter.

Coming to the practices in school where the sacred leaves its mark, draws our attention to the prayer students sing just before they have their lunch. Once the lunch plates arrive and everything included in that day's meal arrives on the tables of the students in their respective classrooms, the whole class, in each room, gets up and says a prayer in not-so perfect unison. 'Thank you God for the food we eat, thank you God for the world so sweet, thank you God for everything'. Sometimes the prayer is sung with great enthusiasm and sometimes the students could be distracted by something else and not show the same enthusiasm. This prayer is a thanksgiving prayer drawn from Christianity and students associate themselves with the thanks embedded in this prayer. There is no issue about it being a Christian prayer because the teachers have introduced it as a concept of thanks to God and do not emphasise on its Christian context. Sometimes students sing it with their eyes closed and hands folded, voice clear and loud and sometimes some students do it as part of a routine school exercise where they are looking here and there, saying the words, hands half-folded. There is no set pattern about this devotion-disinterest zones, that is, the student who displays less interest one day could be praying enthusiastically another day and some would be more regular in what they choose to be. Largely, it is another presence of the sacred in the school where the school wishes them to acknowledge the kindness of a benevolent, transcendental presence.

These are some of the ways through which the school interjects the cultural world of its students by its understanding of how religion can be perceived and experienced. These are not always conscious efforts on the part of the school, as at a more formal level the school does not adhere to any religious ideology and yet its various functionaries, each in their own way bring their private understanding of religion to the public sphere of school. Since these are largely private spheres brought into the public space, they are often not part of the institutionalized rituals of schooling but only partial interventions in the larger scheme of activities.

Aesthetics and Religion

The cultural values that the school intends to impart to its students can often be found to be located in the school's practices of aesthetic education. The choices that school makes here are largely school-specific and are not guided, like the syllabus, by some larger, external authority. Cultural activities in the school are the expressive metaphors that can comment on the meanings that the school seeks to prioritize.

One activity that takes place round the year in the school is the music and dance lessons; art and craft is also regularly undertaken and dramatics start happening closer to the annual day.[3] There are two teachers designated for music and dance; a male teacher takes music lessons while a female teacher takes the dance classes. The approach of the two teachers towards imparting aesthetics education is different from one another, though it must be mentioned that they share an otherwise harmonious relationship.

When the music teacher takes his lessons the students are persuaded to catch the right notes in the music while singing. He cajoles students into getting it right, makes them repeat the notes many times and shouts at the students who are found talking during any such learning session; students have to keep repeating the verses till he finds the performance satisfactory. He does not compromise on the quality of performance in his classes but he hardly ever scolds students. His way of dealing with erring students is to make them do the drill repeatedly and make a student stand at the end of the room if s/he is found talking in the class. The dance teacher however has a different way of imparting education to her students. Though she raises her voice frequently to get across a point, that is only when the students do not get the moves right even after several times of coaching. She is strict and very serious while taking classes and is quite engrossed in her work when she is at it but, despite the strictness, she is not harsh towards the students. Most of the time, her shouting is a 'performance', a mock enactment of a real task-master; she very rarely hits her students but she shouts at them often. She teaches dance with great enthusiasm and painstakingly describes and shows each tiny nuance required in the movements. She does not deride her students but goads them to do their best. She takes her guru persona very seriously and her pedagogic style is therefore influenced to a large extent by the image of the teacher as a guru.

The music and dance room is located in the basement section of the school where the staffroom, Class 7 and Class 8 and the open air auditorium are also situated. This room is as big as the staffroom next door; has a tiled floor in white, is well lit and airy, and has very minimal furniture in it. There are two chairs and two tables for the harmonium during the music lessons and music player during the dance lessons. The walls have a board that carries pictures of some dance forms, largely classical dances such as *Bhratnatyam* and *Odissi*. There is a poster of Hindu goddess of learning and arts, Saraswati, also on the front wall as one enters the room.

The students are required to take off their shoes before entering this room; the teachers also take their shoes off when classes are on. This practice is a non-linguistic metaphor for what these classes mean to the teachers, that is the obtuse link with the sacral is acknowledged and the idea is conveyed to the students through this everyday ritual. The act of taking off one's shoes or footwear before entering a space that is regarded sacred is a common one in Hindu ritualistic tradition. It is a way of showing respect to the religious space and in Durkheimian terminology an act that signals the acknowledgement of the sacred as 'set apart'. There are some markers in every religion that announce the presence of a sacred zone; in Christianity it is not the taking-off of footwear but maintaining silence in the presence of the holy; noise is to be discarded. Among the Muslims, the shoes are removed but it is not essential in case the shoes are clean.

In making it compulsory for students to remove their shoes before they enter the dance room, a cultural value is being invoked but which has a religion-specific meaning in it. It is a gesture of respect for the 'temple' of the goddess Saraswati and it has two meanings to it. The goddess is the reigning deity of the art form which the students learn. In taking off their shoes the students are meant to declare their discipleship and also secure an effective learning. The other meaning is largely religious, she is a goddess from the Hindu pantheon and taking shoes off is the beginning of an act of worship. It is the *first* meaning which is presented to the students because in this context of schooling, her being the goddess of learning better articulates her significance than any other meaning. In addition, the tradition of learning classical dances in India is associated with a religious symbolism associated with Hinduism, so much so that discipleship involves reverence for the teacher who is addressed by the term 'guru'.[4] (guru translates, in everyday usage, to teacher, but its cultural meaning is broader than this. Guru stands for the one who knows and passes on the knowledge to the learner or 'shishya'; the word is derived from Sanskrit where knowledge in all forms is supposed to have been given by the deities associated with that form of knowledge and hence guru gets a status which is half-divine even though human apparently).

The 'guru' is revered as a form of divine and the feet of the guru are touched by the 'shishya' as a form of veneration. It is a declaration of the status of the two, the one whose feet are touched is superior, and it is also believed that feet have the body-energy pass on through them and if a holy person's feet are touched one can partake of some of that energy.

The students sometimes touch the threshold of the music and dance room before entering; they sometimes touch the dance teacher's feet also and often they enter the room sans the ceremony and do not touch their teacher's feet. Sometimes before leaving the room some of the students display a very quick gestured move, a small rotation or a dance posture, as a farewell gesture; this is very occasionally observed. Except for taking off the shoes which has to be done compulsorily, the other gestures are left to the students' discretion and no one is ever scolded or chided for not performing these rituals. The music teacher is not much concerned about these rituals and it is in the presence of the dance teacher that these are observed more frequently. The focus in his classes is only on melody and nothing else. He concentrates on making the craft perfect without going too much into the cultural philosophy of the *ragas* or student-discipleship discourse.

The students practice *ragas* (notes of classical Hindustani music) according to their age-groups, simple ones for the younger lot and a little more nuanced for the older students. Some of the songs that the students practice denote the ethos of the music classes.

One goes:

> Bhagwaan mera jivan sansar ke liye ho,
>
> Yeh zindagi ho lekin sansaar ke liyo ho,...
>
> ... Sunder Swabhav mera, dushman ka mann palat de,
>
> Woh dekhte he kehde, tum pyar ke liyo ho...

Translation:

> (Lord, my life should be for the welfare of this world,
>
> Give a life which should be for the good of the others,
>
> ...my good nature should transform the heart of the enemy.
>
> he should exclaim, you are a loved one.)
>
> They would practice singing Kabir bhajans also.

Another song that they practice is

> Humko jeevan dene wale, dena humko yeh vardaan,
>
> Vidya aur kala hum seekhein, ban jayen acchhe insane,
>
> ...Himmat aur lagan se apni har mushkil kar lein asan,
>
> Gyan ka suraj aise chamke, har ore ujiara ho.

Translation: (The one who gave us this life, bless us with knowledge and aesthetics so that we become good human beings.... With courage and hard work we may resolve our all difficulties; the sun of knowledge should illuminate all directions)

The approach of the music teacher towards teaching music is not replete with the cultural foundations of the teaching–learning tenets and concentrates more on a friendly relationship with the students and on fine tuning their melody-sense; the dance teacher on the other hand considers the background of this knowledge base to be remembered as well. These two different ways of conducting music and dance classes represent two possible orientations that can be taken towards art forms. While religion has links with arts overtly and covertly, the practitioners can choose to highlight the dimension that they find more relevant. It is the choice of the practitioner of these art forms to emphasize upon the beauty and aesthetics or the sacral links of these forms; both will be equally valid.

The students come up with their best in the classes of both the teachers; they learn the art of fine tuning the expressions in both the classes and almost all of them enjoy being in these classes for the kind of experience these offer. There were always a few who would feel a little out of place but they could always hide behind the more interested ones and had their own ways of passing the hour.

The dance teacher believes that 'it is we who have the responsibility of giving the students values, having respect for this art because these are very important in life and sometimes back home, they may not be having this kind of learning happening'.

She was upset with the fact that the students in the main school never take off their shoes while rehearsing or taking dance lessons. She is of the view that recognizing the concept of guru is crucial to imbibing the actual knowledge of dance. It seems on one occasion the students of the main school were practicing some dance using a videotaped version to learn the movements At this she was wondering 'unless the guru is present, unless it (dance) flows through the teacher's self how can dance be learnt and if the teacher is not perfect what will she pass on to the students?' 'My students are taught to touch the stage before they walk on it, without their shoes but the main school students know none of this.' More than the difference in the schools, this distinction in the attitude of the students of the two schools is due to the perspective of their respective dance teachers. While the details of the main school dance classes are not available to us, in interacting with the main school teacher, it is apparent that her attitude is more of a contemporary teacher of dance while the Pratyantar School dance teacher looks at it in the classical tradition of teaching and learning dance and music.

What the dance teacher is talking about may seem entrenched in the Hindu world view where reverence and learning are considered interlinked and where the presence of the guru is essential for learning to take place. This kind of discourse is common to several traditional art forms and is not just restricted to the Hindu classical aesthetic tradition. For instance, Tomie Hahn in her study of a traditional Japanese dance form finds the issue of 'presence' quite intriguing. She writes,

Presence...remains an elusive quality of dance...is vital to a dancer's artistry. I wondered how presence could be transferred from teacher to student—is it in the steps? In the relationship between teacher and student?... Presence is transmitted in the folds of lessons; when the dancers learn to orient themselves via the senses during the lessons. (Hahn 2007: 163)

Such ideas about the essentiality of a direct, face-to-face tutelage from the teacher to the student are reflected in the disposition of the dance teacher, to a large extent.

The dance teacher not only expresses her belief in the philosophy of the art form she teaches but also lives it in her lessons to the students. She observes each one, directs them all throughout and moves with them. She instructs them about their shortcomings with quick repartees such as, 'smile', 'feel happy', 'turn around quickly', 'What's wrong with you' and 'move right and then turn'. She has a peculiar way of scolding where her students stay cool and just accept and follow her instructions rather than feel melancholic or hurt.

The students perform very well under her tutelage. She often jests with the students in her own peculiar way; she exaggerates some act of the students to point out the mistake and makes everybody laugh but the student who is being referred to at that moment keeps the focus on what is being pointed out; the learner mode of the students seldom switches off in her lessons. When the performance is staged before the audience, the toil that went behind it gives way to an exemplary piece of artistic expression. The younger students are more concerned about keeping the moves right while the older students get a sense of what their teacher is giving them but most of them learn this art in a matter of fact way because it is available to them from the first day at school. They are not in awe of this exercise, it is dance to them but some get a sense of the meaning of this work as visualized by their teacher; this shows through in the vibrant performances on the stage.

The kind of values being presented to the students by this segment of schooling is not unique to this school, children learn art forms at their schools all over the world, but once in a while the spirit behind the inclusion of these art forms is brought alive through a teacher's agency; the students may not always inculcate those values as a rule but it nevertheless has an impact. Although, in this instance the referring back to the tradition often, by the teacher seems retrograde but her definition of the 'sacred' in learning is about exploring the expressive potential of the learner. Students who perform during rehearsals or practice sessions often appear to be doing so well that fellow spectators (waiting for their turn) watch spell bound, as if mesmerized. On one such occasion, the teacher asked the spectator students to clap for their fellow dancers, 'They deserve a clap, don't they?' At this they all applaud for the group who had performed. The teacher mockingly says, 'It was the poorest of all performances that's why I asked you to encourage them'. At this, a Class V student promptly said, 'Oh when it is very good you say it was the poorest!' Such repartee is not very common during her classes but this time the performance was so good that it had to be acknowledged, at the risk of talking on an equal basis with one's guru. The involvement of the dance teacher with the training of her students often leads to a transcending of the teacher–student framework. She goes out of her way to bring out the best in them. For this she scolds them, mocks and is unrelenting in the rigour of practice. Once they begin to show desired expertise, she is jovial, witty and appreciative. In both circumstances the usual parameters of teacher–student relations are reconstituted.

Within this zone of schooling the students come across a new form of learning and a new culture of knowledge; they are being familiarized with aesthetic values, which are not entirely free of cultural contextualization. The music teacher represents an orientation towards the acquisition of aesthetic knowledge and the dance teacher forms another perspective on it. The Headmistress of the Pratyantar School finds the art forms to be highly significant for the honing of students' skills; she encourages such expressive art forms as these provide students with an alternate appreciation of their own selves. If students are not very good in studies, she believes they must be good at something and through these arts the students have a chance to explore their potential. Students are encouraged to perform on-stage as it is believed to be a significant confidence booster, by the headmistress. At the same time, a certain anxiety or exclusivity related to the notion of artistic capabilities of all and sundry is absent; that is, arts are not considered the domain of only a few, these fields are kept open for all and students are left free to choose their area of achievement. The opportunities to explore the artistic domains available to the students of Pratyantar acquire even more value in the context of their marginalized social backgrounds. The headmistress is aware of the enhanced significance that such an exposure carries for her students. She actively encourages it for the sake of a comprehensive learning experience and as a means of equipping her students with avenues of self-expression.

Religion is seen to be a part of the students' experience not just through schooling but also through what they carry in their social memory to the school. Notions of justice, worthiness, hope, and the non-mundane constitute the wisdom that young students possess as they go about the business of being educated at the school. School initiates them into another set of values that derive from religions, through value education and aesthetics. Religion makes inroads in a secular space in the form of personal wisdom and beliefs and a rich cultural repertoire and impacts school experiences of the students in ways not always easy to map.

Notes

1. Ambedkar is visualized as an exemplary crusader for the rights and dignity of the Dalits/so called lower castes.
2. Om is considered the core representative sound that encompasses Hindu Trinity of God.
3. The annual day of a school in India is somewhat akin to the founder's day or just one annual event where the school showcases it's academic, co-curricular and any other achievements. It is a very significant day with a celebratory tone to it.
4. 'Guru' translates, in everyday usage, to teacher, but its cultural meaning is broader than this. Guru stands for the one who knows and passes on the knowledge to the learner or 'shishya'; the word is derived from Sanskrit where knowledge in all forms is supposed to have been given by the deities associated with that form of knowledge and hence guru gets a status which is half-divine even though human apparently.

5

Peer Cultures

Avery significant but somewhat less researched aspect of school experience, peer interactions, is explored in this chapter. It emerges that the informal peer interactions are a hub of gender distancing as well as a space where peer relations sometimes overlook the gender difference. School inculcates both these sentiments, but through different pathways, in subtle as well as decisive ways.

Peer Culture in School

A very significant aspect of schooling, as a social experience and practice, is the relationships that students have with their peers in the school. Peer relations hold a special significance for students in schools. At the most palpable level for the students themselves 'having one friend, a circle of friends, groups to talk to...makes life more manageable.... For students, having or finding a friend reduces the chaos of the school' (Gordon et al. 2000: 111). Considering that the students spend much of their significant social time in schools, friendships or peer connections are their source of enjoyment, and provide a sense of belonging and a significant aspect of identity. Unlike other school processes, this aspect of schooling is mostly informal, that is, the school's agenda of educating and training its students in a certain medium (language), a fixed curriculum, the routine practices, the timetable and the calendar of school activities are all laid out formally and the school considers itself responsible for these charted out activities. The space of peer relations, though not totally out of the control of the school management is nevertheless a largely informal space where students apply their criteria and rules of interaction and membership. While it may be seen as a zone of students' choices, in many ways, intra-peer group relations are considered a personal matter of the students where friendship ties and networks are not under the surveillance of the teachers or other school authorities. In this sense, peer relations are primarily constituted in the space of the students. Yet, it would be naïve to imagine that peer relations in school are untouched by the larger school culture or that the teachers are absolutely out of this space and that they do not have any impact on the students' conceptions of peer relations. While the key actors in this space of schooling are indeed the students themselves, they do not act in a priori manner and cannot act without engaging with the world outside, the world of peers. William A. Corsaro (2005) situates peer relations within this space of the personal and the public. Peers are a 'group of children who spend time together on an everyday basis.... It is through the collective production of and participation in routines that children's evolving membership in both their peer cultures and the adult world are situated' (Corsaro 2005: 110). In an earlier work, Corsaro and Eder (1990) defines peer culture as a 'set of activities or routines, artefacts, values and concerns that children produce and share in interaction with peer' and thereby signals it to be a very in-group sort of interaction where children 'produce' and children 'share'. In a later text, Corsaro (2005) understands the peer culture as a dialogue with the adult culture where the children's peer culture 'adopt(s), reproduce(s) and transform(s) adult culture'. It is in both these meanings that the importance of peer cultures is situated. In the context of schooling, 'Pupil culture is thus not some kind of an entity in itself but exists only in relation to the many components of school life: in fact it is an ensemble of relationships' (Thapan 1991: 117).

Even outside school contexts peer groups continue to have the characteristics that are displayed by in-school peer groups, as has been shown in the study of young women in an urban slum in Delhi by Thapan (2005) where 'peer group represents that collectivity…within which identities are expressed, constituted and affirmed. This group provides a crucial forum for discussion and communication for the display and performance of identities through an expression of feelings and experience' (Thapan 2005: 219). In the context of the school, peer groups retain this element of constitution and expression of identities except that, here, in the space of the school, the peer culture gets constituted in dialogue with the school processes, such as classroom interactions among peers, teachers' interventions in their routine, school rules and regulations and codes of propriety, interactive zones facilitated by school, for example outings, cultural events, play time and so on, and the recognition that one is primarily a student here.

In my study of Pratyantar School, peer relations among students are constituted along several of these axes, but what keeps emerging is the gendered nature of peer relations. Kessler et al. (1985, cited in Liu 2006) maintain that each school has its distinct culture and a distinct response to gender issues, that is, each school addresses the gender patterns distinctively, that is how femininity and masculinity come to be constituted in the school's culture (Kessler et al. cited in Liu 2006: 426). Gendered selves find frequent expressions in the space of peer relations and the extracurricular in this school. Curriculum based interaction between teachers and students do not however display significant signs of gender categorizations. There is no obvious discrimination or privileging a particular gender in the classroom culture of the school.[1]

'The informal views and comments of the teachers are also very crucial in gender division of school activities and in directing boys and girls to gender-typed subject choices, and extra-curricular activities' (Chanana 2003: 212). Such a conscious categorization and differentiation is not evident in this school. However, conventional gender imagery is displayed by the teachers sometimes, in extra-curricular interactions.[2] These gender discourses, even among the students, are articulated most frequently in the zone of the extra-curricular, which includes peer relations in these zones. It is in interaction among the peers that gender identities are crafted and expressed most openly, though, perhaps not exclusively.

Significance and Identification of Peers

Students in Pratyantar School value peer relations and consider them to be an important segment of the school experience. During an informal discussion, Class 6 students were jumping eagerly to reply to a query about the importance of peers. The significance of the issue is expressed through the students' eagerness to respond to questions about peers: one boy, wringing his hands and a grave display of sadness said, 'Oh it feels I should return home…nothing feels good when friends are not around'. Another boy added 'It gets very lonely'; a girl said, 'That day, I do not like anything'. Many echoed similar sentiments. A boy thoughtfully replied a little later, 'When your friends do not come to the school on a particular day, that day you realize how important they are for you'. Another boy immediately seconded this opinion, 'Yes ma'am that's true'. Across the age-groups, similar views are expressed by the students in this school on being asked the question: Why are peers important? While Class 4 and Class 5 students consider 'help' to be the strongest reason for having friends; students from Classes 6 and 7 are more expressive about reasons for having peers. 'Help' is a constant and recurring theme for most of the students when it comes to identification of peers. 'They should help us when we are in some trouble'; 'friends are for mutual help'; 'only friends help'. 'Help' is delineated by some students as helping in resolving some difficulty related to school work, sharing information about the instructions teachers gave the day a particular student may be absent from school, sharing things such as pen, pencil, scale and so on, the day one of them forgets to bring it to the school.

The next common reason given for having peers is 'fun'. 'We make friends to stay happy'; 'I will be alone in school without them'; 'no one to talk and play with'; 'alone is sad, with friends it is fun'. The experience of not having peers around is recognized by the opposites of fun, that is, sadness and loneliness. The experience of not having peers accentuates the significance of having them around. It is through experience that students talk about the importance of having peers in school. 'Help' as the prominent, recurring reason for peer group relationships in school indicates the urgency of having such relationships in an ever-looming threat of being helpless and in trouble in school. It is an indirect comment on what school may seem like to the students, left to their own devices. When students of Class 4 and 5 say, 'If I forget to bring something to school, it is my peers who bail me out because school work is halted if some "tool" is forgotten at home.' It could lead to the displeasure of the teacher, probably punishment and a loss of prestige, and the consequent sense of well-being is at stake. Many students mention *mutuality* in the context of help, that is, I may need it and I may need to extend it to others. It is a corresponding sense of responsibility along with dependence on others. It is a simultaneous constitution of oneself as an enabler and a helpless being, in the act of being a peer.

The qualities derided in peers are also another indicator of what is valued by students in the context of schooling. In the case of younger students, 'helpfulness' emerges as the most desired quality in others. A reinforcement of this, as a virtue, accentuates the inculcation of this by the students, more so if peer prestige was expected by someone. Being 'good' in studies and games, and being witty and funny are qualities deemed important in peers, but being helpful surpasses all of these. The virtue of being helpful lies in thinking about 'others' more than self or others as well, if nothing else.

Selfishness and pride are two qualities that are detested in peers, that is, those who are selfish or proud do not qualify as one's peers. These two qualities are exactly opposite of thinking about the others' well-being. This is the opinion of students of Class 5. Class 4 students too consider helpfulness to be the most desirable quality in peers but differ from Class 5 when it comes to expressing what is detested in their class fellows. These students very clearly vote out the non-studious ones as being out of the gambit of peers. Disobedience is another vice that is unpopular among Class 4 students. Being studious and obedient are the virtues that the school as an institution expects from students and when students also reiterate this they reflect the impact of the school's ideology over and above an individual's meaning of schooling. At the same time, they value 'help' in the event of a face-off before the school authorities, that is, the teachers. Peers, in this instance, are being defined in consonance with the school's stand on students and peer relations appear to confirm the school values of studiousness and obedience. The students want to, therefore, project a school habitus—a continuity in their relationship to the school. In the previous instance, that is Class 5, having peers stands as a guard against the potential threats that school practices may pose for individual students. Here the vice is, being selfish, that is, thinking of one's own well-being with no consideration for others' discomfort or fears. Qualification to being a peer in this instance expects a collective acknowledgement of the power of the school and an assurance to each other of all help needed in the event of an 'unpleasant situation'.

As the responses of the next grade, that is, Class 6 emerge, the pattern of helpfulness being the most significant denominator of good peer relations is again evident. But two years later, when the recent Class 6 is asked to spell out the most desirable quality in peers, they no longer express 'help' as a top priority. This time 'sharing thoughts and having personal, heart to heart talks' is put on premium. The current Class 7 also responds in the same manner. Suddenly, the pointer indicates aspects of 'sharing' to be the key component of a peer as against 'helping'. Sharing one's thoughts, feelings and at times, possessions (but the focus was on feelings much more than material things) has a connotation of interacting as individualities open to each other and sharing implies trust. Very often the students mention that with close peers one can freely share one's secrets without the fear of being made fun of or sounding bizarre. A boy responds, 'I can share my thoughts with my friends but anyone else would respond with unkindness towards such expressions, might dismiss those as silly'. All the classes respond in this manner: sharing one's thoughts is an expression of distinctive individualities, and when someone listens, you too have to be available to listen to others. The community of the peers thus enables an expression and constitution of individualities and distinct identities. Sharing in the space of school does not directly place the school as the opposing, threatening power but as a facilitator that enables such groupings. They also share the sorrows and fears that are not always related to school life but outside it as well.

On being asked what sets peers apart from acquaintances, it emerges that the sharing of secrets, follies and indeed everything, without inhibitions, is a luxury possible only with one's peers. Unlike the students of Class 4, who place a lot of premium on friends helping you save your face in the event of an imperfection in the student role, the current students of Classes 6 and 7 value peers for the sharing of problems and concerns other than those of studentship. As grown-ups, there are issues that concern them apart from the school work, and hence, the significance of peers takes on a different meaning as does the school in this context; from being a threat, it becomes a facilitator, a ground for conversing with friends.

On asking students of Classes 4 and 5 about the disqualifications of peers, 'who would you not consider a friend', a pattern emerges, where being unhelpful, non-studious and disobedient draws the line between friends and non-friends. Younger batches of students are able to define even a very personal preference in terms of institution's disciplinary patterns. They internalize school norms strongly so that the personal is replete with the collective. With the students of Classes 6 and 7 the questions are varied and more complex, so apart from being asked what they dislike in people in general they are also asked what causes rifts between peers. The earlier batch of students from sixth and the current sixth show a pattern: while the old sixth blames 'fights' for rift, the current sixth, who are much more expressive in their responses, consider 'rudeness', 'deceit' and then 'fight', in this order, to be the main causes behind rifts between peers. Giving away one's friend's secrets, gossiping about them to others, leaving them for others, not paying attention, death, misunderstandings and one even mentioned 'eating my head with all sorts of complaints and too much talking' are the varied and expressive responses that emerge from the relatively older current batches of students.

The cause of rift is mostly indicative of a damaged trust between friends. Sharing secrets, innermost thoughts and feelings are crucial to students' lives because these are the issues often related to identities, what is wrong and right—morality, subservience and dominance, traditional values and modern lives, and how to carry on despite the follies and hurts associated with growing up. These may be ridiculed or subdued in the adult world that assumes to have a sorted out, fixed way of knowing oneself and defining others. For adolescents, these are issues yet not settled and school, with all its curricular paraphernalia, may not be adequate to resolve these issues; it is an adult's version of what education should be about and it aspires to prepare them for the world out there. Schools teach languages to that end and provide information about history, geography, sciences and so on. However, dealing with life requires some other skills, which come from learning at schools as well as from dealing with peers, learning with them and learning to be with them. Peer group relations are the first lessons in the friendship based on notions of help and trust. These are also the first lessons in an agential acting out of one's identity away from adult supervision. Schools become significant for their peer cultures to many students; the nature of peer relationships may vary from one school to another, from one grade to another but, largely, peer cultures have come to constitute an important aspect of the school experience. What students share with peers is something which they would not be very comfortable sharing with their families. While the earlier batch of sixth grades state that peers in school are primarily significant for help in school work and that the family is significant for other 'important' issues, the new sixth graders and the seventh graders consider peer groups in school to be primarily significant for help in school work while family is significant for other 'important' issues. The new sixth graders and the seventh graders consider peer groups in school as the source of 'guidance', 'identifying human nature', 'personal matters', 'handling troubles', 'being together' and family is significant for 'major decisions', 'financial issues' and sometimes help in studies. There is a reversal of roles of family and peer group in the lives of the school going adolescents in the comparative outcomes of the responses by the sixth graders placed two years apart from each other. The earlier batch of sixth graders responds in a manner similar to the current fourth and fifth graders. As compared to the earlier batch of senior classes, the new senior classes are much more expressive, forthright and value peers as equally significant as one's family.

Gendered Peer Contexts

At one level, peer groups in schools are situated vis-à-vis the school's authority and the adult world's authority, but within these school peer groups, gendered contexts have been of interest to many scholars as potential sites for the emergence and construction of gendered identities. Recent scholarship in this field has moved away from a conception of gender as a neat binary and the consequent essentiality that comes with such binary assumptions about gender. Judith Butler (1990) and Bronwyn Davies (2004) have been two significant post-structural theorists who believe that gender emerges in discourse, in the performativity of self and is not predetermined. Consequently, there are multiplicities of gendered identities that emerge through and in such performatives of everyday experiences.

Gender relations in peer group contexts in schools also show a similar trend. While in some contexts and instances, stereotyped gender differences are visible, in many other situations, these are absent and displace the usual associations between gender and behavioural patterns or social attitudes. For Butler, it is the repetition and disjuncture of discourse that is believed to generate agency, not an identity or a self that people possess (Butler, cited in Lembo 2000: 90). Goffman (1959) too talks about

> the construct of performance to capture the myriad ways that people, no doubt located socially by discourses of role definition and normative appropriateness, exhibit agency in the ways they present themselves to others in specific social situations…gaps and spaces of the normative order…[are significant]. (Goffman, cited in Lembo 2000: 90)

The agential expression of identity is facilitated by the presence of a structure of expression of self, but this structure is not absolute and in its gaps and intermissions agential expression finds its space.

The pathways, through which identities are constituted by individuals, involve knowledge of categories which include some and exclude others, for example, male–female, father–daughter and so on (Davies 2004). Participation in the discursive practices, through which these subject positions are made meaningful, is also necessary. These meanings are expressed through storylines. One creates an identity for oneself by positioning oneself in one of these categories. The position one chooses is associated with the storyline one selects.

The certain stereotypical positioning of gender identities is commonly present within the space of the school. As individuals constitute their identities, they engage with a certain storyline available to them; peer communities provide a storyline which influences its members, though not necessarily in a predictable manner. Our earlier batch of Class 6 students displays a lopsided preference for same gender peers in their responses to the gender break-up of their peers. The girls show only girls as peers and no boys at all while it is the same with the boys of the class. The pattern that emerges here supports the stereotypical segregation of genders and strict same-gender peer relationships. The current sixth graders show a different pattern. The girls have peer relations with boys as well, but the boys from Class 6 and 7 are divided into two segments: one that has girls as friends another which denies having friendships with girls. While girls are not inhibited in their peer preferences and associated with peers across the gender divide, some of the boys from the same grade underline the gender divide by resorting to say that they have zero number of girls as friends. 'Zero' was the response of earlier batch of sixth graders when asked about peer relations across-gender. Zero stands as an absolute; there is a finality and non-ambiguity about this number as it closes all and any possibility of anything else except for this closure. It is a dramatic and excessive response and says a lot by itself. There are instances of boys being made fun of in the new sixth and seventh when the number of girls as peers was more than two or three. The boys would use a whitener to erase the number and overwrite with a zero. Girls appeared not to be under such pressure to deny their friendships with boys denoting an acceptance of cross-gender peer relations, and since the number of girls was less in these sections as compared to the number of boys, girls had a choice of having friends among boys whom they found temperamentally compatible. Boys, however, outnumber the girls and it is the more aggressive, naughtier and talkative ones who deny having peer relations with girls. They are also unlikely to be chosen as friends by girls. Boys in senior classes make fun of the girls while the girls have a tendency to shout back and snap at the boys whom they find irritating. This is not too prominent in the junior classes and takes place in the absence of the teachers. When the senior boys say they have 'zero' girl peers, they may be referring to an imposed state rather than a choice because girls would not want to have them as friends. At the same time, their own dispositions are choices they make about their identity which further reinforces their distancing themselves from girls and in turn gives them a privileged position in peer groups which are all-boys groups. While there are sections of students, primarily boys, who believe in keeping a line drawn between girls and boys; their responses in terms of the most valued quality in peers is largely similar. Boys and girls of the new sixth and seventh classes value sharing of feelings with friends. Here, boys show a preference for friends with whom they can have fun, who are witty and ensure moments of repartee and jest. Boys value trust, but also value a carefree, fun filled time with friends. Another similarity visible across the gender divide in these classes is an expressive, articulate, specific and descriptive style of communicating their choice. The earlier batch of the sixth is monosyllabic across the gender. The girls value lifelong 'trust' primarily while the boys value 'helpfulness' and 'goodness'.

What emerges from this brief exposition is a communication culture in each grade, which is shared by most of the students in that grade. The earlier batch of the sixth was terse and clipped; the new sixth and seventh are expressive and specific; the new fourth and fifth grades are conventional and school oriented in their commentary on peers.

Within the shared communicative style of each grade, there is a thin line that separates the way girls and boys express their preferences about peers. The earlier batch of sixth class girls and boys has a conventional preference for goodness, honesty and helpfulness, but girls differ a bit when they value 'lifelong support' from peers. There is a 'forever friend' promise that they expect from close peers; boys do not refer to this. Carol Gilligan ([1982] 1993) has commented upon this gendered pattern of 'dependent femininity' and 'independent masculinity' as distinct moralities for the two genders.

The new sixth and seventh standard students consider trust and sharing of feelings to be the most important aspects of peer bonding. However, the boys in these classes feel that being witty and having fun as peers is equally important. The new fourth and fifth conform to the school kid image presented by the adults when 'goodness' is viewed as being good at school work and 'bad' is being poor in studies, unclean and disobedient. Here the girl and boy divide is not very sharp. In some responses, boys are more expressive and girls give a general response, in others, it is the contrary. While class 4 boys and girls are similar in what they like about peers, they differ in what is a disqualification for peer group membership. The girls detest 'dirty' people (by dirty, they mean a lack of personal hygiene) and 'untrustworthy' people while boys dislike people who use abusive language.

An across the grades study of peer preferences among the students of this school shows that there is a diversity within one school's culture, as one moves from one grade to the other. 'In this sense, pupil culture is not monolithic: that is, it is not all of one hue and its liveliness is generated by the individual perspectives and activities that constitute it' (Thapan 1991: 144).The individual responses that stand on the margins add to this diversity. While patterns emerge, there are instances of those patterns being unique in some way and different in others.

Peer Performatives: Different Stories

Peer performatives are ways of behaving and believing that the peer discourse of the school culture provides its students with. It is not generated by the school setting alone, but is partially created outside the school and partially within the school setting. It is recreated according to the demands and freedoms that school creates for its students. Peer performatives include close one to one peer relations, within small groups of like-minded students and the larger community of acquaintances who share classroom experiences.

Various discourses available to an individual create the possibilities of identities for him/her. By participating in the different themes, one experiences and expresses a different identity. Peer and gender discourse in the school culture present are two broad zones of possibilities for the constitution of selves for the students of the school. These two discourses involve students' participation in multiple ways. 'Research has established that a wide range of responses to the educational system…occur among students… and that peer group membership and identity is an important mediating factor in shaping response' (Ball and Woods, cited in O'Donnell and Sharpe 2004: 89). Sometimes, for some students, the peer discourse matters more, for others, it is the gendered peer relations which makes their identities meaningful, for some others, it could be a peer identification along with a gendered identification without being taken up by either, or rather being taken up by both, simultaneously either way. Peer identities and gender identities act upon each other in various ways, and a multiplicity of patterns may emerge in a given cultural setting leaving space for both stereotypical and some idiosyncratic ones.

Peer discourse will be taken to be the source point for understanding the gender discourse as the experiences of the two unfold in this particular setting of the school. It is in peer associated performatives that the gendered performatives keep showing up. These are, however, not present without any mediating sites. They are acted out in classrooms when the teacher is interacting with the students, when the teacher is present but not directly engaging with all the students, when the students are on their own in the classrooms, on an educational trip and so on. Playground activities and dramatics/cultural activities are two other significant zones where the two discourses emerge. In this section, educational activities and classroom settings will be our focus.

When the students were asked to number the people in their peer circle, the responses ranged from five to fifty. Some students were ridiculed for counting all the students in their class as their peers in school; most of them reverted by saying that if they think they have all these people as peers, they are peers for them. It is in this range of reference that the concept of peers works, not just in this case but otherwise as well. Peers include very close friends, yet they also include those whom they meet or spend time with due to some regular routine activity; here, it is coming to the same school or class for five days a week. Peers are the others, mostly one's contemporaries, with whom one shares the space of the school on a regular basis.

Privileging Peer Bonding

Ruckus in the School

One of the favourite transition time activities of the students in the school (i.e., when left free between two structured activities such as two lessons), when out of teachers' surveillance, is creating a ruckus, a jolly banter, a chaotic merriment involving running helter-skelter, talking all at the same time, hitting each other, laughing and crafting an utter nonsensical moment for a time being.

This is not a 'must-happen' activity but a mostly happening activity. There are times when students maintain a quiet and workable atmosphere even in the absence of a teacher, but when this sort of melee begins, everyone joins in sooner or later. They engage in such activities when they are happy about something or are worry free. It is not primarily a boys' activity, girls are equal participants. A few students would not take part once in a while but that included both girls and boys. On being asked why you do this, many could not answer; some plainly reply 'it is so much fun'.

On their school sports day, the students are disciplined and well behaved till the time teachers are around but the moment teachers have to leave for participating in the musical chair for the teachers, the students find a reason to cheer and shout.

Corsaro (2006) has tried to understand the meaning of these dramatic fights among school children and finds a cultural situatedness of such peer behaviour. Quoting Abrahams (1975: 63, cited in Corsaro 2006), Corsaro states that such a dramatization of opposing forces is, in fact, a cultural affirmation of community among the Afro-American students who come from a culture that sees constant contrarieties and antagonisms as difficult to eliminate. Its acceptance is expressed through these dramatized mock fights.

The way students behave in this collective revelry is characteristically similar to what Mclaren (1986) describes as the street corner state. He noticed in such acts 'dynamics of peer relations… usually cathartic; indulgently physical; unbound, ungoverned behaviour…overtones of merriment…irregular speech…'. The moment teachers return back to the room or the space where such behaviour is taking place, there would be an instant shift to the 'student state'—'generally quiet, well-mannered, predictable and obedient…very little physical movement…communitas is rare…' (1986: 98). Mclaren states that the street corner state is valued a lot by the students, largely for the spontaneous *communitas* experience that it offers.

The fact, that such revelry is enacted when the teacher is away and stops the moment teacher is around, signifies it to be an act of resistance to the discipline, which is represented in the persona of the teacher. The good-natured friendliness among the classmates is tutored by the teachers when they say 'make sure your desk-mate has also got his/her lunch', 'don't push each other in the line', 'do not talk to your friend while the class is on, you are disturbing everyone' is internalized, but then once in a while this unfettered friendly banter is lived out. Students do it whenever situations are conducive, though not necessarily always, which means they can regulate it if they want to, it is not compulsive in that sense. However, once it starts then only a teacher can stop it; class monitors fail and often join in, the presence of an adult (the ethnographer) does not act as a deterrent, even pleas for taking caution lest they hurt themselves fall on deaf ears. They stop the moment a teacher arrives. So, it is not really against each other that they are acting but together they act against a certain imposed behaviour through sorted out understanding of peer group discourse.

Imitation for Peer Bonds

Imitating the tone of voice, tempo of voice, answering questions and repeating of what someone does by many others instantly is observed in the very junior sections of the school, until Class 3. Imitation does not stop after that, as sociologists believe that people inculcate sociocultural norms and values through some form of learning from others' behaviour. It is only that grown-ups do it more artfully than young children. Peer culture, leaving its impact on the members of the group, is seen through the imitative behaviour of the younger students. They indulge in such behaviour the most when they are clueless. This takes two forms: one, when students are clueless about something they are expected to know/learn. Two, when they are clueless about who they are at the moment and when group behaviour is at work, usually when someone is reading aloud from the textbook and they are to repeat after him/her. Once in a while, there is a third kind of imitation, which is to surpass the other, to compete; students imitate someone's behaviour if that ensures the success of some sort. This imitation, in all its forms, is meaningful among peers; a commonality is acknowledged before and in the act of imitation: 'I am who you are'.

Imitating fellow students acts as a guard against a teacher's unpleasantness or standing out as an ignoramus. For example, on one occasion, Class 1 students had gathered in the music and dance room for the music lessons. The teacher asked them to sing the song about the rainbow, which has been practiced earlier. After one session, the teacher asked them whether they have learnt the lyrics. One girl said she knows the song's lyrics, and all said one after the other that they know the song. Then, one student said he does not know the lyrics yet and everyone repeated the same. Many of them did not learn the lyrics, but in order to save face joined the voice of the one who knew. However, when another student confessed to not knowing and there was no repercussion of that, all those who were in the similar state confessed to it as well. In the same teacher's class, the students, one grade younger than the first (which is called prep/preparatory), happened to call the teacher 'uncle', that is, one student called him 'uncle' instead of 'sir', for a moment there was a pause and then one after the other students started echoing the same. At this, the teacher politely asked them to revert to 'sir' from 'uncle' explaining that 'uncle' is an elder at home while the teacher in the school is 'sir'. It was a mild digression from protocol and when other students saw that no serious harm occurs as a result of this mistake, they too joined in to enjoy the thrill of breaking the norm. It is through the assurance that others are also doing the same that each student gets the courage to handle the new situation in which they find themselves. Class 3 acted in the similar manner in their civics class to save themselves. The social science teacher asked them to name the major airport in Delhi. No one knew the answer. She repeated the question 'the major airport'. On this, the class repeated back in chorus 'the major airport'. She asked again 'so what is the name?' They repeated 'major'. She gave up and told them the name of the airport. This question's answer was something beyond their everyday knowledge, no one in the class knew the answer, all looked at her for it and the first utterance was assumed to be the answer. The whole class imitated what the teacher uttered after posing the question once and they all imitated each other hoping that saying it in unison will make it the right answer.

Imitating others in the peer group (and in one instance, imitating what the teacher utters) is not a sign of laziness or dullness as it may appear like herd behaviour to some viewers. It is one of the ways young learners (in this instance, seven to eight years old) venture into the less known realms and keep themselves safe as well. These students are not imitating the others all the time; they do not do it very often either. However, they do use this device and when they are employing it in their behaviour, it is apparent and used openly. Such apparent imitation is not present in older peer groups (14 to 15 years old 7 and 8 graders). They copy behaviour and traits but are discreet in their imitative behaviour.

There is another sort of imitation that takes place in peer groups at a very young age. It is an act of sheer imitation, with no intention and no particular aim. The text reading sessions are common display fields of this form of pure imitation. One incident is peculiarly dramatic in nature. Class 1 had understood their lesson for the day and in the rest of the time, their teacher asks students to read the chapter from the beginning. One student is supposed to lead the reading; others are to repeat after that student. After reading about five sentences, the 'lead reader' is changed; the change is ordered according to the seating plan in the classroom. The voices of the students modulate according to the voice of the key speaker. One is smooth and reads almost like the teacher—the students copy that to perfection. The next girl's voice is shrill and loud—the class repeats after her in a similar tone. A boy who is next is very, very slow—students try to be that slow as well. Some of them try to correct his speed but the teacher stops them by saying 'let him read'. One boy is even slower than this one—the class almost goes on a holiday—only one tenth of the class is reading with the boy, others wait for him to finish reading. Only a few students react to a tone that is too strange, but otherwise, the class easily shifts from one intonation to the other. The slow ones are not made fun of. The teacher's initiative is intentional, teachers ask students to read aloud the text to improve their reading skills and instil confidence in them. Each child's turn is his/her moment of elocution; teachers discourage interruptions in this process. Students in their imitation are unconsciously getting accustomed to the differences around them.

There is another instance of this reading aloud session in Class 2, where the students are repeating after their classmates and the sing-song manner of some is copied by all; some halt mid-sentence and all students do likewise. These are not conscious imitative acts, but more out of a force of habit, but in that moment, students move along, thereby giving space to their peers to express themselves idiosyncratically. Going along with the key speaker and copying his/her tone, pace and pitch of the voice is an act of reassurance by the peers to that individual speaker. Once in a while, someone may break this norm by asking the speaker to speed up or slow down, but such instances are rare. Students do not repeat in this manner when the key speaker is a teacher; in this case, one can hear multiple tones and pitches. So, this uniformity for the classmate, though not consciously planned, places the peer in a different space than the teacher.

'According to Corsaro, learning the student role is based on becoming a member of the peer culture, which in turn, emerges from children's identification with one another as well as their differentiation from opposition to adults' (Romero 1991: 18). The repetition of the key speaker's intonation by the classmates is the recognition and affirmation of the speaker's identity in the peer society and also an assurance that it is accepted by others. Students like to do these reading aloud exercises and often remember whose turn is it now, if the exercise is continuing from the previous class. In the first understanding of imitation as a peer act, imitation protects the students from harm or embarrassment as imitating what someone has already done makes it difficult for the teacher to single out any one student for punishment. Also, by giving the same response they surpass the unpleasantness caused by 'not knowing'.

Projecting sameness, when being singled out is feared, is the reason why peer relations are so valued. Again, these are not pre-planned acts but signify a sense of togetherness and oneness in the event of a crisis. The other understanding of imitation among peers points towards another way in which peer presence is reassuring in the event of self-expression. Here too, the act is not pre-planned and is not overtly realized or discussed. These are unstated rules of peer cultures in the schools.

There is a third understanding of this imitation of others, where 'getting ahead' of others is the intention. The idea is to do exactly as the other is doing and show how you are no lesser or even better than the other/s. The often repeated act in this segment is when an evaluation is involved, that is, evaluation by the teacher or any other adult. The moment one student's exercise book is being peeped into by some senior, all the students rush to show their notebooks. If someone's craftwork is being appreciated, others too immediately bring along their artwork. If someone's handwriting is being praised, others start opening their notebooks quickly to show theirs. This tendency is more evident in younger students and becomes less and less prominent as students move towards the senior classes.

Here, peer group becomes the parameter along which one is accessed by others. This imitation is for aggressively asking for one's legitimate space in various peer hierarchies. Competition is enjoyable because of the co-competitors; excellence in itself would hold no meaning if there are no one around doing the same thing, but not doing it the way you do it. What makes it an act of imitation and not outright competition is that it happens suddenly; students are eager to show-off their work but do not demean others or never try to harm others in the attempt to prove themselves better than them. Looking into one notebook means to have to look into, at least, 10 to 15 notebooks in the next minute. While surpassing others in the peer society is exciting, the sense of belonging is equally significant. Poor performance is also displayed because it is a sign of belonging to the group, and thus, the students are not nasty to others in order to prove their excellence. Being ostracized from the peer community is avoided, as then the school would become a difficult place to be in, especially when 'help' remains the key sustaining element of peer relations.

Monitoring Peers

Culture patterns prevalent in a society tend to have an impact on peer interaction patterns in the school in that society. Chen et al. (2006) identify certain broad cultural norms found in different cultural contexts, for instance, European–American societies value assertive, self-directive and autonomous behaviour; western individualistic cultures value personal autonomy and individual's freedom; Asian-Latino group-oriented cultures value affiliative and cooperative activities and greater self-control and in Chinese societies, shyness, sensitivity and self-restraint are valued. Peer cultures in these societies too show traces of these values (Chen et al. 2006: 7). This should not imply that every child in these societies would be a replica of these value systems, but the act of doing makes one an agent in a social system. The larger repertoire is given, but how individuals recognize it, how they understand it, how much they follow it and what meaning it holds for them in different circumstantial contexts is determined by the agency of the individual. And simultaneously, these choices and decisions are made from the prevalent value discourses of that social context. Peer groups in schools, when they show a certain tendency to be prevalent, are a pointer towards the social context in which these are acted out and also towards the context from which they obtain their inspiration.

Monitoring is one peer act that is found prevalent among students in Pratyantar School. Monitoring, in this context, basically revolves around keeping a tab on others in the group. It involves a range of acts that can be segmented into taking care or showing concern for others; checking out for some social misdemeanours and either resolving them by themselves or by complaints to the teacher; assessing others and commenting on that. Since, it is in the school that these peer acts are performed, they have a meaning in the context of schooling but these are also related to the cultural context outside the school. School inculcates these ways of being when teachers tell students in the class, 'make sure all your classmates have got their lunch' or when they ask some students to actually monitor the class, as in keep an eye to maintain discipline, in the absence of the teacher or when students are encouraged to help their desk-mates with small difficulties or when teachers point out a mistake committed by some student (in this case, they do not only mark out the wrong act, but also the wrongdoer and the students read it as 'some people break rules', and thus, keep an eye on any repetition of the unruly act). It is through this culture of competition, comparison and acknowledgement of differences, for good or for bad, that monitoring becomes a part of the fabric of peer culture. However, as stated earlier, peer culture monitoring is not just about pointing out the follies, but it is also about getting to know others and even assisting them in crisis. While the school culture of monitoring, tutoring and disciplining plays a role in its prevalence in the school peer culture, some of it could be inspired from the culture back home.

During a parent teacher meeting (PTM) there was an instance where a boy's mother complained about the behaviour (non-studiousness and talkativeness) of her son's fellow student who is also their neighbour. She complained not so much against him but was assisting the teacher in looking for the reason behind his poor results. This sort of involvement (and somebody would call it 'meddling') in other's issues is a very culture-specific behaviour. Similarly, at the same PTM, the teacher asked two boys to inform their classmates, who live near them but were absent from the school that day, to definitely attend the meeting. This informality and involvement with neighbours are a cultural trait not common across all the neighbourhoods in Delhi. However, monitoring as an element of peer culture in school cannot be stated to be formulaically linked to these sources in predictable manners, but the possibilities of links are indeed present.

Monitoring to Assist Peers

Peer culture acts, where monitoring results in a concern for others, are not restricted to any specific gender. The focus is on the space where peer relations are privileged and not gender-centred peer relations. For example, the prep section was in the music room and a girl from the class was punished and made to stand away from the group for talking in the class. When the class was over, the teacher directed the students to form a line and move to their classroom. All the students started moving out, that girl's three friends, two girls and a boy looked worriedly at her, they advised her 'say sorry to the ma'am'. Then a student came running 'ma'am is calling everyone, come hurry up,' the three of them went away, but soon the teacher came herself to call the girl standing alone. Her friends had informed the teacher that she was still left in the room.

In the same section, on another occasion, a young boy came up and said, 'This boy *Yash*, he is a very bad boy, you know, he calls the aunty (caretaker staffers) his *nani* (maternal grandmother)'. At this, a young girl walked up and said, 'This boy (you are talking to) is a naughty boy and the teacher has punished him that's why he sits alone'. The girl was concerned about Yash being maligned for no reason, so came up and gave the facts that would protect Yash, who was not present during the conversation. The well-being and reputation of peers are guarded on several occasions and the senior sections too display such gestures.

Class 2 was practicing music with their teacher, and some students were not clear about the lyrics. One girl, who was good at the song, sang the lyrics for them and once again provided the lyrics by a recitation of the words for the benefit of her classmates. She had a clear and instructive voice; the students who were confused could now recite the song well. She began by singing the song for them but on her own, without any instruction from the teacher, and changed the tutoring from musical expression to clearly stated lyrics. This concerned mediation is often visible in several instances in the school's everyday practices.

Brief warnings such as 'ma'am is coming'; 'keep quiet or you'll be taken to principal madam's room'; 'don't dance like this, you'll tear your legs apart'; 'last warning before I put your name in the monitor's notebook' and so on are some other ways in which the peer structure tries to prevent harm coming to its members. Class 8 students were being asked to fill up their options for subject preference; the choice was between Hindi and Sanskrit. All the students kept opting for Hindi and no one opted for Sanskrit. The teacher kept asking each student, and one boy murmured 'nobody is going to take Sanskrit'. One boy explained to the other 'if you take Sanskrit you will get good marks initially but later (i.e., from next year) you will have to study some subject called French... then it would be very difficult. It is better to take Hindi'.

Class 6 was discussing their results for the first term when a girl reported that one girl is crying. It seems she is the one who stood third in the class last time, and this time, she was pushed to a lower rank as two boys stood third in the class. One of those two was sitting closer to her desk and smiled as he said gently, 'Look ma'am, she is fighting with me for taking her position'. Everybody came around her for a while and consoled her; the teacher too spoke indulgently to her and asked her not to cry over such a small matter. The boy next to her, whom she was angry with, also tried to calm her by playing down the issue through jesting comments. Eventually, she was fine. The girl who stood first in the class was sitting quietly at her desk at the end of a row. Two girls walked up to her, hugged her, pulled her cheeks and said, 'Look at this one, she always gets the best rank'. She smiled back with some shyness.

The acknowledgement of success by others is also important for success to be meaningful. Just as peer support is essential to overcome the failures and the resultant pain, it is equally essential for success to look like success. Others, in recognizing the good work, actually support the person. In other words, success also needs support, just as failure does. Participating in the friend's happiness makes it meaningful for the person who has earned the success. Just as the boy who stood third but the sorrow of his classmate took the attention away from his success, and marred the pleasure of success for him. Similarly, acknowledgement of success achieved by the girl who stood first by her friends certainly enhanced the pleasure for her.

Later in the day, when the parents were to visit the school for the PTM, students were at their best behaviour. Parents of the classmates were greeted with respect and cordially offered seats. The moment a parent or a set of parents enter the classroom, the student concerned was informed quickly so that he may be alert that his parents are here. Students tried to diffuse the tension created by the results of the tests by being funny and excessive about the treatment that awaits them at home on that day. Girls, as well as boys, contributed to this pool of wisdom. One girl repeatedly kept saying, 'Oh god please do not send my mom today. I'll have a very bad time if she comes; may be she will lose her way around the school...' It was all excessive blabbering because once her mother came, she was one of the most benevolent of parents, had an easy smile on her face and gently patted her daughter's back on meeting her. When I asked that girl later about this episode, she just smiled back sheepishly. That day's excessive muttering about being beaten blue and black at home by the classmates was part-real and part-ritualistic.

The usual chatter and rowdiness was missing and they were joking about how there will be 'a rainfall of blows at home'; 'unpunctuated thrashing'; 'I'll be killed'; 'oh, other people's moms will also beat me up'. The mock dramatized articulation of trouble that awaits them after their poor performance in school is a sign of support to one another. For some, it is real and those (like the girl mentioned above) for whom it is not real, nevertheless, participate in the collective acceptance of insults that come with poor performance. In the excessive jocular articulation, members of the peer group were reassuring each other that they all are in it together and thus making the insults bearable. They are monitoring the possible situations their classmates may find themselves in, and making fun of the situations before they actually materialize. This collective bearing of insults thus makes them less hurtful and easier to endure.

On one occasion, a Class 7 student was scolded by the teacher for something in the class. Once the teacher left, students gathered around that boy and cracked jokes about how the 'clouds that make a lot of noise go away afterwards without doing much'. They were thus indirectly pointing towards the uselessness of such scolding, and in this way, the peer group takes away the pain of the punishment. The younger peer group response to the punishment given to friends is one where they advise conformity with the rules to absolve the pain. The older peer groups also give such advice, but in some circumstances, they blow away the impact by making fun of the whole exercise or making fun of the person who caused the pain.

Monitoring to Ensure Conformity to Norms

There is another aspect to the monitoring of others' actions and feelings among the peers. Junior classes are more monitoring-prone in some senses. In some ways, their sense of being with each other, being fellow students to each other, is very strong. They react more quickly, more animatedly and immediately to what others around them are doing, especially if it is out of the norm. It includes breaking of rules, antics, somebody getting a scolding or punishment, announcements and so on. Older students behave in a different manner. Younger groups are much more particular about normative behaviour. If somebody has not spread their napkin during lunch, it is announced by a class fellow; if someone transfers the contents of their lunch plate into someone else's plate or hides it inside the bag, that is loudly proclaimed; if somebody tries to copy a person's unique skill in doing something then the original performer shouts aloud that it was his/her idea they are trying to copy; she replied first, he spoke later (while answering in class); your belt is going towards the left; he came running to the class; he is chewing the food with his mouth open and so on. Small incidents become matters of transgressions of stated and unstated rules, and complaints are fired against those indulged in 'trespassing' the norms.

A class 1 student dropped her halwa (a sweetmeat made with classified butter and flour) on the floor and her desk-mate Jaya, who is very vocal and perceptive, announced aloud in the direction of the teacher, 'Ma'am, she dropped the halwa on the floor, she was trying to cut it like a cake, I started this style of cutting halwa as cake' and went back to her meal. This is the other aspect of monitoring which culminates in complaining primarily to the teacher or to others. When a class monitor is on duty, younger sections' students take it upon themselves to report trespasses of others. They believe in rules and in their effectiveness in ensuring justice for all, so they very eagerly appeal to the authority (teacher, monitor or the group) and they are also at a stage where they are learning the ropes, so, in complaining about the others they also observe what sort of punishment this trespass results in. They are also more worried about their own well-being in the face of the rules and authorities that implement them. They are yet not very confident about the devices they can employ to be safe and thus pointing out the follies of others assures them that, at least, for now they are on the right side of the rules.

The norm about 'finishing your lunch properly' is one such issue that leads to complaints to the teacher or comments from peers. The teacher of Class 1 was reported about a boy putting the banana, that he got for the lunch (apart from other things), in his bag, and the teacher asked him to eat it now and then was busy with her work. Students take it upon themselves to deride the act. One boy said, 'It will smash in your bag and spoil all your books', and there was a glee on his face at the prospect of the mess that would be created. A girl commented, 'Why are you stealing the banana?' as though eating it then and there, with or without any pleasure, is the dutiful act and preserving it for a better opportune time and enjoying it later is 'a steal'. Another proudly claimed that he has already finished his share of the fruit, thereby having a laugh at the one who was trying to duck the 'onerous task' and was boosting his self-esteem while making the other appear silly and incompetent. The boy who had put the banana in his bag sat confused for a while but since the teacher did not instruct him, he let it be. The singling out of the norm breakers is instant and intense, but episodes do not linger on and within the next few hours or days, peers are incorporated into the group again.

Class 2 students were waiting for the teacher to come when this conversation started with me. They (some of them) suddenly pointed towards a boy saying, 'He is the naughtiest boy of the class'—several others joined in. The boy, who was being talked about, stood explaining how it is not true. Girls and boys came up to explain how he is a 'bad' boy as the teacher punishes him often and that he has no friends in the class except for one, who himself is very naughty, and they pointed in the direction of a boy who was doing some sort of acrobatics with his desk. The 'good' students claimed that they are not his friends. Meanwhile, the teacher returned and they went back to their seats. While the teacher was settling down, I ask that boy, Abhishek, to tell me who his friends are. To my surprise, he pointed out to those 'good' students who have just refused to be his friends. One of them, seeing this, nodded quietly indicating disapproval. Teachers often tell the students that no one should speak to the student who does not listen to the teachers. That acts as a major pressure on peer relations. Some students are sympathetic towards such ostracized students, but deriding them comes more easily. This strategy of punishing the rule-breakers works well in younger sections, but not in the older sections where teacher-recommended boycott is not taken seriously.

Older students also complain about the unruly behaviour of their peers, but it is not as frequent as it is among the younger lot. The older ones see through some of the façades of the rules and authority. They assess the situation of the authority figures, and if found to be at fault themselves, they do not pose a serious threat to the students; at least the rules lose their sanctity. When students move to higher classes, they have already explored the strength and support of peers, and thus, are not easily taken in by the teachers' suggestions about ostracizing a nonconformist. Students judge on their own who is worthy of punishment and it is rare that they go to the teacher with a complaint against someone.

Ridicule amongst them constitutes a control device that students use if they find their peers transgressing a boundary. When Class 6 has been shown their text sheets, students scurried towards different corners of the room to look at their sheets in private. One boy came up and said, 'Look ma'am, that boy has failed and yet he is saying "oh wow! I got such good marks"'. The one he was complaining against was one of the naughtiest boys of the class—he commented on all that was happening around and was bursting with an urge to say or do something out of order, something that surprises others and breaks normative barriers. The boy who complained meant that despite failing, instead of feeling sorry or ashamed, the errant boy has inverted the norm by expressing happiness and pride in his achievement. In this act of 'rejoicing' over failure, that boy was deriding the norm related to the prestige associated with passing the exams since he could not pass and has devices available to him with which he could subvert the embarrassment of failure. It caused the other boy to complain, as he had to study and pass the exam to feel this but the other was also "feeling" thus without the effort.

Incidentally, the school sometimes asks the naughtiest students to be the class-monitors. It is a successful formula for reining in the unruly. Once they are made in charge of discipline, they are quite good at establishing it, and the students obey them as well. The same boy was made class-monitor in Class 7 and was doing his job quite seriously, although he has not left his talkativeness and repartee characteristics entirely. He was given the right to complain against the rule breakers. Grown-ups, the older students, are much more on the side of their peers than the authorities, as the monitors would also give several warnings before they actually wrote somebody's name in the 'black book' of mischief makers. The ones warned argue their case, explain their situation and just take a minute more to continue with whatever talking or moving around that they were doing. Largely, when the senior sections' peer groups had some issues worth complaints, they would mostly resolve them by their own devices of making fun of the wrongdoer or shouting at them or not talking to them. It was very rare that the complaints would reach the teachers through the students themselves. Teachers, if they found unruly behaviour, would punish or admonish the concerned students. Many of the problems were not related to school rules at all and were more personal in nature. The younger lot was more school-rule oriented in this sort of monitoring of peers.

Monitoring for a Recognition of the Peers

The last form of monitoring that remains is neutral—largely objective assessment of the peers and their performances. These acts of evaluative monitoring do not aim at complaining or assisting as was the intention in the earlier two forms of monitoring. It is less subjective and somewhat collective in nature, that is, these assessments are made by a group or the whole class and are not limited to one or two individual peers. These are prestige inducing when positive, and the other side of it signifies an ordinary existence.

Class 2 was having a poem recitation session. It was a poem about *Ibn-battuta*, a Persian traveller known for his penchant for journeys around the world. The poem is written by an Indian poet, adding a comical element to it. It describes how he started his journey amidst great storms and how it was tough to carry on. He, eventually, lost one of his shoes and was left stranded at the cobbler's shop. The students were to recite the poem, standing before the class, one by one, and they had to appropriately enact the events.

Responses of the students to each presenter were different. One girl was too inaudible and the students remarked 'louder-louder', they kept saying 'we can't hear you' and so on. It is important what they were doing since all of them knew the poem already, so when they say that she should speak louder, they are not worried about them missing the story but know that at this moment they are the audience and this girl is a presenter and are playing their role to the hilt. She was being told about her short-comings. They did not deride her but were clear about what was missing in her presentation according to the norms of such presentations. Another performer was a boy, he recited the poem with a staccato tone, his hands did not move though he wanted to do some actions about the traveller. He stood straight and kept moving to and fro, and the students patiently bear with him. No one made fun of this, but they all sat without much interest, although they all were looking in his direction. He completed the task and everyone applauded. Next was a little girl, who tried to add some action to the recitation but was abrupt and inconsistent. The class laughed a little at her attempts, but she herself was smiling shyly making the class too feel free to laugh along. After her, a boy came up, and somebody shouted from the back 'He will take off his shoe,' and the whole class started watching attentively, anticipating the fun that this presentation promises. The boy started the act with great gusto, actions and modulation of voice. All eyes were on him; a few even sang along with a smile. Finally, the moment came, he took off his shoe and the whole class roared with laughter, and then, he threw the shoe a little away to show that the shoe has fallen in Japan (that's what the poem states). Finally, he gave a very sullen expression to express the angst of Ibn-battuta. The class loved his performance; they knew he would perform in this way so he already has earned recognition for himself and this is an encore of that recognition and appreciation.

Another boy came forth, he too wanted to repeat the same antics, but at the moment of taking off the shoe, his shoe did not come off. He tried hard but it did not move, the class laughed at it. He completed the poem and went back to his seat. Later, a girl recited a long, difficult worded poem on the benevolent nature of trees, but kept faltering and repeating the same action of flaying her arms in a semi-arch and continued beyond the allotted time. The class tried to pay attention but was more enamoured by her resilience than the content of the poem. It inspired awe but not admiration. A little girl came next, she was holding a paper chit in her hand and tried to read out of the paper, but her voice got stuck and she could not speak a word; the teacher cajoled her, but then she was sent back. The class did not react in any demeaning manner and let her be. The class sang along with the students who performed well. They laughed at small faux pas but were not dismissive to someone who did not perform well. The appreciation by peers enhances the confidence of the good performers and silence from peers makes the not-so-good ones realize that they have not made it to the select few ranks.

When the teacher is not present, other skills are talked about among the peers. Class 2 and 3 have dance talent which apparently is recognized by all the peers for their performance of popular Bollywood dance numbers. Such students are known to be skilled dancers and are appreciated for their brief acts presented in free time, in the absence of the teacher.

In general, students know the academic standing of their peers and monitor, who is ahead of whom, who has lagged behind and who has improved or gone down the ladder. These assessments show their influence in indirect ways. A Class 6 boy who was asked by the teacher to work much harder, to improve his academic skills, was jocularly reprimanded by a fellow boy, 'so, what have you been doing all this while?' And when his mother came to meet the teacher on PTM, the students of his class went berserk greeting her with false salutes, 'Namaste auntyji'; 'have a seat'; 'how are you?'; 'namaste'; 'aunty namaste'. She understood the jest hidden in the greetings and was not very pleased by this show of mock-reverence. On the other hand, when parents of an academically successful boy enter, they are greeted by students with genuine respect, especially the girls make it a point to go closer and talk to the mother of that boy. The parents too are accustomed to this respect and behave accordingly, showing pleasure on meeting their son's classmates. Apart from being good academically, he is good looking, well-mannered and gentle that adds to his popular status and more so among the girls.

Assessment of peculiar traits also happens among the peers and students appreciate these though sometimes assessment comes out in the forms of nicknames that the group accords them. However, because of their uniqueness, students mostly love their nicknames and almost never reject them. One girl in Class 6, who has a temper and is a little dark complexioned, is nicknamed *kaala toofan*, that is, black thunder; another girl in Class 5 is nicknamed *chuhiya*, that is, a she-mouse for her small build, rapid movements and a mild resemblance to the species. In the same class, another girl named Tulsi Devi is called TD—her long, serious sounding, mythology inspired name is reduced to a curt, anglicized denomination. One boy came up to announce his nickname and with great pleasure informed me that he is called *kalajamun*, that is, a spherical black sweetmeat, by his friends because his face is round, sweet looking and he is dark complexioned. Nicknames are assessments made by one's peers of one's unique traits and are half jocular half endearing. Though students would sometimes be embarrassed when called by their nickname in front of an outsider, these are accepted as they signify some special recognition among peers.

On the whole, the dramatized, unruly, collective display of 'mucking around', various versions of imitations and differently intended monitoring among peers are some of the aspects of peer culture of Pratyantar School, which privilege peer group membership over anything else. These performatives are not gender restricted or gender specific and are displayed by both girls and boys. Thus, not all spaces in the school are gendered spaces, but there are zones where gendered peer group membership show up, that is, there are certain contexts where the gendered nature of peer relations is evident, mostly stereotypical, but these exist along the earlier mentioned largely peer-centric relations.

It was observed by Marion Underwood (2008) that 'if girls and boys are observed in the same social contexts, many of the gender differences in children's discourse become smaller and boys' and girls' conversations appear more similar than different' (2008: 26). There are contexts where peer group membership or studentship or other human vulnerabilities and aspirations take centre stage in the everyday performatives. These contexts and zones have significance for gender discourse because to a large extent, they signify the shift that has come in the way schools are becoming a space that can be seen as a possibility for generating multiple gender codes that are not sunk in the stereotypical binary codes that are, in fact, restrictive and discriminatory.

Gendered Relations in Peer Groups

Peer culture in school is not completely dissociated from the gender stereotyping, though in the present contexts, it is not normatively binary and is not absolute in its impact. There are significant performatives of peer relations that are not structured around or governed by gender differences as they were prevalent several years ago. Studies in the different parts of the world, that focused on the gendered peer relations, primarily in classroom interactions, found that girls are marginalized in these contexts through various ways (Rajagopal, S. 2009, Thorne 1993, 2002, Wazir 2000). Teachers' blatant privileging of boys over girls, through praise, encouragement, presumptions and differential behaviour, contributes to a gender conceptualization that influences the peer relations also. These obvious discriminations may have been checked in schools, in some cases, but what remain, despite conscious efforts to bring in gender parity, is unconscious perpetuations of these discriminatory binary codes by the educators and the students themselves.

Attempting to Overcome the Bias

Girls in Class 1 of the school are not at all shy or inhibited in their interactions with the teacher during class. They are alert, sharp and well organized. They are quite clear about what are the correct answers to the questions the teacher poses and are competitively aware of providing the answer before their peers. Class 3 students also show a similar pattern. Girls participate in discussions, give their comments and observations and are treated by their teacher as equals. The only students that are scolded are those who do not pay attention. Students in both these classes sit in mixed pairs and in gender-specific pairs as well. Class 4 is managed by a girl monitor and everyone recognizes her authority. There are other sections as well that have girl monitors who are as effective or ineffective as boy monitors.

Classroom behaviour of the teachers is not discriminatory in overtly gendered terms. The school imposed gender segregation practices are not evident; they are not asked to sit separately, no girls versus boys competitions are held in classrooms, and girls are paid as much attention as boys by the teachers and others. These are the attempts that the school makes in keeping opportunities open for girl students. The teachers are conscious of the overt perpetration of gender bias. However, covertly, sometimes teachers display gender-centric behaviour in non-academic associations with the students.

On one occasion, Class 7 boys were asked by their teacher to open the windows of the basement so that their class could get some fresh air. The teacher associated tough work with boys and asked them to look into it. On the face of it, there was nothing in it that would be called discriminatory, but the assumption that girls are not suitable for this work that needed some labour is indicative of an underlying remnant of bias, despite the overt efforts to erase discrimination. Similarly, the Class 6 teacher asked a boy of the class to run an errand for her, where he was supposed to call some tall boys from the senior sections as they were needed for putting some files and folders in the upper segments of a cupboard. The assumption that boys are taller was working in the subconscious of the teacher, though otherwise, she is one of the most supportive teachers and is appreciated for her sincere efforts towards the students. There were tall girls too, in the senior section, but her preference was for the tall boys.

These assumptions are considered harmless on the face of it but are some of those perceptions that need to be checked in the everyday contexts of interactions. 'The gender regime is a state of play rather than a permanent condition. It can be changed deliberately…' (Kessler et al. cited in Liu 2006: 426). Students sometimes carry deeply embedded notions of gender segregation from homes or other contexts, such as popular culture, peer talks and so on. One day, the dance teacher was supervising the preparatory section as their teacher for that period was on leave. A boy found a small shiny sticker shaped like a dot from somewhere in the room and brought it to the teacher. The teacher, in jest, put it on his forehead like a bindi (an ornamental mark that Hindu women and girls apply on their foreheads). The boy jumped back in shock and removed it instantly from his forehead. The teacher was surprised and asked him, 'Why did you throw it away…What happened?' The boy replied, 'Girls put bindi, I am a boy' while the other students watched him. The teacher asked, 'How do you know you are a boy?…Who told you?' The boy replied, 'I know'. A similar incident, reported from a preschool in Ohio, showed a four-year-old boy who had playfully applied red nail paint on his nails and the next day was sent by his father to the school with an angry note about this. The boy explained to the teachers that boys do not wear nail paints and insisted quite strongly that he should be recognized as a boy (Davies 1989: 136). The boys, in this instance and the one at our school, both displayed a serious concern over the 'confusion' being created by the teachers about gender-specific behaviour; both students vehemently resisted such attempts. They were already familiar with a certain gender coding prevalent around them and though not overtly engaged with the masculine–feminine issues, were nonetheless, drawing from this discourse of binary opposites.

On the sports day of the school, the preparatory section was to participate in an event where four girls would stand at one end of the small race track and four boys partners of theirs would have to race down to them where girls were to put dots and other stickers on the boys' faces and make them up as clowns. Here, the boys had no problem with coloured dots put on their faces because the role was that of a clown. Being perceived as a clown was acceptable to the students but appearing to cross the gender boundary was unbearable. Many of the sports events are gender segregated since boys and girls are not considered as equals in terms of body strength and stamina, and it is considered a fair play to keep them in different competitive zones. However, girls and boys participate in all the events without discrimination.

Gender Stereotyping in Peer Contexts

Playgrounds and classrooms are as significant social spaces for the constitution of gender identities as other formal spaces and sites. Peer group interactions and attitudes of the classmates act as a serious interjection in the process of construction of one's gender identity, as it happens in the space of the school. Reay (2003) finds an association between academic success and bullying among the boys. Boys doing well academically were subjected to bullying and name calling. They were called 'sissy', 'gay boy' and 'queer'.[3] Being a clever and high achieving student in the class has implications in terms of gender identity. High achieving boys stand the risk of being labelled 'geeks' or 'swots' while high achieving girls are accused of being 'bossy', 'arrogant' and 'selfish'. In this sense, both boys, as well as girls, face similar reactions from their classmates, that is, of being off track in their gendered identity.

It is mostly in unsupervised contexts that gender stereotyping among the students is more prominent. During a poster making session in Class 6, when the teacher was gone for a while, the students displayed a typical girl–boy differentiated behaviour in the class. The girls did their work quietly and diligently while the boys walked around, played pranks, passed comments on each other and so on. Even when the teacher returned and the class realized that it is not a proper lesson, continued with the same behaviour though they are somewhat subdued now. The teacher was admonishing the boys while the girls did their work quietly. It was a classic instance of 'boisterous boys and quiet girls'. The teacher has to communicate more with the boys, but as noticed in some other studies too, it is mainly a communication in the form of rebuke, correction, asking them to behave and do their work; and the girls often have more work related issues to discuss with the teacher.

This gender construction of 'silly/sensible dichotomy' is prevalent in many classrooms across the world and constructs the two genders as oppositional. '[While for] the feminine construction, maturity, obedience and neatness are valued "sensible" qualities… the masculine construction involves, "silly" qualities of immaturity, messiness and naughtiness' (Francis 1998 quoted in Paechter 2006: 368). The gender stereotyping often moves through seemingly innocuous binaries. There is a 'construction of femininity as sensible/mature and self-effacing; and the contrasting construction of masculinity as demanding and assertive' (Francis and Skelton 2005: 99). However, this sort of dichotomy is not without its exceptions, which are gradually growing. In the school, such an obvious silly/sensible divide is more prominent in the senior classes, but not always. As mentioned in earlier sections, naughtiness is not gender restricted and girls, as well as boys, are equally engaged in cheerful chaos creating sessions once in a while.

Rituals of pollution, teasing and chasing are some of the other forms of interactions that take place with members of the other gender as students enter preadolescence (Thorne and Luria, cited in Underwood 2008: 21). Thorne identifies border work as these intense and brief interactions between genders as girls and boys get 'interested in exploring the world of the other gender' (1986: 21). We can observe a similar phenomenon in this school. In Class 8, three pairs were sitting as mixed pairs and the rest of the class sat in gender specific pairs. Those sitting next to each other constantly fight with one another. On being asked why they need to sit next to each other if they fight with each other so much, they just continued with their complaints 'he is so bad', 'she is unbearable'. Another pair is jostling about the space boundary—the invisible line drawn on the desk that separates their 'areas'. The boy kept his bag between them and pushes it in her 'area'; at this, the girl would scream and push it back. Another pair—the boy made a wisecrack, the girl totally unimpressed, said loudly, 'You better not talk to me, okay?'. These are the rituals of pollution, which are believed in and followed among pre-adolescents sometimes. Discrimination is sustained by talk of 'boy germs' and 'girl germs' polluting one another. A boy in Class 6 responded during one informal discussion on peer relations 'It is bad if your friend does not come to school but it is such a relief if your desk partner does not come', he added, looking at his partner, a girl slightly bigger than him, '…as that day you are saved from all the "falling down on you" acts'. The class laughed and the girl made a mocking face.[4] During an educational excursion, some girls complained of boys pulling their ponytails. The younger ones complained to the teachers while the older ones shouted back at the boys trying to tease them.

One Class 7 boy complained to the teacher about his classmate, a girl, who was running after him to see his exam sheet. He said, 'I have got very poor marks, but she insists on looking at my answer sheet and would not budge'.

These acts of teasing, fighting, keeping the other away, running after one another and so on are gender conscious acts, where gendered differences are played out much more than gender parity or peer relations. Here, gender distinctions are highlighted, but in the context of a discourse which segregates and forbids camaraderie. The younger students interact relatively freely though they too have their conceptualizations of gender segregation, but this segregation becomes more expressive in older sections of students. The younger peer groups are very particular about personified gender codes and the material representations; about the dress, hair, name, accessories and so on. The older peer groups are more conscious of the behavioural and communicative codes of gender like, the physical distance between genders, patterns of communication, physical comportment, attention and non-attention and so on. The preadolescents are somewhat overt in their attempts to segregate the gender groups while the adolescents carry some of that sense of segregation along with a deliberation towards being with the other.

Jesting Masculinities

Jesting, playing pranks, repartee and puns are performatives appropriated by boys' peer culture. This is one zone where girls do not compete or figure very frequently. Laughter as a subversive tool has been associated with masculine subcultures of schools in the work of Willis (1977) and more recently in Kehily and Nayak (1997). Willis (2011) has described 'laff' as a multifaceted counter school act that is taken to be a panacea for the problems schooling creates for working class boys and laughing, 'having fun' are very macho acts. However, in this particular school, what seems to emerge is a culture of witticism, leg pulling and dramatic one-liners that are appropriated largely by the boys and that too, boys from 6th standard onwards, but laughter is not always a device used by macho, anti-school boys, it is often used by some of the more studious boys who simultaneously want to look smart and sharp. So, laughter inducing phrases or acts are used by three sorts of boys— studious and well-placed in the school's academic culture, not too studious but aspiring for a status among the peers nevertheless, and studious but sharp-witted ones who do not want to be known only for their book knowledge or as 'nerds'. The nature of humour is such that they try to display their worldly wise attitude, a 'know-all' sort of attitude, a pattern that shows a refusal to be treated like imbeciles and easy to fool. Basically, it is an expression of being prepared for the world out there and represents a masculinity which must know how to deal with several levels of existence.

One very common query that boys across classes have is if they could write girl and boy both when they were asked to mention on the questionnaires whether the respondent was a boy or a girl. Someone or the other, among the boys, would ask this question and were very pleased with this existential dilemma brought up by them. No girl ever asked this question. This question was asked mostly by boys in older sections and usually by those who tried to act flamboyantly at other times. They always moved around a lot, were always trying to be dramatic and spoke in Hindi film dia-logue-style and were constantly trying to set themselves apart from the ordinary others, including the not so flamboyant boys. Not all of them were academically marginalized ones but had a tendency to be up to some acts that would make them visible and noticed.

Class 7 boys were asked to open the basement windows high up on the walls. At this, several boys asked one of the shortest boys to open the windows from inside the room 'Why don't you try opening the windows from inside the room, you can do it easily'. The windows had to be opened from outside as this is a room in the basement and the boys asked their classmate to open it from an impossible height. The boy being targeted replied, 'Yes, of course, why not'. This sort of leg-pulling is common among peers, more among the boys. In Class 8, a short boy is one of the most studious and sharp students of the class. He has answers to all the questions put up by the teachers and jumps with energy while such ques-tion–answer sessions are held in the class. When he was replying to a teacher's question in the science class, one boy from the last bench murmured, 'At least stand up before you reply to the teacher, have some sense'. At this, another one added, 'he is standing, what do you expect'. Meanwhile, the small built boy looked back with a smile and said, 'I am standing'. Such witty teasing among the friends is a sort of a daring that only friends are allowed. Enduring these and recognizing these as fun is part of peer culture. A Class 7 boy, on being asked, what was his experience of the annual day program, replied, 'It was wonderful because I did not come that day to the school to watch it'. This too is another form of being witty in the event of a lack or when trying to camouflage a not so pleasant expression. The boy did not participate in the annual day events and gave it a miss and has a response that exaggerates the usual comment supplied for such questions.

Peer Acts in the Playground

The playground is another site in the school's space, which is distinct from the rest of the school in some ways. Playgrounds are used during recesses and games periods. There are legitimate spaces for playing, an activity that is orchestrated by the children and not so much by the teachers and adults. Playgrounds in school are spaces where peers interact with each other, largely, free of adult supervision. Playing, as an activity, is an act that involves role play-ing, rules, fantasy and creativity. Given these aspects, playgrounds in schools are significant spaces that may present peer interaction in a different light.

Meaning and Significance of Play

The playground is a part of the school and yet is not like the formal spaces of the school. In this space, students, as children, explore their own ways of learning and relating to other children. It is not a distinction made by the adults or the researchers but is a distinc-tion that children recognize as well though they may not articulate it in a detailed complex form. As noted by Romero,

> Children appeared to equate work with having to conform to teachers' specifications of the tasks to be done...Activities labelled as play, in contrast, were voluntary and self-directed...the same activity was labelled as play if children had chosen it for themselves, whereas it was classified as work if teachers had assigned it. (Romero 1991: 126)

Playing games on the playground during the games period or occasionally in a free period is a much-cherished act among the students of all sections in the school. Students do not sacrifice their games period for anything. Beresin notes in her account of recess studies in schools, 'the children chose to play rather than eat'… (2010: 9). The older students are as playful as the younger ones during their visits to the playground. It is not an enormous space but is not small either. It has grass on the surface and a tiny basketball court in one corner. The other corner has a few swings and some other structures made of steel, iron and plastic for younger students to climb upon and manoeuvre.

With the shift in context, the performatives of peer relations also change. In the playground, the students do not perform in front of the teachers, so the fear of the authority and careful conduct is given a backseat, and they feel free to do what they want. Playgrounds are places of knowing what the children would want to do when allowed to be with their peers, but they also know that this is a window space and they have to return to the discipline again. In this context, playground activities are significant for understanding peer relations of school-goers. This section will focus on the games, playing and other activities that students indulge in during their stay in the playground and will also explore the gender axis in these activities and how it emerges.

Camaraderie during Play

Class 6 was enjoying their games period. It was noon of early summer time, but the enthusiasm was at its highest. Not even a single minute has been wasted doing nothing, and it was so across the genders. The students were improvising their games constantly; if they were bored of playing one game, they generated another. What collectively decided, though, an unstated agreement, was a complete freaking out or a collective hanging out without any restrictions or inhibitions. It happens very often. Such sort of absolute involvement with playing on the field is common and observed when classes younger than 6th standard are observed during play time. In all these observations, with all these classes, a shared understanding among the peers is that one should not rest during this period—every moment here is meant to be completely active. The constant concern was how to not let the action stop. The children seemed intoxicated with laughter all this while. They did not have much in the name of play gadgets, but a time out with their peers with a shared understanding of what it means to be here and now. As soon as they were informed about the time up in the field, the mood shifts; they queue up, so much quieter but happy.

In the playground the 'children's game playing has its own momentum' (Tucker 2008: 109). The transition in their movement from the playground to the classroom captures the significance of play for them. While at play, they were using their cultural skills of which they were largely sure and over which they have certain mastery but in the movement towards the classroom, they were again going to be positioned as learners, something they were not confident about. As peers too, a lot of learning and proving oneself has to be accomplished, but the rules can be negotiated then and there very easily. In the classroom, peers do not decide the rules of the game, teachers do, and are not so easily malleable. Playground is a different place in this sense, and the games are played according to certain rules, but the observation of the playground activities shows that rules of the game are charted out in the field, and rules are changed midway but with a consensus of peers. Often, rules are not adhered to, or changed abruptly by one person who is placed in a disadvantageous position because of a certain rule and sometimes rules are totally forgotten. What is significant is that during such times when the game is being enjoyed by all, playing around with rules does not create any sourness. Somebody who has a complaint about this rule-bending would go to the accused and very rarely to the unspoken leader of the moment, discuss the matter and then continue with the game. When students inform that peers are valued because they 'understand us' this is one of the meanings that understanding takes. The need to give the rule a backseat for the sake of having fun in the game is possible and recognized by one's peers. The call to go back to the classroom is a reminder of the shift to the space where rules are not changed for comfort that easily. In fact, getting back to the classroom because the time is up is one of such rules which are not so easily negotiable. This camaraderie is valued because it is not so readily available in other spaces. Not to say that peers do not have disputes or quarrels, but what is more significant is that they still belong to the realm of play. As Romero (1991) remarks, children identify all those activities which they control as play, the rest is work, so the disputes, differences during play are nevertheless counted as play.

The students of the school, from preparatory section to 8 are fond of their games break. The younger sections, including the 6 standard, particularly tax their bodies in the play area. Till younger sections, the girls and the boys indulge in an almost euphoric manner with running around, jumping or falling acts, but the older sections, 7 and 8, are not so frenetic, although they too are very actively involved. As many students from older sections reported, peer relations are significant for the sharing that happens, the heart to heart talk that is possible most easily with one's peers, and so the playground does not mean a space where self-expression finds its outlet for them. They are not restricted to the explorations of the body in its most active possibilities; they have narratives that are to be explored to their active possibilities. They, as grown-ups, have other ways of negotiating the rules, by humour, by habit, by a cultivated irreverence for some rules and so the playground is valued but not as much as by the younger peer groups who are coming to terms with the restrictions school poses on bodily movements. These distinctions between the older and the younger peer groups in terms of their interest in playtime are not absolute. There are younger students who sometimes play quietly, calmly and sometimes older ones indulge in hyperactive behaviour. Most of the time, it is the younger groups that are more adventurous. Even if somebody gets hurt during the play (not serious injury), through a ball hitting them, someone pulling or shoving, falling, getting breathless due to constant running and so on, nobody complains. They do not even sneer at others, except sometimes when the hitting is deliberate and understood to be with a malice that an instant 'revenge' is taken. Otherwise, the bodies are extended to their endurance limits and all participate in this act according to their individual potential. Once in a while, one or two of them would come and sit on the stairs close by and take some rest, then rush back to the heart of the action. Carmichael notes in her study of peer cultural explorations, 'the students' creativity in entertaining themselves during recess was admirable, some of their play on the equipment seemed dangerous....some children didn't appear to know their bodies' capabilities and got hurt doing things that were not safe for them physically' (2008: 177). The students in schools are trained to keep their bodies in discipline because the curriculum is primarily transmitted through listening, seeing and thinking; the body must stay in control and these senses have to be supported by the disciplined body. In the play, these senses are also at work but this time, the body is also allowed to be a part of the whole exercise and allowed much greater freedom than it gets anywhere else in its everyday existence.

Gender as an Axis

Playtime is a favoured form of activity among the students. They maintain a shared understanding of its utmost utilization, that is, sometimes students would laze around and play games that do not require frenzied activity and sometimes some segments of the class would be behaving in a very different way than the others so that if most of them are playing relatively quietly, others are jumping around, shouting, laughing and vice versa. What is shared is an understanding that this time and this space is for the students, and they set the pace, create the rules and largely do whatever they want. However, within this shared discourse of playtime, there are gendered peer performatives coexisting with the classroom performatives in some significant ways.

In the classroom, students sit together in mixed pairs of boys and girls, though largely they show a preference for same gender pairs. Teachers do not consciously display a bias for or against girls or boys. But the moment students enter the play area, a clear segregation according to gender is visible.

Boys play basketball while girls are into the jump rope. Three girls dribbled a basketball a little away from the boy's group. At one point, the smaller group from the boys' teams tried to take away the new, better basketball from the girls by mixing up the two during the play. The girls soon noticed this and threatened the boys to return it or else they will report the matter to the games teacher. At this, they promptly returned the ball. While most girls were engaged in conventional girl games, one of which is the jump rope, and some were busy racing, three girls were sharing the space with the boys on the small basketball court, but were playing at their own pace. Girls needed the assistance of the teacher to make sure that they retain their status quo in the face of being cheated. Two boys, bored of the basketball game, were watching the girls playing the jump rope and were impressed by the dexterity of the girl players and showed interest in joining in. Girls taught them the procedure, but they could not do it for long and moved aside laughing at their own failure. Meanwhile, girls continued with a relative ease. The ease with a game shows a longer association with it. Girls' slow pace in basketball and boys' failure at trying the jump rope shows the divide; however, the distance is not insurmountable because neither girls were ridiculed for trying out basketball nor the boys for trying their luck at the jump rope. They do not play these games as mixed groups which point towards the gendered nature of playground performatives.

The other favourite games of the girls were *kikli* (where girls clasp their hands in a criss-cross manner and turn around in circles in a fast encircling motion), catch-chain (where one girl runs after the others and whomsoever she touches will have to join hands with her to touch the others, gradually the chain gets larger and it becomes difficult to continue) and cuckoo game (where girls stand in a circle and one in the centre, all the girls prompt her to touch them but if they start flapping their hands, making a clucking sound and stand on one leg, that girl cannot touch them).

Boys play a different sort of games. An all-time favourite was a game that drew inspiration from a crime-detective serial on television, C.I.D.[5] Snake-water-gun, hide-and-seek, catch the ball and run and catch are few others to count. C.I.D is played with great involvement. The roles are distributed and great debates ensue over who takes which role. During one such enactment, a leader of the group decided, 'I will be the doctor and you (pointed to one boy) be the one who gets killed' then continued, 'I will drive the car, all of you sit behind me'. The group adjusted itself behind the driver's 'seat' as though they were travelling in a car, 'applying brakes' at appropriate intervals. Suddenly a shootout was enacted by them. The one who was to be the murdered man was falling over other children playing their games. The details, of who will get shot in what parts and in how many shots, were being meticulously discussed, the 'dead' one lay still. In another such enactment game, the 'murdered' one was writhing in pain when others called the special investigators though a 'mobile phone'. In the course of this, the 'murdered' boy tried to suggest some move related to the game when his friends shouted, 'Oh you are dead, don't talk!' It is played by boys largely for it involves a confrontation with murders and mystery. Fiske notices that '...violence is an element of masculine popular cultures' (1989: 129). It is associated with the difficult situations out there in the real world that they will soon need to confront and hence an involvement with this game.

While girls' games are about dexterity, keeping the chain of people together while running around, hopping on one leg, doing several things at one go, boys' games are about chasing, guns, fights, killings, a display of courage and so on. Much of these are stereotypical images that the students come across at their homes and in the everyday consumption of the popular soaps on television and films, constitute the discourse through which these typifications get coded for them. The school's attempts to bring in gender parity fall weak in the face of more persuasive and prevalent gender stereotypes available in everyday life. The school's efforts towards promoting some measures that counter the stereotyping, along with the parallel discourse of gender issues in televised programs and voices raised by associations engaged with concerns around gender biases together, have created a counter-discourse. This new discourse is generating possibilities of not just gender parity, but also multiple performatives of gender. There are, therefore, confident girls who are leaders of their groups during the games, there are girls confident of themselves as they reclaim their space in the playground, there are boys who show interest in 'girls' games and there are girls who act like bullies. These are minor shifts, though significant, but the dividing discourse is more prevalent and often permeates through apparently harmless mediums.

As Thorne notes, 'the gendered worlds children inhabit are far more complex, shifting and fluid than the separate cultures thesis would indicate' (2002: 291) and '…Girls and not just boys sometimes play in larger groups and negotiate and argue about rules' (Thorne 2002: 296). While girls in the playground sometimes appear to adhere to the dominant model of femininity, by playing in encircled groups and playing non-aggressive games, there are instances of girls taking over the playground through their 'chain' chase. In this game, a group of girls line up and moves aggressively, without concerning for others on the ground. This poses a non-conforming feminine image. As Paechter observes, 'while the majority of girls construct their femininities more or less in conformity to the dominant conceptions of femininity within their particular location, many do not' (Paechter 2006: 371). In the emergence of leaders among the girls whom girls turn to for decisions about the rules and players, there thus emerges another expression of a femininity that can 'read' power and is learning to lead. Moreover, the presence of the 'bully' girl shows that bullying is not masculine only and feminine is not always about being 'nice'.

Proving the hunch right, this section, through its enormity and diversity, brings out some of the richest accounts of meanings that being in school can generate, not necessarily always along the expected lines. Peer relations, as informal segments of schooling, hold immense potential for imparting learning to the students, sometimes more relevant and empowering than the usual 'lessons' and textbooks. Students as children script their own strategies of learning and coping in these informal, untutored spaces within the school. In many ways, these sites of peer interactions and play are sites where knowledge is practiced, and where participating in the throes of life imparts learning and wisdom. This valuable part of schooling perhaps needs greater acknowledgement in our under-standing of schooling in the contemporary society.

Notes

1. As studies of classroom cultures in schools in African countries show, girls were assigned duties that were domestic or clerical in nature while boys were given mana-gerial tasks by the teachers. Also, a study of some Chinese schools by Liu (2006) shows clear segregation of genders, by teachers, in the seating arrangements, codes of conduct and play areas.
2. The extra-curricular are the activities held and promoted in and by the school but are largely non-academic in nature.
3. See also Thorne (1993), Redman (1996) and Epstein (1998) for understanding gender equations in the school context.
4. David MacDougall's film 'Some Alien Creatures' is about gender relations in Rishi Valley School, where girls and boys treat each other as some *alien* species. See http://www.roninfilms.com.au/feature/620/some-alien-creatures.html (Accessed on 12 October 2010).
5. C.I.D. is a crime detective series aired on Sony channel. It is one of the longest running television series on Indian television (from 1998 till date).

6

Extracurricular Activities

This chapter explores the formal extra-curricular activities that the school undertakes for its students as well as the outcomes of such engagements. The significance of these activities for the students, as mundane or extraordinary, are important indicators of their world views extending beyond the school world and their ordinary daily experience.

The Extracurricular in School

A segment of the cultural life of a school is invariably linked with the popular culture that the students experience outside their school. The school's location in the larger social space determines the form of popular culture that its students engage with. In this context, that is, in the case of this school, the popular culture is present in the television programmes that the students watch by choice or circumstance. The choices that the students make in the consumption of televised tales are, to some extent, significant in the context of their peer relations as these stories, imageries, issues are discussed by students among themselves and thus peer relations are also about knowing these stories and events. The gender stereotyping or, sometimes, attempts at undoing such binaries (that emerge through some of the more gender-centric stories and representations), constitute the repertoire from which children draw meanings.

During an outing to the Nehru Planetarium,[1] the older students stood at the end of a long queue of the school students. The boys were together and the girls were within their smaller groups. The planetarium is called *taramandal* in Hindi and this was written outside the main hall. The boys were teasing one of their friends, who is Bengali and his name is Gaurav Mandal. The teasing was centred on the pun situated in the intonations of *mandal*. The boys said to one of the younger teachers, 'Ma'am this looks like Mandal's house as it says taramandal'. Another small, thin boy added, 'We are going to learn a lot about the future of Gaurav Mandal in this hall'. The boy who was being teased was smiling and trying to shut them up simultaneously.

This sort of leg pulling, teasing, repartee and poking fun is not so prevalent among girl peers. Although the girls are at times funny as well as witty, the boys behave in such a manner more often than girls. This may be seen as an indicative of a less strict cultural distinction between the expected behaviour of the girls and the boys now in some contexts, but a significantly apparent distinction persists, despite the attempts to bring in gender parity.

During the tour of the museum, some of the boys from the older sections kept commenting on what they saw. They commented with jest and some sort of mockery. The younger lot was awestruck and kept commenting on how huge and beautiful everything was. The older ones, especially the boys (some of them), took great delight in having a different perspective on it all. In the guest room, they commented, 'So this is where the tea was had'; in the inner lawns, 'This is where the IPLs, that is, Indian Premier League (a recently established, novel pattern of holding cricket matches and have no association whatsoever with Nehru and his times) must have been conducted'; to the rose beds, 'This is the source of his rosebuds, all right'.[2] When they reached the room where Nehru spent the last moments, before passing on most students kept quiet, younger ones bowed reverentially and, an older boy commented, 'Move along, the soul could still be here'. As they were lined up for leaving for their buses these boys spotted a foreigner couple who were taking pictures of the place and jumped out of the slow-moving line, bunched up and had themselves photographed and came back commenting, 'Now tomorrow our photo will be everywhere…see us on Facebook'.

Many among the older students are sceptical of being reverential towards all the norms and rules of the school just because these exist and everyone is supposed to respect them. The younger ones are ready to believe the narrations that they come across.

Shared Narratives among the Peers: Television

Television as a media that brings the world to home and as a source of a world of representations can unfold significantly, some ways in which identities of school going children are constituted through it. A multidimensional perspective is recommended that recognizes the importance of the subject's position in commenting upon the way television creates an impact. 'The sociality of television is shaped by the spatial and temporal contexts in which viewing takes place, and by the presentational structure of the medium itself' (Lembo 2000). Television viewing encompasses practices of meaning-making and the imaginative dimensions of those practices. David Buckingham (1993), commenting on contemporary societies, claims that media constitute one of the major leisure time activities and children spend as much time watching television as they spend in school. This new entrant in the lives of the people in urban areas has been found to be influencing the relationships with others in the family, in the school and in the neighbourhood, and also plays a role when it comes to constituting a certain identity or identities. The nature of influence, however, is rather difficult to identify.

In order to explore this relationship between television and the audience, what needs to be acknowledged is the diversity and the particularity of the social situations in which the subjects find themselves. The act of watching is thus made into more of a process than an act. Besides this, it would help to let go of any presumptions about this relationship. It cannot be assumed that watching television is a mindless pastime in the same way as it would be a flawed judgment to believe that television has the power to persuade. It could be entertaining and could elicit a serious thought and a discussion.

Ethnographic accounts of children watching and talking television would be the creators of a pathway for this exercise, for it is in these everyday details that the process of identity construction is worked out. At times, issues related to gender, power, religion, community and class are addressed and influenced through these the most.

A certain pattern of preferences regarding the television programmes emerges among peer groups from different age cohorts, but it is not a stable and uniform sort of pattern. Students of different age groups show their preferences for certain sorts of programmes on television, but it is difficult to say that the choice centres on a certain programme. There are considerable variations and some similarities as well. Students of Classes 3 and 5 largely prefer cartoons and animation serials. Class 3 especially focuses on cartoons whereas Class 5 boys have a special preference for a crime-detection based programmes which girls of the class do not seem to prefer. The pattern that emerges in the responses of Classes 7 and 8 (the first batch of the school, i.e., the earlier batch of Classes 7 and 8) is a common dislike for melodrama for unreal, overdramatized TV serials and a common preference for real-life television, contests and cartoons and some serials/soaps which they find credible. These broad patterns indicate a peer factor at work. Students talk to each other about the television watched at home, games are sometimes inspired by television stories such as the CID game popular among young boys; singing and dancing during free time is inspired by the same as seen on television (during such times, poems or songs learnt in classrooms or music classes are not used but popular culture as experienced through television is evoked). Television, across the grades, is seen to be the primary source of entertainment. Students comment that what is shown in soaps, films and so on on television is largely drama, that is, unreal and yet they claim to be influenced by it. A large number of students in Class 7 asserted that they like watching films and television soaps; news does not have many takers but reality shows have a popular following. On being asked what they learn from television, the first instant response was 'nothing' and then gradually some chipped in, 'domestic feuds', 'fighting' and 'dance'. At the mention of 'dance' many more joined in, and some of them broke into a brief jig.

There is a consensus on the kind of programmes a peer group watches as patterns vary from class to class. Class 3 showed a great liking for an animation series *Chota Bheem*. Class 5 did not mention it; their preference is Doraemon, Shin-chan and Power Rangers Reign Supreme. Peer groups, therefore, influence television choices but there is no predictable and fixed link between the two. There are variations in these choices which must be recognized. Apart from some of these apparent associations between peer associations and television choices and a few observable influences these programmes have on students, the nature and extent of the impact are not easy to decipher. These engagements with visual culture may remain as a memory in the minds of the children/students and may influence their thoughts and expressions in ways which even they would not always be able to identify. As John Fiske (1989) states, ([T]he) activation of the meaning potential of a text can occur only in the social and cultural relationships into which it enters' (1989: 3). The patterns of choices of television programmes favoured by students of different age groups show an impact of peer communication. What is selected out of the available choices by the students reveals its meaning when associated with their age and gender. The concerns these programmes address for the students play a role in these choices. In the context of schooling, television viewing becomes significant in terms of peer cultures as well. What is watched and how it is valued makes for one of the ways in which peer group connections are reinforced. The notion of what is 'in' or 'cool' may seem frivolous from one angle, but it is one of the markers of belonging or being excluded from a group. In schools, peer groups constitute one of the strongest strategies through which life in school becomes easier and enjoyable. And belonging to a group is connected to being in tune with what the group cherishes. Not getting it right can have consequences.

Are Gendered Patterns Present?

In locating some interconnections between television as a source of cultural coding and an aspect of students' lives, their gender conceptions, the issue of real or drama must be addressed. If students say that most of what they watch on television (apart from some real life documentations) is unreal/drama, perhaps, can one assume that they thus do not associate with it? It is the association between the real and the mythical/fictional/imaginary that needs to be understood, if only at a very preliminary level. The engagement with the make-believe, drama and myth does not take place in television watching alone, it happens, in this case, during play as well. As Carmichael notes, '([C]hildren)...get into play, and as they play sometimes they get into the role so deeply that they forget...who they are...they become something else' (2008: 177). The impact of make-believe entertainment is not insignificant although, the audience may be well aware of the fictional nature of it. 'Despite their working knowledge of television's unreality, people continue to turn to it to derive something more than merely entertainment' (Lembo 2000: 170). These are two associations that point towards how people engage with the unreal with great meaningfulness. In the case of television, when students collectively say that television programmes are mostly imaginary, and yet in the next moment they claim to have learnt something from watching those programmes, the issue of 'plausibility' (Lembo 2000) comes to the fore. It is also related to what they choose to watch on television because they choose it,

> [W]hen they find something to be plausible, it usually means that one or another aspect rings true with what they take to be their own experience and because of that, such programming usually merits their sustained attention...In distinguishing plausible from implausible, people relate it...to one or another aspect of their own lives...In doing so, they supply a referent or referents to the television discourse...they actively transform what television provides for them. (Lembo 2000: 168)

This perspective on the significance of television as a cultural medium is being used in the analysis of the relationship between students' choices in television programmes and their social agency.

When Class 3 students opt for Chota Bheem,[3] they are therefore indicating their preference for the experiences that a nine-
year-old boy, who is brave, strong and intelligent, goes through.
Bheem has a rival in *Kalia Pehelwan*, a jealous eleven-year-old
bully who is envious of Bheem's popularity. Bheem moves in a
group of friends that is made up of a monkey, a very young boy
and an older girl while the rival moves around with two boys who
are not very wise. Bheem is helpful by nature. The serial draws
inspiration from an epic character from the Mahabharata (Bheem
is one of the five *Pandava* brothers and is the strongest of them).
While the association with the mythical figure of Bheem is not
very significant, the serial does remind one of him. In its impro-
vised version it refers to an imagined childhood of Bheem and it
keeps bringing in very 'modern' elements and issues such cricket,
birthdays, friend visiting from Mumbai, aliens, the Mask (the Jim
Carrey starrer Hollywood movie as inspiration), fashion show, a
day at the beach, *Shaolin* (a form of Kung-fu), circus and so on.
The depictions are often highly implausible but young students,
both boys and girls, of Class 3 are very fond of it. In showing their
appreciation, they point to their concerns about friendships, difficulties, small-time rivals and modern day interests; it is of as much
significance to a girl as to a boy. However, there are gendered preferences too. The girls are drawn more towards Doraemon, the
gadget cat from the future, a science fiction comedy drama about
an earless robotic cat who travels back in the time from the 22nd
century to aid a schoolboy. It is of Japanese origin. It caters to
values such as honesty, courage, perseverance, family and respect
for elders. The boys prefer Power Rangers, a series about the polic-
ing of the earth by a group of power rangers who have an alien as
their leader and the group values teamwork apart from skilled
commando actions and weaponry. In choosing Bheem's narrative
commonly and going separate ways in the next choices, the students are displaying a gendered perception that knows certain
common grounds between girls and boys, but in choosing the
other two narratives differently, they are showing their susceptibil-
ity towards the gender norms prevalent in their everyday life and
in other discourses that exist around them.

Class 7 students collectively dislike melodramatic representations in TV serials and vote mostly either for 'real life stories' or cartoons. In rejecting the melodrama in these televised stories, they are rejecting the over reactive, unreal parodies of women and men and call these implausible, but are open to 'real' stories whose plausibility is undoubted or for cartoons which are licensed to be fantasies, and are imagined as a genre. Boys of Class 7 totally reject TV soaps of all kinds and show their preference for sports, Discovery channel, cartoons and reality shows related to dance, music, or comedy. Girls choose between the melodramatic girl bashing serials and the 'realistic women-centric' serials, enhancing the latter. They too reject melodramas where girls are tortured and they whimper and weep, instead they prefer narratives that are dramatic but are about the empowerment of women, within the limitations of being popular. As Lemish (2010) notes,

> Popular culture seems to be involved in an ambivalent process, wanting to depict strong girls in a manner such that they do not pose too dramatic a challenge to the traditional association between men and toughness, while growing in scope and condoning in character.... (2010: 4)

Class 8 also shows similar patterns when gendered choices are involved. Girls prefer cartoons, adventure knowledge-based programmes; boys prefer Discovery channel, music and dance shows; both, the girls and the boys, prefer foreign channels and reject Indian melodramas. Girls, here too, are against girl bashing serials and boys are averse to 'overreactions' as they call it. Class 8 boys, as a peer phenomenon, deviated towards dance reality shows. Pallabi Chakravorty (2011) states that '...dance reality shows are opening up new public spaces for contestations and reaffirmations of identities in contemporary India' (2011: 137). She further elaborates that such dance competitions that began during the 1990s, 'started the trend of showcasing a new kind of commercial dance genre in which Bollywood, classical folk, rap, break disco were packaged for consumption by the young...released dance from the more austere conventions of classicism' (Chakravorty 2011: 145–46) and became significant for their high possibility quotient of granting fame to ordinary folks.

Despite a shift in the way television choices reject domestic melodramas that tend to exaggerate gender oppositions, certain stereotypes nonetheless emerge. Class 8 girls describe gender traits as follows: a girl is responsible, caring and sweet while boys are the opposite, irresponsible and careless. The boys describe boys to be talented and naughty while the girls are described as helpful, nice, hyper and angry. Interestingly, the adjectives boys and especially girls used to describe themselves are much more idiosyncratic, where girls refer to themselves as happy, caring and cool. Class 7 boys describe boys, as a category, as handsome, intelligent and crazy/noisy/lost, but when referring to individual selves they see themselves as honest, intelligent and loving. Girls as a category for them have positive attitudes. Girls describe, girls as a category, as sweet, beautiful and emotional, but individually talk about their own selves as smart, best, curious and helpful. Boys, as a category for them, have positive qualities such as being intelligent, handsome but are largely negatively portrayed as proud, selfish and overconfident. Gendered perceptions play out differently in different contexts. When referring to an image of the other gender, stereotyping comes easily, but what emerges when referring to actual individuals is different and not categorized or, at least, categorization does not come easily. The television programmes that the students dislike are actually pointing towards a departure from certain fixed categories in the portrayal of genders. A revolution of sorts has not really occurred, but a certain shift in the way stereotyping has been checked is visible. When extremes are rejected, their plausibility is being rejected, which then suggests that multiple portrayals, closer to what is perceived as 'real', is being given credibility and hence some approval.

Dance, Drama as Gendered Expressions

Cultural events in the schools, especially the dramatic and dance events, in which students participate during competitions and the significant days of the school or public calendars, have implications for the portrayal of gendered identities. Schools, through these events, become contributors to the repertoire of gender conceptions available to their students. These events also become the sites of gendered expressions apart from impressions. The annual day celebration is a sort of a culmination of these year-long efforts.

On the Stage: Who are You Today?

The annual day of an educational institution, especially schools in most of India, has broadly three segments to it, but before that, it must be mentioned that it is a big day for a school because here, on this day, the school showcases its achievements through its students. So, the three segments include: the presence of some significant people as chief guests and the presence of the board members; the principal of the school announces the achievements of the students in various academic and extra-curricular activities held around the year; and a cultural programme towards the latter half of the scheduled time. Parents and family members of the children/students are also invited to watch all this. It is a big event for most of the schools and preparations begin at least a month in advance (for the cultural programmes and other arrangements such as invitation cards, annual report and so on).

Through this event, the school exhibits itself to the 'outsiders' present. Here, parents and families of the students, the board members and the chief guests, that is, people of some significant standing in the society.

The students' on-stage presence through various art forms is of deep interest to them. The school had been preparing the students for a whole month, one hour every day had been declared the zero period (from 1–2 pm) when students from all the classes were trained for various performances. There was a dramatic presentation, an elaborate musical, a song, a Sufi song, a welcome song and a yoga performance scheduled for the D-day. Except for the grand musical prepared by the dance teacher of our school, the practice sessions of other programmes were not very visible because some rehearsals were held in the main school and some took place in small sections over a period of time. The drama, for instance, was enacted with the help of a teacher from the main school. Almost 70 per cent of the students of the school from across the classes were involved in some presentation or the other. On the day of the event, the pre-presentation activities were in full swing. Students were getting dressed up in their respective costumes, hairdos and character specific makeup. Three makeup artists were called from outside, some parents (mothers) have pitched in, the teachers responsible for various acts were working non-stop for the last hour preparations. That day the school did not have a single student in it; there were fishermen, tribal women, *Kathak* dancers, little pink fairies, dacoits, *Shiva*, sari clad miniature ladies and others, but not a single student.

I was moving across the corridors when two gun-toting dacoits crossed my path, they had already 'got into the character' and for a second looked scary, and then I heard them wish me 'good morning ma'am!' The main school auditorium was allotted for their annual day celebrations. The pathway to the hall was decorated with white strings of flowers and blue orchids with some floor designs on the sidewalk. Two students stood welcoming the guests; all were given a printed copy of the programme. The auditorium was full to its capacity of around eighty to hundred seats. The chief guests were from the field of art. There was an eminent *sitarist*, a *Mohiniayattam* exponent and a Kathak artist. The proceedings and announcements were made largely in Hindi for the benefit of the parents of the students, even the chief guests, two of them are non-Hindi speaking, spoke in a broken, halting Hindi to keep up with the spirit. There were lighter moments too when a teacher by mistake announced in Hindi, '*Ab principal sir aapke samne kuch prastut karenge*' (now principal sir will be performing in front of you all). There was a faint murmur in the audience. The principal walked up to the dais, and in his characteristic quiet style stated, 'First of all, let me make it very clear that I am not going to "perform" anything, I will only address the audience'. There was a loud applause. In short, the school was upbeat about the important day and as described by the Headmistress in an earlier informal interview, the chief guests were from the field of creative arts as well.

The auditorium is well-equipped with gadgets that help change the colour schemes on the stage, so while a programme is being presented, light and sound effects could be played with to accentuate a certain kind of background. There was a chorus song by around fifty students from all programmes to welcome the guests; many have camouflaged their elaborate costumes. The song was in Hindi, which was followed by an elaborate and impressive presentation by Class 2 and 3 students, a variety of simple and complex yoga postures (yoga is a form of physical exercise that bases itself on a holistic understanding of the elements of body and its postures are alignments of body in various positions for health and wellbeing). Students were dressed in pink costumes having pink roses in hair, and there was a huge pink lotus prop in the centre around which students as young as 6 and 7 years performed various easy as well as difficult yoga exercises. It was a western, fairy sort of get-up while the yoga is about a different sort of world view. The play of light and sound made the event look a little ethereal. This was followed by a Sufi song by some boys. The song has been penned by Amir Khusro, a well-known Sufi saint. Each event has a commentary introducing it to the audience.

What came next was a riot of laughter; it was a play based on one of the popular stories from Arabian Nights—Ali Baba and Forty Thieves. The play was presented through *Kissangoi*, a tradition where stories are passed on through the oral tradition of storytelling. Another feature of the hilarious play was the intermixing of another plot in it; a story of a Hindu boy who is well-known for his deep reverence for his blind parents—story of *Shravan Kumar* was brought in the Arabian Nights plot, and Shravan Kumar created comic effects, as one very thin, *dhoti*-clad small built boy in the tale of a robust, gung-ho, heady dacoits. Smart one liner, Shravan showing interest in *Marjeena* while others from her community were interested in her and dramatic improvisations of character play by the students themselves had the audience in splits.

The last presentation was a musical—a grand musical on the river Ganges' journey from its source to the cities. The song was a depiction of the river Ganges (one of the biggest rivers in India; apart from its geographical significance, it has religious significance for the Hindus as it has mythological associations with Shiva, one of the key deities in Hinduism). The river is travelling incessantly and gracefully over the centuries for the good of the mankind. The musical traces Ganges' journey as it touches the lives of various communities, villagers, tribal people, fishermen and cities, its mythological context and finally how it is being mindlessly polluted by the very people for whom it brings life. The song asks, 'Why do you flow o *Ganga* amidst all this?' The presentation was planned and coached by the dance teacher of the special school and was indeed spellbinding. One of the chief guests, the Kathak practitioner, was moved to tears. She extended her assistance to any of the students who wish to pursue further training in this field.

Through this participation, students were engaged with an experience in the aesthetic transformation. As Schutz has described it, 'aesthetic experience suspends the belief in common sense but still remains in a communicative relation to the world of everyday life…[and]…[in a sense]…is closer to religious experience' (Schutz, cited in Knoblauch 1999: 13). This experience was a 'playful embodiment of multiple identities' (Hahn 2007: 155). It requires a special training in multitasking to remember who you are at the moment and embodying that character and enact a life of that character. It must be done with great dexterity and only then it touches the audience. In their comments later on about their experience of the whole event, the students were very glad to have been a participant in the big event. Many said that they were nervous in the beginning of their performance but soon coached themselves into courage. Some of them got confidence through audience applause and laughter. There is a peculiar trend observable in the students' responses; some of them loved their own performance so much that they reinvent the context of their play or dance. For instance, the boy who played the role of Shravan Kumar stated that it was Shravan Kumar's play in which the story of the forty thieves got mixed up while actually it was the other way round. Similarly, a boy from the group of dacoits remembers his role as the role of dacoit *Mangal Pandey* while there was no such role in the play. Many of them said, 'I was this', 'I was that', rather than saying he/she was playing the role of so and so. Many report that it was a memorable experience. They experienced something new either as a character or as having realized that they can act or sing or dance and that they look forward to another such event. Overall, it was a transformative experience for the students, made available through the presence of their school. Although it was one day in the year, it engaged them with new disciplining of their embodied selves and in that disciplining opened up other ways of being to them. In the performative, they not only learned new ways of being but also secretly expressed their selves through the performative.

Philip A. Woods (2009) has employed the concept of re-enchantment in relation to the impact of creative and expressive endeavours and associates it with what Peter E. Woods (1993 as cited in Woods 2009) has called 'critical events' in primary and secondary education. School activities and undertakings where teachers and students work together, '…have the features of educational processes that are not reducible to rationalized procedures and outcomes' (Woods 2009: 129).

> Critical events,…have something of the spirit of what Turner calls 'Communitas'…it has something magical about it…a quality both intensely real and intensely unreal. Latent or suppressed feelings, abilities, thoughts, aspirations are suddenly set free…a new collective spirit….uncommon excitement and expectations are generated. All this is something special, though exactly why is difficult to explain. (Woods P., cited in Woods P.A. 2009)

Philip A. Woods (2009) suggests three possible ways of explaining this, though the idea of

> [E]ducational entrepreneurialism (enterprising initiatives by teachers that brings out and make a reality successful, ambitious projects that engage number of students and adults); the passion of individuals that critical events attract and that goes beyond (is distanced from) the confines of work aimed at achieving just measurable achievement; the immediacy of artistic expression, enjoyed and appreciated for its intrinsic value. (Woods 2009: 129)

The event remains registered in the memories of the students, months after its actual occurrence. It is fondly remembered for the self-expressions it facilitates, for the barriers overcame in the process. It registers as an exercise that allows for a transformation from being a student to being somebody other than that, someone grand, or foolish, or divine, or ferocious or malicious. The body is allowed to jump over to other formations of self within the field of school. Transformations to other selves are for once not punished but are rewarded and appreciated. In enacting the profane myths, the new possibilities of becoming someone else are being actualized and the experience is being cherished by the students for its uniqueness.

From a theological resourcing of values and its significance in directing a world view, the students interact with a school that has a little different take on theo-cultural values and a memorable engagement with the culture of performative brings out a different self for the students. The impact is not homogenous for all despite the structural contouring being defined socially, and each zone has its own peculiarities and capacities vis-à-vis human agency.

Some very young students, girls and boys, were trained to participate in a musical presentation of yoga postures. In the green room, two girls (dressed in pink leotards and t-shirt with pink roses in their hair) were making fun of a boy participant dressed similarly except for the roses. They said, 'You are dressed like a girl, in pink', and laughed mischievously. He was offended and complained to the teacher, 'Look ma'am she is saying that I am dressed like a girl'. The girls were hushed up.

The girls were much larger in number for the dance–drama, a musical on the river Ganges. It depicted the journey of the river and the nurturing and giving nature of the river, which is believed to be a goddess, a deity. Girls represented the Ganges in its various stages namely, the beginning, the mid-course and in the cities. Girls represented all that was good in the musical. Boys either had a brief entry as fishermen or as lord Shiva,[4] but their most prominent role was that of 'pollution' that harms the river Ganges.[5] The song's lyrics say, 'Why do you still keep flowing o mighty, graceful, powerful, grand Ganga…why don't you just retaliate?' It was meant to portray several cultural codes—the various classical dance forms; girls in their finest get-ups; Ganges as a river, a lifeline; Ganges as a religious figure; Ganges as an enduring feminine power who can but does not unleash its wrath; on the other hand, boys as the dark, negative influences (they actually wore black dresses and black war paint and masked their eyes). The girls portrayed as the finer forms and the boys as rogues was another axis. For the drama, boys were in a majority while there were hardly 4–5 girls. The drama was a witty portrayal of the well-known Ali Baba and the forty thieves from the Arabian Nights. What was significant in the terms of gendered expressions was a multitude of gendered persons—boys as thugs, dacoits, honest, funny, romantic and wise, and girls as intelligent, cunning, greedy, quick witted and romantic. Later, each of the boys told how they liked what they were portraying; the dacoit loved being the dacoit, the small, funny romantic boy liked his role, the people who were 'killed' liked their role and all seemed to say that the play was centred around their role, though peer participation and peer applaud were also acknowledged. In a way, there was no one hero but several, each significant for what they were. Girls in 'Ganga' were portrayed more as a unified identity, so in their responses, the individual differences did not come up, they talked in terms of 'our group' (different groups of girls performed different forms of dance) did well or faltered somewhere.

This chapter has assessed the significance of peer contexts in their multiple hues, especially for the students of the Pratyantar School. The peer relations mediate the schooling sometimes by socializing the students in the culture of the school and also by helping them overcome the anxieties that the school tends to induce in its students, intentionally or unintentionally. Peer cultures of a school are the informal aspect of school experience but an integral part of the process of schooling. In this study, a very significant link emerges between peer performatives and the gender identities. Peer contexts seem to support the gender stereotypes in some situations while simultaneously providing gender neutral spaces as well. In fact, the most prominent display of gender-segregated activities is provided in and through the peer interactions, at least, in this school. The formal school activities attempt to come through as gender sensitized no matter how preliminary these may seem. Gender constitution, as formal schooling facilitates, as extracurricular aspects of schooling lead to, as peer stereotyping creates and as peer relations tend to, disregards the gender differences. All these discourses generate several pathways for gender identity to be constructed and reconstructed for the students.

Notes

1. Nehru Planetarium is situated in Delhi at *Teen Murti* and is part of the Jawaharlal Nehru Memorial Museum and Library. It has a sky-theatre with a huge dome shaped screen that simulates a travel into the universe and provides knowledge related to astronomy. It is a popular place for schools for an educational trip for their students.
2. Nehru used to adorn a rose bud in his jacket lapel as a regular practice.
3. The animated series is produced and set in a village of India. It revolves around the everyday life of young children and the concerns it caters to are of friends, rivals, insults, cleverness, victory, 'giving it back' and is interestingly modern in its intertextuality, that is, though it is set in a village background and this Bheem is the childhood portrayal of the Bheem, one of the five Pandava brothers (and here too, he is assisted by *Krishna* the Hindu god who assists Pandavas in the Mahabharata)
4. He is one of the prime deities from the Hindu pantheon, who is believed to be carrying Ganga in his mane.
5. Over the years, the river Ganges has been polluted enormously by the industrial effluents and city waste.

7
Reflections and Possibilities

This ethnographic study, given its spatio-temporal boundaries, substantiates some of the key indicators of life at school. A reading of the variations of interpersonal interactions informs about agential actions that take place in the everyday life. Schooling practices, formal and informal, are often found to be cross-cutting and interrogate each other. Students' experiences in and dialogues with schooling show up some stereotypical patterns, but these are those of conformity as well as of resistance. There are other kinds of responses as well, ranging from making the most of an opportunity to a calculated apathy to schooling. These strategies of interpersonal interactions in different contexts, though enacted within the school, are nonetheless not only informed by the social contexts outside the school, but also have implications that go beyond the school. This study did not seek to measure the impact of the school in some quantifiable way but sought to mark the various activities and perceptions that play out in the process of schooling in order to bring out the vital multiplicities that make school meaningful. School processes are social situations and thus what transpires through these processes have complex, deeper meanings in non-school contexts and in the constitution of students' identities to some extent.

The state exercises its influence in creating the structural framework within which the school must function; this happens through the prescriptions of curriculum, textbooks, rules of teachers, recruitment and other directives. What emerges is that while the Pratyantar School follows state directives, the management of the school, instead of being restricted by them, goes beyond and emphasizes the value of schooling. Instead of a routine way of operating a school, the management of Pratyantar takes a keen interest in involving marginalized children in their project of teaching and learning. The emphasis on schooling and its signifi- cance for the children are realized by the management and in this school, the structures privilege learning, as it were. Structures are not necessarily constraining, they could, therefore, create possibil- ities as well. The school, with all its emphasis on discipline and order, offers space to its students and emerges as an enabling school. Pratyantar is not an alternative school by usual standards and yet, within its framework of mainstream schooling, the school attempts to make a difference to the lives of the children who come to study here. I cannot claim that the institution operates flawlessly and is entirely bias-free; however, small islands of good intentions take it up several notches on a scale of school achievements.

Contexts of Research on Schools

Schools have been seen in relation to various social formations and categories, be it gender, religion, ethnicity, caste, popular cul- ture, language or ideologies of various kinds. Schools act out the categories of social existence through the processes of schooling. Language, especially English, in the context of India has a classed connotation with implications that are as disabling as they are enabling. Gender is seen as reinforced through classroom dis- courses and interaction patterns, in choices of subjects and in peer perceptions. Religion colours pedagogy and codes of disciplining. Schooling is deeply associated with one or more of such aspects of social existence. The ways in which these aspects of social exis- tence play out in the space of school, however, cannot entirely be presupposed. For instance, in this study, gender stereotyping has been more evident in the non-formal zones of schooling while the formal classroom interactional behaviour appears to play this down. Religion also does not find a place in the official agenda of the school, although strong allusions to religion find expression in the aesthetical representations and the moral discourses chosen by the school practitioners, that is, students and teachers. This study also shows that the school's agendas and the sub-themes in the agendas do not remain uncontested by the students. The school's agendas leave an impact, but the nature and extent of this impact are not always measurable.

Fieldwork and Some Improvisations

The prescribed fieldwork techniques were extremely valuable and indispensable; however, improvisations had to be devised during the course of the study. Each field poses its unique problems and leads to equally suitable ways out of those problems. In this case, the keen observation mode was the most helpful tool that could be used, least unobtrusively. School management, teachers and students were also very eager to know what was being studied. Any directed attention on a particular event or activity or set of activities caused them to erase any traces of error in their presentation. Under these circumstances, maintaining an overall interest in all that was happening around and feigning non-attention to something that needed attention were some of the ways that had to be employed to diffuse overzealous interventions from the school participants. This is not to say that the school was dishonest in what it was doing, but it was keen on showing itself as absolutely error-free. Acceptance as a researcher was more forthcoming when teachers believed that I was not there to assess their teaching skills and students felt reassured that I was not spying on them on behalf of their teachers. Informal conversations were the other more suitable sources of information as formal interviews suddenly put the interviewee in a politically correct mode which could hinder the emergence of the 'real' picture. Informal conversations and casual, overheard remarks played a crucial role in completing the picture to a larger extent, although it can never be complete.

The students' responses too had to be elicited in a similar manner. They were difficult to engage with in a group discussion as they would all start jumping out with responses that created chaos. It was much better to get them to respond to open-ended questions in a questionnaire format that allowed them to express themselves anonymously in a manner that they liked. The same point was asked through several differently framed questions to ensure a well-rounded response and to look for discrepancies in the responses. One word metaphors were also elicited from them in response to certain categories, such as gender, peer, school, home, self and so on. Gordon et al. (2000) use the technique of 'use a metaphor' where the informants are asked to write the first association that comes to their mind for the things listed in the form of a questionnaire. Metaphors are not objective details; they are culturally informed and by using them in this quick response questionnaire mode the intention is to capture the cultural response in simple terms that would not have come up otherwise (as sometimes the thought out response may not highlight the key sentiment). Metaphors are quick answers, not very carefully thought out, and perhaps reveal the key signifiers that the mind uses often in relation to the category concerned.

I found the observational mode to be very helpful as compared to the interaction mode as I could observe and note any aspect that I wanted to focus on without there being too much pre-empted behaviour from the actors. For instance, many a times, while I would be noticing the gendered nature of classroom interactions the teacher and the students would, in fact, be focusing on presenting a picture of a well-informed class. Sally Anderson privileges the observational mode as a preferred one over the articulated expressions and states, 'I used detailed observation of social interaction as a basic technique in all venues, and, thus, intentionally placed myself in a rather passive participant role' (Anderson 2008: 33). She further elaborates, 'my work explores the usefulness of nonverbal, physical data in gaining understanding of the "doing" of "being" a child. It also questions current culturally biased approaches that privilege verbal articulation over physical action as the most authentic expression of *real* individuals' (Anderson 2008: 36). School settings sometimes pose a restriction on the formal verbal expressions as those are tutored in the classroom interaction mode of giving a right answer and from the prescribed forms of knowledge. The students would often provide predictable responses to direct questions. 'Interviewing students poses special problems since they generally find it difficult to go beyond institutional habits' (Simons as cited in Okano 1993: 51). 'A previous empirical study documented difficulties experienced in eliciting views from Japanese high school students through interviews: students gave similar short answers to the questions posed by the short term visiting researcher, and as such the replies were of limited use' (Horvath as cited in Okano 1993: 51). Formal, verbal and direct responses from the students to the queries of the researcher are not always forthcoming. The discipline-centric and image-conscious atmosphere of schools is one common reason for an obstruction in the flow of information which has been observed by other school researchers as well.

Anonymous, open-ended and multi-layered questions helped in generating relatively freer expressions and those were then discussed informally whenever possible.[1] These responses were also seen in the context of their everyday actions and expressions. Pia Christensen (2010) discusses the significance of 'cultures of communication' as ways of conducting, interacting and communicating that benefit ethnographic research.

> [I]t emphasizes the importance of seeing fieldwork...as a practical engagement with local cultural practices of communication. Thus, by observing children's language use, their conceptual meanings and their actions, the researcher is able to piece together a picture of the social interactions and the connections between people. (Christensen 2010: 151)

The field presents its peculiar situational contexts which need appropriate combinations of methodological techniques. The value of detailed, expressive and multiple natures of responses to the questionnaires became even more apparent when, on one occasion, a teacher was left with the questionnaires and her very young respondents. The first half of the questionnaire was full of diverse responses by the students during the time I was present in the classroom. When I left the classroom for some other work, the other half had identically worded responses, except by one or two student. The freedom that the students had in responding to anonymous questionnaires with no tutoring from the teachers or even fellow students created a space that was not replicated in my formal discussions with them.

Patterns that Emerged at Pratyantar School

While classroom observations play out the classed nature of school interactions, the spaces outside the classroom but within the school display religion and gender at work in the school. This finding has several implications. While the formal school with its focus on pedagogical training is an important aspect of schooling, it remains one of the several axes of school experience. There are other places within the school that are relatively non-formal and yet very significant for the students. In fact, at times, 'formal' becomes less meaningful as compared to the 'informal' in the school. We may therefore conclude that within the school there are zones which have different meanings for the students and the teachers.

Gendered Perceptions in the School

A significant implication of this finding is that it points towards a tendency of a preponderance of particular experiences in certain school processes. Peer relations emerge as a zone where gender relations find their multifaceted expression, both in stereotyping and surpassing the stereotype. The formal classroom interactions, the attitudes of the teachers in the formal curricular settings and the students' assessment of themselves in such settings were largely devoid of gender stereotyping. Gender inequity as often observed in classroom contexts is not as markedly present in this case as it is present in the peer interactions and peer perspectives. There are the usual complaints about gender discrimination in classroom contexts, such as privileging boys in allowing them to respond to teachers' questions, paying more attention to boys, boys dominating the discourse, and boys opting for math and science and doing well in them. These were not found to be present in classroom interactions. A studied sensitivity towards these aspects was observed in the classrooms. Gender stereotypes are present outside the classrooms, in informal interactions among the students. In the contexts of peer interactions gendered perceptions prevail many a times. However, there were activities which are common and where peer relations are privileged over and above the gender differences. There is no doubt an imperceptible shift in the way girls and boys are beginning to relate to one another in this kind of a school in urban India, but this shift must be acknowledged.

The informal or non-curricular activities in the school were sometimes found to be regressive despite a new alertness against the prevalence of gender discrimination. It emerges that the hidden and less apparent inequities remained undetected and were perpetuated through apparently innocuous acts such as the distribution of stereotyped roles to girls and boys during the stage presentations of cultural events. The roles of dacoits and the 'evil' characters were handed out to the boys while girls got to play roles of kind, nurturing, graceful personifications of the river Ganges. Girls were given detailed and delicate dance moves on the stage while boys were provided macho movements and less of dance forms. The students too, on their part, accepted and approved these identifications. The young boys, who were given a pink costume for yoga presentation, were defensive when the girls made fun of them for wearing pink. Older boys took great pride in dressing up as dacoits and as 'pollutants' dressed in black, with black masks and face paint. It must be mentioned that stage presentations were meaningful for the students for several other reasons which played a constructive role for them and that gender stereotyping was one aspect, but not the only aspect of the activity.

Class Expressions

Classroom interactions resonated much more with the issues related to social class identities. Curricular knowledge, handwriting, proficiency in English, cultural presumptions of teachers and subject preference are issues that repeatedly point towards the classed experiences of schooling for these students. These experiences were, however, not homogenous. Teachers face a dilemma in relation to educating these students. They are expected to maintain a certain prescribed standard in their pedagogy and are often upbeat about the impact they have on them. However, there are times when these teachers face a barrier in their efforts which they associate with the students' homes and their belonging to another social class. The routine classroom interactions become sites of contestation of class identity. Informal conversations about these aspects bring out the attempts towards adaptation and resistance to these by the students, as expressed by the students and their teachers as well.

Religion and Its Contexts in the School

Pratyantar School is secular in its pronounced status, and thus religion is an issue that is treated with a studied sensitivity. In such a context, religion makes inroads through some other channels and in the non-formal zones within the school. In this case, it enters through representational tools and through the 'cultural legacy' path. There are two significant aspects of religion in the school that have been explored in this study. One, the ability to talk about religion in a social space in India without referring to the communal element so often associated with it. Religion as a site of conflicts has critical significance and there is a valid reason for its recurrence in the scholarly works in the Indian contexts, but there are other significant ways of referring to religion. This study focuses on religion as a perspective, a philosophy and a cultural system. This study suggests that even in a 'secular' social space, religion can make inroads as it permeates the cultural paraphernalia of a particular society.

An attempt has also been made to understand students' patterns of comprehending religion through their conceptualizations of the notion of God. This reveals how the children relate to religion, what meanings they draw from it and how they are well-versed in the philosophical arguments about the 'god-figure'. It emerges through this study that school does not provide most of this knowledge that, by and large, remains an education that students receive from home. School has its own way of presenting religion to the students though not through indoctrination but in cultural practices and through extracurricular aesthetics. In the absence of any structured practices specific to religious pedagogy, the school's intervention in students' perspectives on religion does not take an evident form. At the same time, in the absence of a strong secularizing discourse and a covert reliance on idioms of religion as a source of aesthetics and values, school emerges as a space that is not absolutely free from the impact of religion.

Technologies of school practices reveal how the transmission of knowledge is perpetuated, resisted, negotiated and incorporated. Schools cannot be linked with a singular agenda though such an intention may be expressed at some level. As the implementation is carried out, the people responsible for the implementation interpret the agenda/s in their own ways and ultimately it changes forms at different stages.

There are certain sites that privilege certain kinds of social expressions. A classroom in an urban school may downplay gender inequity but may not be able to erase inequalities of social class. A secular school may stay away from the indoctrination of students but may not hold back religion from entering the portals in its cultural avatar. Informal interactions in the schools may encourage coping with the school issues but may perpetuate gender perceptions. The awareness of the diversity of school experiences within the space of the school opens up possibilities of exploring the potential of the school in constituting the identities of its students. The everyday practices mark a significant point, which can be taken as the smallest unit in actualizing a shift in perspectives.

All that happens in and through the school is constantly being influenced by the non-formal zones in the school and the other social contexts that are situated outside the school. Schools need to be situated along these tangents if their significance is to be assessed in a comprehensive way.

Note

1. See Appendix for a sample questionnaire.

Appendix 1
School Culture: Conceptual and Methodological Locations

Theoretical Perspective

[T]here is no single best way to reconstruct and represent the social world.

—Hammersley and Atkinson (1995: 240).

Theoretically, this search for diversity in social reality finds a place in orientations that recognizes the agency of individuals in the realm of the social. Perspectives such as symbolic interactionism, through its different proponents, and more recently post-structuralism, which draws attention towards the performative aspects of social existence, are significant. The prevalence of social structures and their commanding presence is not denied but it is suggested that the everyday execution of the formal principles of these structures gets mediated at several stages and is implemented differently in different contexts. A symbolic interactionist perspective would be one of the basic standpoints of this work. The symbolic is present in all the interactions among the human subjects. Recognition of this aspect of human relationships and the consequent implications these entail for a sense of self is explored in this study. The premise held at this point is that different individual students carve out distinct personas for themselves within the broader structural frameworks of school processes. Though there are several exponents of this paradigm, this work has relied on a few concepts presented by some interaction theorists and is not based on the work of any one particular theorist.

The New Sociology of Education was initially a combination of 'three orientations: Neo-Marxism, interactionism and the sociology of knowledge' (Ball 2004: 4). While the neo-Marxists were concerned with the reproductionist element of school processes, the interactionists, through the ethnographic studies of the schools, were concerned with the issues of identity construction through school processes and the sociology of knowledge dealt with the issues of curriculum. As Green and Whitty (1994 as cited in Ball 2004: 4) have put it, 'they were less willing to accept that nothing could be done about it', that is, about the 'unequal distribution of social possibilities' (Green and Whitty 1994 as cited in Ball 2004: 4). What emerges here is that a certain eclectic pattern needs to be considered from among the theoretical perspectives present today. While reproduction theories can gain from interpretative ethnographic analysis through observations of day-to-day school processes and practices to see how they do or do not contribute to reproduction; to locate the spaces of subversion, the agents in that and the implications therein. Alternately, the other theoretical perspective, that is, the interactionist approach, could gain greater depth in its analysis of situational contexts by not neglecting a perspective that relates these with the outside social world. The teacher–student ratio, the school infrastructure and resources, peer culture and academic and extra-curricular activities have a complex relationship with the world outside the school that is equally significant to explore.

In its most basic assumptions, as conceived by Blumer (1969), symbolic interactionism believes that human beings' behaviour towards the things depends upon the meaning those things hold for them and that those meanings arise as well as alter during the interpretive process that human beings engage in as self-reflective individuals. The interaction between human beings is symbolic (Blumer 1969: 2). Symbolic interactionism with its focus on inter-subjectivity and creation of meanings through everyday interactions of the individual actors deals with the thoughts and actions in and through which reality exists for these actors. Interactionism understands the relationship between the individual and the social as a dialectical one. Berger and Luckmann (1966) have focused on this aspect in great detail through the concepts of social processes, culture and symbolic universe. The concept of identity puts it in a relational aspect.

> Identity is formed by social processes...it is maintained, modified or even reshaped by social relations. The social processes involved (in this)...are determined by the social structure...the identities produced...(similarly) react upon the given social structure, maintaining it, modifying it, or even reshaping it. (Berger and Luckmann 1966: 194)

'Definition of the situation', a concept developed by W.I. Thomas (1923) of the interactionist school, accords greater agency to the subject/actor/agent in creating an understanding of the situation according to his/her perspective and stand. Similar objective, structural conditions can mean different things to different actors depending upon how they choose to define those structural elements for themselves. Meaning emerges as the core concern of the symbolic interactionist approaches placing greater significance over the creators of meaning, that is, the human agents and simultaneously over the situations of meaning construction, that is, the larger contexts. What emerges consequently is an approach that points towards multiple levels of meaning-occurrence. A self is created in this process; not a singular fixed self but several selves contingent upon the other interacting selves and the contexts of interaction. These elements associated with identity formation would constitute a major segment and a key area to be explored through this research on school processes.

While symbolic interactionism has an eye for details and nuances of everyday interactions, Hammersley (1980) suggests that it would further enrich the perspective if it rechecked its margins. Hammersley suggests that, with its commitment to details and actors' views, everyday interactionism must involve itself with interrelationships among the institutions of a society, if not with an overarching framework of societal structure. It can lend significant insight into these areas since it is not deterministic in its methodological orientation. As members of different institutions, the behaviours of individuals during interactions can add a significant dimension to these studies.

This concern for engaging further with the contexts finds resonances in another theoretical paradigm. As Rob Moore has put it 'current post-structural approaches follow on from earlier ones grounded in symbolic interactionism in arguing that differential outcomes reflect the degrees to which different groups feel the school to be relevant to and to value their identity, experience and heritage' (Moore 2004: 9). Bronwyn Davies' study of discursive practices in school settings (Davies 2004: 128) gives a distnict format to the emergence of subjectivity in relation to the contexts. Post-structuralist paradigm has been identified as proclaiming that the individual is not a fixed product of a socially constructive exercise but is, again and again, constituted in the discursive practices that they participate in. Davies has used this paradigm to focus on the processes or discursive practices through which identity emerges and re-emerges in school settings. It involves learning the meanings of the various categories available for creating an identity through 'storylines'. Taking up or not taking up a discursive practice shapes our identity. 'Images, metaphors, narrative structures, terms of address, teaching practices all have a strong role to play in creating various discourses which when appropriated by the pupils, shape their identity' (Davies 2004: 137). They are not passive recipients of what the school has to offer them, they already have 'a personal baggage of images and metaphors based on their own experience of being positioned within the many and contradictory discursive practices that they have encountered' (Davis 2004: 138).

In *The Logic of Practice* (1980), he describes,

> [T]he *habitus* is an infinite capacity for generating products—thoughts, perceptions, expressions and actions—whose limits are set by the historically and socially situated conditions of its production, the conditioned and conditional freedom it provides is as remote from creation of unpredictable novelty as it is from simple mechanical reproduction of the original conditioning. (1980: 55)

The possibilities of agential improvisations have thus been acknowledged in Bourdieu's perspective.

Significant Contributions from School Ethnographies

Since the emergence of the internalist approaches to school and the qualitative, ethnographic researches inspired by the New Sociology of Education in the 1960s and the 1970s, works on schools have seen a growing interest in the processual dynamics of the school cultures. The orientations may have been towards pointing out the reproductive agenda of schools, or the impact of ideology on school, or the resistance within the reproductive workings of schools or catching the identity dimension of school processes, but an involvement with the cultural frameworks has found favour with most of the studies. Paul Willis (1977) through his well-known ethnographic account of working-class students, in his *Learning to Labour*, has focused on the school education's reproduction agenda and resistance that it faces from the working-class 'lads' through their counter-school culture. The dynamics of this counter-school culture were recorded in this study through the workings of cultural behaviour. The way these students embodied an overtly, heightened masculine identity in their talk, mannerisms, dressing and attitude was a response to the demeaning undercurrents of the school that in its class biased framework placed them at a disadvantage in the beginning itself. The cultural practices that these students endorsed were drawn from their own social culture and they played it against the school culture. Refusing to be showed down by the school in their subversive witticism, they downplayed the seriousness of the academic endeavours. It is through paying attention to these culture attitudes that the resistance to production line develops and this is a definition of a situation by a group that exists not despite, but because of these straining conditions.

In the foreword to Peter McLaren's book *Schooling as a Ritual Performance*, Henry Giroux locates this work as 'an ethnography in a theoretical discourse that critically appropriates and combines the methods and insights of ritual and performance theory...and the new sociology of education' (1986: xi). McLaren's work also identifies the reproduction cultural codes prevalent in the school processes and he looks at the students' cultural codes as they come in contact with the school's dominant culture. In displaying the ritualized dimensions of these interactions, McLaren brings out the various 'states' that the students are capable of creating for themselves and how those 'states' are identified by cultural practices and attitudes. The non-literal aspect of social interactions has been explored and showcased in this neo-Marxist reading of the school culture. Overcoming the binary projection of 'ritual: practical=sacred: profane', McLaren places ritualized behaviour on a continuum where one extreme is formalized ritual ceremonies and then there are several other forms that ritual takes, mostly as embodied symbolic meaning. The interpretation of ritualized behaviour would be contingent upon historical and situational contextualization of the act. Everyday rituals in the schools can be carriers of the cultural hegemony of the dominant ideology (here, class). It is not easy to interrogate these as these are meant to be perceived as natural, universal and right. McLaren discusses several metaphors in describing the teachers' instructional rites such as 'performatives', which do not simply describe but bring a state of affairs into existence; 'indirect speech acts', give the impression that the source of statement is sacred and permanent; and 'power spots', in which each teacher had a favourite place and position in the classroom where they feel powerful and safe. McLaren has analyzed the processes involved in cultural reproduction through the concept of 'root paradigm'—the dominant theme in a range of activities. The dominant themes of this school for the students were 'becoming a worker' and 'becoming a catholic'. The former was promoted through putting a premium on the 'student state' marked by instructions, such as work hard, sit still, copy your work, be silent and so on. The resistance to this theme came in through those who were deeply engrained in the 'street corner state'—unpredictable, boisterous and playful.

An ethnographic study of a school in India, involving the work of an ideology, by Meenakshi Thapan (1991), *Life at School*, (through the theme of culture as an ethos of the school, present in its rituals and ceremonies), brings out the multi-layered complex interrelatedness of school processes. The ways in which the foundational ideology of a school gets negotiated through the teacher cultures, student cultures and teacher–student interactions put a focus on the interpretive element of social interactions in the school. Cultural practices give substantive ground to the transcendental order and the local order to come through in speech, body practices, consumption culture and values. The two orders that stand for the ideological world view and the ordinary respectively create multiple definitions of the situation for the subjects involved. Since the two orders are quite different in their perspectives a possibility of conflict pervades the school's processes. Thapan's ethnographically grasped and culturally schematized analysis of the everyday activities of the school lucidly brings forth the multiple ways in which the conflict comes to be identified by differently situated subjects and how it gets resolved through broad routing through either exclusion, or absorption or a dialectic. And this exercise of observing the everyday life through the theoretical framework of interactionism addresses not just the polemic question of power and its dissemination but also the intricate significances of the tools that get employed in it. It also brings out the implications of social processes in negotiation with human subjects in the context of schooling.

Sheila Riddell's (1992) ethnographic study of school processes, *Gender and the Politics of the Curriculum*, focuses on the curriculum as representing the school's agenda towards reproduction, especially gender and class identities. As she herself puts it, this work is a combination of social reproduction approach and social action approach. She interrogates why gender codes tend to keep women in a disadvantageous situation in the labour market (as mediated by the curriculum design and choice-making) and also whether the situation is changing now. How school, home and teachers have a role to play here, that is, school ethos and the gender codes promoted and accepted by home and teachers. As an interactionist endeavour, it also places significance on the people's understanding of social situations as a determining factor in creating an identity for them. Her work shows that gender and class sometimes intersect each other and have uncommon implications, for example, the working-class boys were found to have the most stereotypical views on gender roles while middle-class girls had the least stereotypical views.

Peter Woods' (1979) *The Divided School* is an ethnographic study that understands school through the theme of 'division', that is, the division between the external factors and the internal factors. The former, for example, may mean the class condition and the latter the institutional elements (of the schools). This singular theme has been located in various practices and perspectives within the school through some of the most interesting interfaces in the workings of humour; how it may stand for conflict or control or solidarity or release, and how all of these, none of these or some of these may be involved and have different implications. Woods confers significant transformational potential on the institutional order of the school and the teacher's perspectives in the difficult-to-surmount conditions of social differentiation. He maintains that not all divisions in society, equally deep-entrenched for all, and the intensity of dividing factors can be moulded at various levels during a lifetime; the school and the teachers have a possibility of altering the situation of division. As he puts it, 'though Paul Willis argues that teacher style to likely to have little effect on disaffected working-class kids. This might be true with extreme intransigent or rebellious groups but...at low field, teacher style was important for all groups' (1979: 297). The various forays into the ethnographic, interpretative and interactionist studies of school and the other structures of the society have identified various circumferences built by structural conditions and have simultaneously mapped the workings of these vis-à-vis the human agents. The view that structural conditions get substantiated and actualized through human agency and there is an interactive link at work and not an imposition link, creates the space for emergence of a diverse range of possibilities that can contest the image of structurally dominating discourse.

In all the works discussed above, the turnaround in the orientation towards the subject matter and definition of the subject matter is evident. There has been a shift from an objectivist study of things as they are to the representation of the subject's position and the acknowledgement of the subjects as not just active participants but also active interpreters of their worlds. It clearly marks a shift from the notions of structural imposition of dominant discourses to contested discourses; from singular determinants such as class, family, ethnicity and gender exercising influence over educational prospects to intersecting, multi-layered discursive practices and from either 'school's prime responsibility argument' or 'family main culprit' argument to a difficult to point out one influential factor. As Mehan sums it up, 'the emphasis in the interpretative tradition…is on social agency, cultural mediation and constitutive activity' (Mehan as cited in Ball 2004: 1). Identity will constitute a key segment in this work, and almost all the researches with a qualitative bend and an interactionist orientation have dealt with its various dimensions substantively. Any discussion of agency would have to incorporate the issues surrounding identity construction. In choosing to study the school processes as mediated by students' experiences at three levels, namely, class, gender and religion, I will need to address the overlaps and contradictions that these three categories of identity construction will inevitably present. Within the school, the practices specific to school regime would be scrutinized, primarily, the cultural values promoted by the school management. Its interpreted versions at the hands of the teachers, peer group cultures and the students' embodiment and cultural articulation of these will also be significant.

Students' Identities in Works on School

The relationships between schooling and students' identities have been explored in studies on schools. Paul Willis' (1977) work stands out as a descriptive account of the counter-school culture exhibited in the expressed selves of the working-class students. Within the school culture, deviant labelling theory (Becker 1963 cited in Rist, 2015) assumed that consistent labelling of students by teachers may lead to deviant behaviour as students may take these seriously and over the time may internalize them. Cathy Bird (1980) observes through her study of schools in London, that though such an argument has credibility, the generalization assumed herein is problematic. Such assumptions are removed from the contexts. And contexts lend a very significant meaning to incidents and practices of labelling by the teachers. Sometimes a certain labelling could be in the context of a particular teacher and not everyone and that labelling may not get communicated or even accepted. However, in a more sustained, structurally emanating context, labels could be internalized, but again the impact is not fixed. Similarly, encouragement of certain ideological (Thapan 1991) or religious (Kumar 2000) orientations by schools does not smoothly translate into the imbibing of these orientations by the students. Thapan's study of an ideologically oriented school shows that its impact on students' identities was ranged on a continuum of the deeply inspired 'sensitive students'; the moderately influenced ones; the indifferent ones, that is, those who participated in the practices associated with the ideology but did not practice the ideology otherwise; and many who were averse to it, interpreting it as something that 'can be practiced only by the "rich and retired"' (1991: 152).

In a study of schools in Banaras, Nita Kumar (2000) goes back to the historical data on Annie Besant's endeavour to Hinduize the students and observes that despite the zeal and impositions or inclusions of practices that were meant to keep the students on a Hinduized Indian path, the project failed to impact the students due to spatial and practical reasons. '[T]hat the appearance, layout and location of spaces changes habits—of living, working, playing, socializing—and following upon habits, expectations and idealizations. The school building is a reality to which the child is required to mould himself' (Kumar 2000: 103). A building structured on the colonial architectural model coupled with 'a selective and reduced version of Hinduism' that neglected 'the body language, attitudes towards space and time, cosmology...life and death, work and leisure' countered the impact that was intended (Kumar 2000: 154). The students imbibed the other messages but a cultural interaction with this scheme remained ineffective.

Jeffrey remarks that students are not interacting with a neat, bracketed value system; the reality that they encounter is diverse and often contradictory. 'Little is known about how children respond to such learning regimes or how these discourses relate to children's behaviour in schools' (2005: 30).

Peer group relationships have also been found to be significant in affecting students' identities as peer groups constitute an important aspect of the experience of schooling. In a study by Paul Willis (1977), the peer group culture among the working-class students gave energy to their resistive approach towards the school. Identity, to a certain extent, always assumes the conception of the 'other' and in this case the others were the girls and the conformist boys. They identified a strong, masculine self for themselves. Mike O'Donnell and Sue Sharpe (2004) in their analysis of peer group subcultures and the implications these may have for identity in school contexts have found Paul Willis' (1977) version of peer group identity of working-class students to be an extreme version. While Phil Brown's work (cited in O'Donnell and Sharpe 2004), *Schooling Ordinary Kids,* shows that there are very few working-class students who were found to be resistive and macho. A larger proportion was more involved in the culture of 'getting on', that is, neither rejecting the school nor getting too involved, but somehow getting through. They further researched peer group impacts in different studies on schools and outside schools as well to find that, in itself, by virtue of a certain 'generational belonging' and as a 'mediator of other influences on them, such as class, ethnicity and wider youth culture' (2004: 89) peer groups were influential. But this work does not place much significance on school processes per se, though the schools' attempts towards creating a non-racist, non-extremist identity for the students has been recognized to be creating an impact to some extent. Larger commercial and patriarchal tendencies have been considered more significant in this study.

Robert Meyenn (1980) finds Willis' work to have focused on peer groups of the male students and in an anti-school mode. He advocates discussing girls' peer group subculture and not just as absent/present but on its own terms it could be very similar to or distinct from that of boys. Lambart's study of girls' peer group (cited in Meyenn 1980) showed that while a group of girls was identified as deviant by the staff members they (i.e., the girls) were academically sound. A cultural norm that guided their construction of self was not being too poor in academics and having space for fun as well. While one study (Blyth as cited in Meyenn 1980) found girls' peer groups to be smaller and close knit, another study (Coleman as cited in Meyenn 1980) found them to be elaborate and complex.

Sara Delamont (1996) has looked into the peer group structuring and impacts in the context of co-educational schools. She finds that 'even in mixed schools, co-educational friendships or working groups are rare; pupils get little school experience of cooperating with those of the other sex' (1996: 26). They usually interact only when the teacher forces them to. Thapan's (1991) study found similar attitudes among the students. The interaction between girls and boys was restricted to some extent due to the teacher's attitudes against 'deep friendship' between a boy and a girl and peer pressure on not interacting across sex groups (1991: 145). This strain in the relationship between the boys and the girls got evident during dances, drama performances and even in classroom activities, such as girls responding to the teacher's question sometimes led to scoffing by the boys.

Teachers' stereotypical views can often influence the peer group cultures. We cannot assume that students accept all that is proposed or imposed on them, yet if the teacher stereotyping coordinates with students' views on certain matters then the impact on the students is significantly enhanced. Delamont (1996) observes that many studies on peer group gender stereotyping have shown one trend, that is, children are relaxed about their own gender-related behaviour, somewhat stereotypical towards their same-sex peers and highly rigid about opposite sex peers. It was also found that if a 'differently' believing teacher tries to change such conceptions, it gets rejected by the students as they feel that it is against the normal way of being. 'A whole-hearted intervention' might work successfully, but a 'half-hearted' may make things worse.

Ramya Subrahmanian (2005) has commented upon the impact of teacher perspectives on students' identities, especially on the Dalit students. He is wary of the 'normalization' of the practices of inclusion and exclusion through the routines of schools. The teachers' constructions of the learning potential of certain students in the classroom interactions leave an impact on their identities; in this case, Dalit students performed poorly in academics because they were constructed in the teacher's discourse as being academically poor. The family background, locality and every other thing were included in the construction of their identity by the teachers though the discrimination was never articulated explicitly in referring to them as Dalit or tribal. Except for one school, where students were referred to as strong or weak students without direct or indirect references to their background, where the discrimination took a back seat, many schools exhibited the other pattern.

A recent ethnography by Nandini Manjrekar (2013) on the schooling of urban poor in India in the discourse of hard labour (*kadi mehnat*) through classroom interaction brings out a disjunctive tendency of education. The content of the textual knowledge, orientation of the middle-class teachers and urban middle-class understanding of 'education' are represented through the school. While the recipient of this discourse stands outside it, on several accounts, there is a 'hope' of belonging to it soon through a successful internalization of all that school represents. A de-contextualized discussion of what constitutes 'work' plays out the possibility of realization of this dream by neglecting 'labour' that constitutes the actual life conditions at home.

In another context of schooling and racial identity, Victoria Ward and Robinson Wood (2006) find that racism does not emerge in the form of overt use of racial language or discriminatory practices but comes up in 'coded racial signifiers' which 'reproduce racialized images and racial myths in our collective psyches' (2006: 377). McLaren (1986) discusses the implication of reification of the students as some type, as in the case of the Portuguese students who were reified as culturally deprived, leading to turning them towards basic level, below average academic activities, assuming them to be academically poor and incapable. What was 'believed' in the ritual structure of the school state was rendered insignificant in the ritual structure of the street-corner state by the students. The students had to tolerate the irrelevant school work, despite the fact that it devalued them because they were aware of the necessity of getting enough education that would see them through their workplace.

Teacher's perspectives have been considered to be carrying less significance in cases where it is believed that non-school factors are responsible for stereotypical identities of students, but wherever the responsibility of the school has been recognized in this, efforts towards addressing those have been undertaken. Riddell's (1992) study of gender codes at work in schools as well as outside it, especially in the media's representations of these codes, family and friends, as reflected in subject choices by girls and boys, has found these external elements and schools' and teachers' ideologies too responsible for continuation of gender stereotyping. The subject choice option available to the students seems open, democratic and unbiased when it leaves all the options 'open' to all the students irrespective of gender or class. And yet, there is discrimination working at the school level when physics is presented as dealing with volume, speed, mathematics and so on and home economics as about keeping good homes. As one teacher corrected this view—home economics is about what you eat, dietary habits and worldwide food distribution, why is it presented and operated the other way then? Though there has been a shift in the way girls' and boys' futures are visualized by others as well as by themselves, yet, boundaries continue to exist. In mapping the routes that these identity constructions take, they may get interrogated.

Two works in different contexts have concentrated on the issue of identity construction in ethnic terms (Connolly 2003) and in the sphere of religion (Gupta 2008), notably among the very young schoolgoers. These two works are similar in certain manners, in that both have not really looked into the school processes as mediating factors. The role of family, community and memories of a past or even everyday has been highlighted in both the studies. Connolly's (2003) study focuses on the recognition of ethnic markers among very young Protestants and Catholics to find out whether the children recognize these markers, the extent of

identification as one and not the other and whether it get impli-
cated, then, in a distrust of and hatred for the other. The initial
quantitative measures of showing them pictures and items belongings to the two ethnic group identities followed by a qualitative
in-depth conversations led to certain conclusions: the very young
(three—four-years-old) are aware of differences, but these do not
translate into prejudices for them and even over the years the identification with one group may not necessarily translate into a
hatred for the other. Connolly was concerned about the problem
of ethnic characteristics as being presented and imbibed as natural, unchangeable for this is not their real nature. These issues
need to be brought up in 'mono-ethnic schools', especially since
the possibility of children taking their ethnic identity and associated features as natural and of others as 'strange or inferior' exists
(2003: 180). Gupta's (2008) study also came across similar response
patterns where distinctiveness of the identity (religious) is available to the very young children, but the prejudices are not very
strongly visible though not entirely absent either.

School Processes as Sites of Interactions

School processes could be generating a very authoritative scheme
which would clearly expect the students to toe the line; however,
socialization in other zones of social life tends to create varying
impacts of these processes on different students. McLaren's study
reveals that 'domination is not simply reproduced but is constantly
being "worked up"' (1986: xii). Such activities often have a tendency to order, control and subdue the experiences that students
bring with them to the school. His work is located in a school that
is an urban public school which has economically disadvantaged
students. While the school's structural values aim towards making
them 'good' workers and 'good' Catholics, the students resist these
gestures as they assert their experiences that constitute their being
outside the school. Their identities outside the school's framework
are different and often in conflict with the dominant structural
aims of the school.

McLaren has presented a very perceptive analysis of everyday practices of the students inside the school and just before and after the school. His study shows that identities are not fixed, they keep shifting as space and the structural contours change. For instance, the 'street-corner state' flourishes just prior to the school and its setting is school playground or neighbourhood nearby the school. Here, the peer group is the stronger collectivity, the rules of interaction are of bonhomie, unbound and ungoverned, but these are rules nevertheless. Imaginary, creative, taking roles, experimentation with what all one can possibly be and a strong sense of emotionality are the features of such a state. Once inside the school, the shift is visible. The gestures are formal and relatively rigidly structured. The control is now in the hands of the teachers. Predictable, disciplined and obedient existence is perceived here. The rules and rituals are conventional, invariant and powerful.

A student who is prominent in the street corner zone may try to extend that prominence to the school state zone also, although the authorities would find it objectionable and would suppress it. And often a student who has a poor status in the street corner zone may feel better in the school state zone. The operational rules for the two states are very distinct from each other and someone who is central in one state may get marginalized in the other state. But again, this is one of the several possibilities when students shift from one state of being to the other. The 'sanctity state' is the zone of religion and prayers, but because it is not understood to be imposed, the students' mood is that of reverence and subservience to the concept of some power that is beyond rational bounds. It is unlike the school state despite invoking reverence because here the students perceived a possibility of going beyond the constraints of being human through certain connect with the divine. The home state was a sort of a mix of street corner freedom and controlled student state.

In the school, studied by McLaren, the classroom behaviour and classroom mannerisms, as expected to be practiced by the school authorities from their students, were conveyed to be the ideal way of being, but in the street corner space, those mannerisms were not valued at all.

The school rules were to be followed unquestionably; the students conformed to them but they did not necessarily believe in them. Much of the school processes were seen to be of not much significance by the students, but a complete rejection of school was also not viable. Hence the tussle between how should one be in the school from the school's perspective or from the working-class students' perspectives. Religious classes in the school were the only exception to this discord; the students were encouraged to develop a critical attitude towards dominance, and though this was also a part of the school process, it was never resisted as much by the students.

Student identity is not singular as it does not exist by itself. It is identifiable nevertheless because it is a result of the choices that one has made and in that sense selection has happened and some ways of being have been picked out of the several available possibilities. Even then, such identities correspond to various associations they may have with religion, gender, market, class, nation, values or several such social contexts.

Another significant aspect of the school processes is the physical space of the school. The school's space gives a context to the processes that take place within. Veronique Benei in her study of a military residential school in Maharashtra observes that the attempts of school's processes of making their students certain kind of people were contested. The school aimed at 'turning young boys into proper men who will serve their country dutifully' (Benei 2005: 146). The family or home became the space that does not care much about this identity projection. The families were not defying school's expectations from their children, but neither did they comply completely with the school's ideology and processes of accomplishing the same. The school expected its students to shed all association with the family, and the home and its comforts, both physical and emotional. The idea behind this was to inculcate a strong male-regimented patriotic identity among the students. It manifested in rules such as getting up very early in the morning, taking a cold water bath, doing one's work on their own, having the meal cooked for all without consideration for one's taste and preferences, having a regimented schedule, and being strong and fearless. The home space was not only distinct from this but it also did not completely subscribe to the school's vision. Families indulged their children once they were home for holidaying and did not care much about the school instructions regarding how the child should spend his day at home while he was on holiday. The school instructions followed its students till home but the home space, it seems, was not open to that agenda of identity construction. And there was another binary association at work here. The students who did not feel much attachment to their home for various reasons felt at home in their school. Besides this aspect, the school tried to generate a home-like atmosphere for the students by occasionally preparing sweets for them, celebrating their birthdays, creating personalized bonds with them and so on.

As McLaren's study (1986) depicts, the students' resistance to the school state and the associated instructions were a 'reaction to the separation between the lived cultural meaning of the street corner state and the thing-oriented, digital approach to learning of the school state' (McLaren 1986: 144). It was not acceptable to them as it overlooked their class identity and rendered it less significant; besides, it also often turned oppressive. In the classrooms, school instructions were resisted through 'buffoonery…open disputation…anti-teacher verbiage (usually muttered in muted or whispered tones), constant carping at the classroom rules…incessant jabber, insouciant slapstick, engaging in conversations with pears unbeknownst to the teachers…threatened to make hay of established codes of classroom propriety' (McLaren 1986: 145).

Veronique Benei (2009) comments that the dominant project of Hinduization through state and schools in the state of Maharashtra is visible in the routines that the schools follow in the prescribed texts and in the larger sphere of media as well that influences the public. Yet, in so far as the identity formation of the students studying at these schools is concerned, the project does not pass on unmediated. First, the teachers were active social agents and not passive transmitters of the dominant ideology. Their mediation had a range of impacts as far as the outcome was concerned. Second, the process of negotiation of who one is or of identity formation is not determined by a single factor, no matter how dominant it is. A range of significant influences such as, the school, home, the 'public' sphere and several other structures are involved in this procedure of self-formation. This 'negotiation...is always fragmentary' and ever incomplete (Benei 2009: 264); although the structures give it a ground to emerge, the project of self-formation need not incorporate some of the most prominent structures and may, at times, recognize less dominant structures. '[E]ven the most "efficient" state schooling cannot preclude the eruption of the unpredictable in daily routine' (Benei 2009: 265). Such negotiations of school agenda are a significant aspect of schooling and should be accorded importance whenever the impact of school education is being scrutinized.

A study of the RSS (*Rashtriya Swayamsevak Sangh*) education project shows that what passes off as 'cultural heritage' in an English medium school for upper and middle classes is found to be different from what it entails in a vernacular medium school for the non-English speaking classes. While the former focuses on the classical tradition of music, dance, mythology and deeper philosophical issues from the past, the latter is far removed from this perspective and instead receives a more superficial overview of the past, with the focus on memorizing the factual details and not so much on the critical appreciation of the matter therein.

In this case, the 'cultural heritage' has a religious component to it too. A certain religious identity is sought to be promoted by the school. [T]he RSS educationists adept and redeploy religious symbols, working towards a uniform Hindu-nationalization of young minds...metaphors of chariots, charioteers, horses, reins abound in *Vidya Bharti* language' (Advani 2009: 36, 40). One of the values that are constantly inculcated in these students is that of submission to the traditional authority and a sense of on-going struggle against *adharma* is implied through various discourses. In identifying the *adharmic* forces, dharma is being defined by the school. The adharma that the school is cautious against is broadly divided into three segments; one, the Marxist influence in the field of education; two, the Muslims blocking a view of history and society; and three, the westernized corrupting values (Advani 2009). Despite a clearly stated interest towards promoting a certain orientation towards religion, the school's project must meet halfway with several other orientations towards the issue of the religious identity of its students.

In the case of the RSS school, while the school's being a vernacular-medium institute coordinates well within the class situation of the students and their parents due to its accessibility, the religious orientation of the school is not so smoothly coordinated within that of the students. The definitional axis of dharma and religioun makes it not a smooth exercise for the school.

> On the one hand, the term *dharma* can be understood as 'religion' in a way similar to the book religion (Islam and Christianity)…*dharma* has also retained connotations of socio-religious moral order, law and duty… 'The right order of life and worship…'. Therein lies the ambiguity and consequently the difficulty of drawing a line in everyday life between obvious *Hindutva* militancy and a Hindu overview providing an idiom of morality. (Benei 2009: 59)

The school's agenda of transforming its students through their education may or may not coordinate with the social dispositions of the students. Many students from this school, studied by Benei, did not foresee a future for themselves along the lines they were being trained. Many parents chose the school more for its easy availability and not so much for its religious training. What they appreciated was that the school fostered a respect for authority (which includes parental authority as well).

The meanings that emerge from of these interactions can never be predicted. In the school studied by McLaren (1986) the twin agendas of the school of 'making workers' and 'making Catholics' were not accepted by the students in totality. While the school wished to incorporate values suitable for making them 'good workers' by its regimes of discipline, obedience and rote learning, the students resisted it through their own culture of street corner state. On the other hand, the school's project of making them Catholics was redefined by the students through readily accepting the values of freedom and power that those lessons gave them. However, they did not necessarily imbibe the Catholic values.

Veronique Benei's (2009) study of schools in Maharashtra observes that the *Maharashtrian* official version of history in the contemporary situation was renegotiated in at least three different manners by differently situated schools. While the Marathi medium schools valourized Shivaji's role in making the state free from oppression, the Urdu medium schools hardly mentioned his contributions and the Marathi speaking Muslims did not shy away from claiming Shivaji as theirs too. Another significant observation made by Benei in this study was that very often the reconstruction of the dominant discourse, resistance to it and, for that matter, the imposition of the dominant discourse does not always emerge in a recurring, cyclical manner. Those may have to be observed in small, seemingly innocuous interactions or utterances. For instance, while the formal discourse in Maharashtra usually is not openly anti-Muslim, but in the confines of homes, such expressions find their way out.

Peggy Froerer (2007) in her study of the *Saraswati Shishu Mandir* primary school explores the relationship between everyday practices of the school, especially the disciplinary ones, and the school's agenda of promotion of a Hindu nationalist ideology and finds that the students do not see this as an education on Hindu nationalism but as a pedagogical exercise which they must master if they have to succeed academically. Disciplining of the body, as visualized by school through its aim of a Hindu nationalist identity forging, was not taken as that by the students; they took it as an ordinary classroom practice of chastising the erring students.

Sara Delamont (1976) observes with the help of several studies conducted in the UK during the 1970s that since pre-nursery a subtle segregation and stereotyping of gender roles for the students begins to emerge. While many schools 'tried' to foster a sense of equality of sexes, their ingrained behavioural expressions quietly undid those. The girls, for instance, were appreciated for their appearance while boys were not thus commented upon. The boys were appreciated if they showed valour. Divisions of tasks in the schools are often gender stereotyped, not just by the teachers but by the students themselves. In one school, students (nine-years-olds) were to write an essay on their favourite place; the boys had imagined jungles, ships and adventurous places and situations while the girls talked about beautiful homes, fairgrounds and so on.

During classroom interactions too, many studies show that opportunities to participate in classroom talks are given largely to boys while girls are not really given much space. This may happen consciously or unconsciously. In fact, studies during the 1980s suggest that despite an intention to treat both girls and boys equally, teachers often end up allowing more time to boys and let them dominate classroom talks. However, a study of classroom interactions by Sunderland (cited in Litosseliti 2013: 82) shows that although, at times, the teacher may seem to be paying greater attention towards boys in the class since they tend to dominate the conversation through their pitch and aggression, the teacher could be communicating more often with them over the issues of discipline and not so much about academics. On the contrary, girls were found to be less dominating, but their interaction with the teachers was centred around more academic queries and not so much about maintaining discipline in the classroom. Baxter (cited in Litosseliti 2013: 83) observed, during her research in a mixed-sex classroom in the UK, that the obedience in girls makes them provide interactional support while they do not get as much for themselves from the others. They are valued for their 'collaborative talk' (Baxter, cited in Litosseliti 2013: 83) but, at the same time, they are then forced into a stereotypical role of being good listeners. What is supposed to be their strength in classroom discourse, in a way, subscribes them to this value forever and makes them powerless in the process.

Research in various societies, from a period approximately around the 1980s to 2006, by different scholars, have repeatedly generated data that exhibits a certain trend in mixed-gender classroom interactions between students and the teachers. Girls are assumed to be academically successful only through hard work while boys, when they do so, are just being natural. If girls fail, it is not alarming, but if boys do, they must not have been attentive or careful enough. The stereotypical image of girls is that of being indecisive, lazy, gossipy, laid-back, good at memorizing and good at observing. On the other hand, boys are projected as the opposite, they are sharp, intelligent, clever, good at analysing, have an innate capacity to do the maths and have the potential to take on the hard sciences and difficult subjects without much effort, but are naughtier. These images are reflected through everyday conversations and interactions in the classrooms. Since this travels in a very innocuous way, often these comments would pass off as ordinary remarks on the students.

Students may not 'innately' show such signs, but over the time, they internalize these assumptions and may begin to actualize those presumptions. Maths and science and even computers are considered subjects better suited for boys while arts, humanities and languages are considered suitable for girls. Teachers support this view, parents too do not counter it and students gradually take this to be true. Many girls, despite being good at the subjects that boys are considered to be better at, shy away from pursuing them as choices for higher studies and career options.

Discourses and metaphors of everyday practices quietly generate identities. Participation in seemingly innocuous activities in social contexts lends a certain character to the participants. The already learnt ways of being a girl or a boy are not easy to challenge even in the place called the school where learning is supposed to be the prime activity. MacNaughton (1998) presents the instance of an educator who tried to persuade the girls and boys in her class to play with toys from an un-segregated pool. Earlier, the boys' toys and the girls' toys were kept segregated. Her attempt to undo that segregation, extended over a period of several months, could not change the way the students perceived which toys 'belonged' to them. Davies (1989) shows how attempts to reconstruct the fairy tales, where the stereotypical imagery of 'beautiful princess' and 'brave prince' were replaced by a more equalizing imagery, were met with resistance by the students.

Peer group associations define gender for many students. A monolithic, uniform conception of what being a girl means or what being a boy means usually does not exist. While it has been observed that certain gendered peculiarities constitute the domi-nant discourse in the space of school, variations in the discourse are equally powerful. One dominant construction of genders as oppositional shows girls to be 'sensible and selfless, boys as silly and selfish' (Paechter 2006: 368). Another prominent moral compulsion associated with being appropriately feminine, especially among the middle-class schoolgirls, is that of being 'nice'. This niceness is associated with the middle-class values about femininity. It involves keeping away from any disagreement and a denial of being different especially being academically excellent (Walkerdine 2001, cited in Reay 2006).

A collective response to participation in sports as girls grow older is another expression of peer group induced norms of gendering. A gradual increase in passivity towards sports as girls move up from the primary school stage is to a great extent caused by the presentation of sports as the zone of male aggression and domination. The construction of an appropriate, acceptable femininity in the school space demands girls to declare a difference from aggressive sports. On the part of the male peers and to some extent the teachers (sports), girls are sent out subtle signs that sports is not for them. And if at all girls want to participate, they must position themselves as non-feminine (Nespor 1997, cited in Paechter 2006; Reay 2010; Skelton 2006).

While a generalized femininity gets constructed in a local context, in this case, school. However, within that larger framework, agential interventions keep emerging as well. They could be in the form of conformation to the generalized and in the form of denial or opposition to that.

Research on schools from various parts of the world shows that school peer groups or classmates tend to keep the sex-segregation alive. Interestingly, they would play together as neighbours or at home, but in school the attempts to challenge the segregation would be met with mockery, ridicule and ostracization.

> One of the most unforgettable memories of my middle school years in the early 1980s was that girls and boys in my class were hardly on greeting terms. Anyone who ventured to talk with anyone from the other sex would cause a 'quihong' (roars of mocking laughter) from the boys. (Liu 2006: 428)

The same was noted by a more recent research on some Chinese schools as well. Teachers also reinforce this segregation by dividing groups for tasks on the basis of gender. The teacher-imposed segregation becomes more evident as students enter puberty. The idea is to avoid romantic involvements between girls and boys as it is believed that such interests would take a toll on the academic work.

At this point, it must also be remembered that there is a possibility of the incompleteness of any and all social processes in the construction of identities (Benei 2009: 123). Castells has distinguished between roles and identities where roles are institutional and are structured according to the expected norms of that institution, such as the role of a teacher, a girl, a mother and so on, but identities are what an individual believes he/she is (Gewirtz and Cribb 2009: 135). It may mean creating versions of a single role, or resistance to the role or incorporating other structural roles to create a certain sense of self. The space of school vis-à-vis the space of home can interact in various ways with various consequences in terms of gendered selves. A study of Bedouin girls shows that the girls were not allowed to attend school for the fear of loss of honour in case the girls get involved with boys from other tribes (Abu-Rabia-Queder 2012). In another instance, Benei (2009: 125) remarks how a very strict teacher of a Maharashtra school, who was very particular about sticking to the dress code prescribed by the larger traditional patriarchal values, was not at all disturbed by the dress code followed by her daughters at home. At other times, tradition may be used to counter the sexism and assaults that girls may experience at school.

Identities have been found to emerge in various ways within a given structure. This often happens through negotiating the possibilities within a structure as every structure gets mediated by the intricacies of another one and by individuals belonging to several spheres at a time.

Students' Content Selection
Patterns from Television

Television features several kinds of programmes ranging from soaps to news, sports to reality shows, and movies to sacred dramas, cartoons and documentaries. So television is situated somewhere between a free run of fantasy and a projector of real events. Its impact is also situated somewhere between its work as a representer and a persuader. This gets exemplified in an excerpt from Gillespie's (1995) ethnographic study of the Indian community in Southall.

> *Diljit*, 17, is expected to speak Punjabi at home and when he and his siblings speak English together, their father blames the television for influencing them to become 'more English'. He also believes that his children will eventually copy the behaviour they watch on screen.... *Diljit* disagrees with his father, dismissing as absurd his fears about the potential of soaps to inspire imitative behaviour; yet he does admire the way in which young people in 'Neighbours' assert themselves to their elders. I will sit there thinking, yeah I should have done that...I should learn to talk back to my dad, but, you know, it's very bad to show disrespect to your Father...but it is good to see how someone can. (Gillespie 1995: 97)

So, while the father fears for a certain loss of the Indian Punjabi identity because of the English television's impact, the son finds this fear unfounded and yet somewhere lives out the possibility of being unlike the Indian children who are not supposed to talk back to their parents or elders.

Similarly, 'news talk' by the young boys manoeuvres through a discussion of the way events are projected in the news, and the way such projections create an image of India which intervenes with their life as immigrants here. It holds significance for them in terms of their individual selves and group identifications. 'Strong resentment is felt at the circulation in the west of images of poverty, underdevelopment, death and disease, images which are [then] seen to be linked to the "degradation" of Indians in Britain where they "get racist harassment"' (Gillespie 1995: 83). Boys were found to be much more disturbed by the 'negative' representation and images projected through news as well as films from India. Most Indian parents encouraged their children to connect with their Indian culture through these films and soaps as these not only imparted knowledge about the moral ideals of their culture but also train them about their mother tongue. Not all children, however, are keen on following this advice. For many of them, watching English or western soaps holds greater significance as it gives them a sense of participation in the western youth culture. *Neighbours*, one such soap, is watched by 67 per cent of the Indian children in Southall (Gillespie 1995).

There is a gender distinction in the way Indian soaps and films are perceived. Boys were wary of these films that played too much on absurdity and fantasy as for them this projects Indians in a poor light as compared to the westerners whose films are closer to the real. Girls, however, watched for the social and moral values inherent in these films and were not found to be critical of these. This distinction works in two ways. Girls are supposed to stay indoors while boys are relatively free to pursue many more kinds of leisure activities. Homebound girls, while watching these soaps and films coming from their 'homeland', are tutored into a certain evaluation of these. Boys go out more often, their peer connections are not censored, they are allowed for various free time pursuits and they interact more with the westerners, thus, do not see much value in moral injunctions presented in their native programmes. Boys dissociate themselves from this moral universe while girls almost emulate it. The same television projection has different meanings for the two genders and further constructs their differentiated identities through their attitudes towards these. Gillespie noticed another clear gender distinction in the patterns of television viewing. Boys were more interested in 'science fictions, science programs, game shows, documentaries and crime serials than girls. Girls report watching pop and quiz programs, soaps, cartoons and children's television' (Gillespie 1995: 77).

This, however, is not the only way television is perceived by the Indian children in Southall. In another case study of a Hindu Bengali family, the religious identity of the members of the family gets reinforced through a rejection of a westernized version of the

Mahabharata legend and a complete devotion to the iconographic version of the same. They displayed distaste for the version that did not reinforce their version of what the Mahabharata is about. In this case, television programme is not seen as a representation but 'synonymous with the ancient Sanskrit texts' (Gillespie 1983: 52). The western context and life in it get mediated through television viewing with significant consequences for identities at the level of gender, community, religion, nation, by the children of Indian parents.

Television, through its various forms of content presentation, that is, films, soaps, news, sports, game shows and so on exposes viewers to a range of value systems that come associated with each of these presentations. A preference over some has been found to have consequences for identity formation. Identity is not just about what one thinks one is, but also about what one imagines being in some deferred time. For instance, viewing the iconographic version of the Mahabharata and not having the patience to watch Brook's version of the same, places the viewer in a certain situation as far as religious identification is concerned. The traditional version prioritises the sacred and the moral elements while the version by Brook is more philosophical, moral and relatively modern in representations of the characters (Gillespie 1983).

The teaching of history in the schools in Maharashtra, especially the story of Shivaji has been supplemented with showing films on him. And, several textbooks that tell his story derive their framework and detailing from these Marathi films on him. The narration of these historical events in the classrooms takes place almost like a film version. National identity and patriotism of a certain kind get generated through these narrations (Benei 2009).

Even the so-called non-fantasy programmes, such as news are not without some selective presentational tendency. Arvind Rajagopal (2009) observes how the vernacular news, especially which is produced for the local and provincial population, has an element of narrowness that restricts these to the immediate cultural moods of their locale. The English news is comparatively less 'impassioned' and is presented in a less localized, less regionalized and less sentimentalized manner, so to say. The audience of these

two types of news stories would eventually be identifying ideologically with very distinct frameworks. He particularly discussed
this point with reference to the *Ayodhya* issue.[1] While the vernacular television, especially in the north Indian belt, posed it as an
issue related to communal tension in India, the English television
presented it as a constitutional issue, the issue of political stands
and legal rights.

Returning to our key concern, how school processes get mediated by student's experiences of religion, class and gender with
consequences for the questions of identity, agency and structures,
it has been observed in the previous pages that first, the categories
of experiences move in an intertwined way; class with gender,
class with religion, language with religion, gender with religion,
and television as a representational resource too influences as well
as reinforces constitutions of identities. Second, what appear as
structures are not always uniform in their impact. Subject positions, interpretations of structures and intervening impacts shift
the way structure appears in different conditions. This chapter has
attempted to present school practices and processes as constituting and being constituted by various social categories in different
contexts in order to highlight the social character of schooling.
During this, it emerges that the structures of school are experienced through agential interpretations too. This chapter has
attempted to present the various processes of schooling as carriers
of various structural messages and the implications these have on
the students as discovered in studies specific to schools, both in
India as well as abroad. A presence of several situational logics
and multiple meanings within the space of the school makes the
analysis of school as a social institution a complex task. Locating
individual agency amidst this remains contingent upon the
negotiations of meanings in a situation.

Note

1. A dispute over a piece of land which the Hindus claim to be the birth place of the
   Hindu god *Rama* but the Muslims claim it to be the site of a *Masjid* built by the
   Mughal emperor Babur.

Appendix 2
Sample Questionnaire

Questionnaire A

Age: _____   Girl: _____
                        Boy: _____

Father's Occupation:

Mother's Occupation:

Siblings:

Where do they study?:

What do you want to be?:

How do you spend your leisure time?:

One word for your school:

One word for your home:

One word for yourself:

Who selected this school for you?:

How is this school of any significance to you?:

Two famous people whom you admire:

Your favourite television program:

One television program you dislike and a reason why:

Which stream would you select in the future and why?:

One wish for your school:

Write one word for: _____

Girl: _____

Boy: _____

Vacation means: (Pl. select one)

- A time to enjoy
- No school friends
- No fun
- Should never end

School's most significant contribution: (Pl. mark as preferences)

- Good education
- Good behaviour
- Self confidence
- Good values
- Proficiency in English
- Anything else

Bibliography

Abu-Rabia-Queder, S. 2012. 'Between Tradition and Modernization: Understanding the Problem of Female Bedouin Dropouts'. In *Learning from the Children: Childhood, Culture and Identity in a Changing World*, edited by J. Waldren and I. Kaminski, 35–50. Oxford, USA: Berghahn Books.

Advani, S. 2009. *Schooling the National Imagination*. New Delhi: Oxford University Press.

Altheide, D. L. and J. M. Johnson. 1994. 'Criteria for Assessing Interpretive Validity in Qualitative Research'. In *Handbook of Qualitative Research*, edited by N. K. Denzin and Y. S. Lincoln, 581–94. Thousand Oaks, CA: SAGE Publications.

Anderson, S. 2008. *Civil Sociality: Children, Sport and Cultural Policy in Denmark*. Charlotte, North Carolina: Information Age Publishing.

———. 2011. 'Going Through the Motions of Ritual: Exploring the "as if" Quality of Religious Sociality in Faith Based Schools'. In *The Study of Children in Religions*, edited by S. B. Ridgely, 139–56. New York and London: New York University Press.

Assmann, J. 2006. *Religion and Cultural Memory: Ten Studies*. Stanford, CA: Stanford University Press.

Austin. 1962. *How To Do Things With Words*. Harvard University Press Cambridge Massachusetts

Bakaya, A. 2004. 'Lessons from Kurukshetra: The RSS Education Project'. In *Education and Democracy in India*, edited by A. Vaugier-Chatterjee, 27–54. New Delhi: Manohar Publications.

Ball, S. J. 1980. 'Initial Encounters in the Classroom and the Process of Establishment'. In *Pupil Strategies*, edited by P. Woods, 143–61. London: Croom Helm.

———. 1981. *Beachside Comprehensive: A Case Study of Comprehensive Schooling*. Cambridge: Cambridge University Press.

———. 2004. 'The Sociology of Education: A Disputational Account'. In *The Routledge Falmer Reader in Sociology of Education*, edited by S. J. Ball, 1–12. London and New York: Routledge Falmer.

Beck, G. 2006. *Sacred Sound: Experiencing Music in World Religions*. Waterloo, Ontario, Canada: Wilfrid Laurier University Press.

Benei, V. 2005. 'Serving the Nation: Gender and Family Values in Military Schools'. In *Educational Regimes in Contemporary India*, edited by P. Jeffery and R. Chopra, 141–59. London, Thousand Oaks, CA and New Delhi: SAGE Publications.

Benei, V. 2009. *Schooling India: Hindus, Muslims and the Forging of Citizens*. Ranikhet, India: Permanent Black.

Beresin, A. R. 2010. *Recess Battles: Playing, Fighting and Storytelling*. Jackson, Mississippi: University Press of Mississippi.

Berger, P. [1967] 2011. *The Sacred Canopy: Elements of a Sociological Theory of Religion*. New York: Open Road Integrated Media.

Berger, L. and T. Luckmann. 1966. *The Social Construction of Reality*. Doubleday, New York: Anchor Books.

Berlak, A. and H. Berlak. [1981] 2012. *Dilemmas of Schooling: Teaching and Social Change*. Abingdon, UK and New York: Routledge.

Bernstein, B. 2004. 'Social Class and Pedagogic Practice'. In *The Routledge Falmer Reader in Sociology of Education*, edited by S. J. Ball, 196–217. London and New York: Routledge Falmer.

Bidlake, E. 2007. *Language Learning as a Gendered Experience*. Available at: http://research. ncl.ac.uk/ARECLS/volume_4/BIDLAKE.pdf (Accessed on 27 January 2015).

Bird, C. 1980. 'Deviant Labeling in School: The Pupils' Perspective'. In *Pupil Strategies*, edited by P. Woods, 94–107. London: Croom Helm.

Blumer, H. 1969. *Symbolic Interactionism: Perspectives and Method*. Berkeley, Los Angeles and London: University of California Press.

Bourdieu, P. 1990. *The Logic of Practice*. Stanford, CA: Stanford University Press.

Bourdieu, P. and J. C. Passeron. 1990. *Reproduction in Education, Society and Culture*. London: SAGE Publications.

Boyatzis, C. 2011. 'Agency, Voice and Maturity in Children's Religious and Spiritual Development'. In *The Study of Children in Religions*, edited by S.B. Ridgely, 19–32. New York and London: New York University Press.

Brown, P. 1987. *Schooling Ordinary Kids*. London: Methuen.

Buckingham, D., ed. 1993. *Reading Audiences: Young People and the Media*. UK: Manchester University Press.

Burgess, R. G., ed. 1985. *Strategies of Educational Research*. London: The Falmer Press.

Butler, J. 1990. *Gender Trouble: Feminism and the Subversion of Identity*. New York: Routledge.

Carmichael, C. M. 2008. On the Playground: Discourse, Gender and Ideology in English Learner Peer cultures. PhD Thesis: Department of Language Reading and Culture, The University of Arizona, USA.

Chakravorty, P. 2011. 'Global Dancing in Kolkata'. In *A Companion to the Anthropology of India*, edited by C. D. Isabella, 137–53. UK: Wiley-Blackwell.

Chanana, K. 1988. 'Social Change or Social Reform: The Education of Women in pre-Independence India'. In *Socialization, Education and Women: Explorations in Gender Identity*, edited by K. Chanana, 96–123. New Delhi: Orient Longman Limited.

————. 2003. 'Gender Inequality in Primary Schooling in India: The Human Rights Perspective'. In *Education, Society and Development: National and International Perspectives*, edited by J. Tilak, 197–219. New Delhi: NIEPA.

Chappell, T. 2014. *Knowing What to do: Imagination, Virtue, and Platonism in Ethics*. Oxford, UK: Oxford University Press.

Chen, X, D. C. French and B. H. Schneider. 2006. *Peer Relationships in Cultural Context*. New York: Cambridge University Press.

Christensen, P. 2010. 'Ethnographic Encounters with Children'. In *Educational Research and Inquiry: Qualitative and Quantitative Approaches*, edited by D. Hartas, 145–58. London and New York: Continuum International Publishing Group.

———. 2011. 'Foreword'. In *The Study of Children in Religions: A Methods Handbook*, edited by S. B. Ridgely, ix–xiv. New York and London: New York University Press.

Clarke, P. 2001. *Teaching and Learning*. London, Thousand Oaks, CA and New Delhi: SAGE Publications.

Connolly, P. 2003. 'The Development of Young Children's Ethnic Identities'. In *Social Justice, Education and Identity*, edited by C. Vincent, 166–84. London and New York: Routledge Falmer.

———. 2004. *Boys and Schooling in the Early Years*. Abingdon, UK and New York: Routledge Falmer.

Corsaro, W. A. 2005. *The Sociology of Childhood*. London, Thousand Oaks, CA and New Delhi: SAGE Publications.

———. 2006. 'Qualitative Research on Children's Peer Relations in Cultural Context'. In *Peer Relationships in Cultural Context*, edited by X. Chen, D. C. French and B. H. Schneider, 96–120. New York: Cambridge University Press.

Corsaro, W. A. and D. Eder. 1990. 'Children's Peer Cultures'. *Annual Review of Sociology*, 16 (1): 197–220.

Davies, B. 1989. *Frogs and Snails and Feminist Tales: Preschool Children and Gender*. London: Allen and Unwin.

———. 2004. 'The Discursive Production of the Male/Female Dualism in School Settings'. In *The Routledge Falmer Reader in Sociology of Education*, edited by S. J. Ball, 128–37. London: Routledge Falmer.

Davies, B. and R. Harre. 2001. 'Positioning the Discursive Production of Selves'. In *Discourse Theory and Practice: A Reader*, edited by M. Wetherell, S. Taylor and S. J. Yates, 261–71. London, Thousand Oaks, CA and New Delhi: SAGE Publications.

Delamont, S. 1976. *Interaction in the Classroom*. UK: Methuen.

———. 1996. *A Woman's Place in Education: Historical and Sociological Perspectives on Gender and Education*. Aldershot, UK and Brookfield, VT: Avebury.

Denscombe, M. 1985. *Classroom Control*. London: Allen and Unwin.

Denzin, N. 1992. *Symbolic Interactionism and Cultural studies*. UK: Blackwell Publishers.

Durkheim, E. 1895/1982. *The Rules of Sociological Method*. Tr. W. D. Halls. New York: Free Press.

———. 1912/2012. *The Elementary Forms of Religious Life*. Mineola, NY: Dover Publications Inc.

Eck, E. D. 1993. *Encountering God*. Boston: Beacon Press.

Everhart, R. B. 1983. *Reading, Writing and Resistance*. Boston: Routledge and Kegan Paul.

Faberman, H. A. 1973. 'Towards a Social Theory of Mentality'. In *Towards the Sociology of Knowledge*, edited by G. Remmling, 261–70. London: Routledge and Kegan Paul.

Fiske, J. 1989. *Understanding Popular Culture*. London: Routledge.

Foucault, M. [1969] 2005. *The Archaeology of Knowledge*. UK: Routledge.

———. 1977. *Discipline and Punish: The Birth of the Prison*. New York: Pantheon Books.

Francis, B. and C. Skelton. 2005. *Reassessing Gender and Achievement: Questioning Contemporary Key Debates*. UK: Routledge.

Froerer, P. 2007. 'Disciplining the Saffron Way: Moral Education and the Hindu Rashtra'. *Modern Asian Studies*, 41 (5): 1033–71.

Geertz, C. (1973) 1993. *The Interpretation of Cultures*. London: Fontana Press.

Gewirtz, S. and A. Cribb. 2009. *Understanding Education: A Sociological Perspective*. UK: Polity Press.

Giddens, A. 1986. *Constitution of Society: Outline of the Theory of Structuration*. Berkeley and Los Angeles: University of California Press.

Gillespie, M. 1983. 'The Mahabharata: From Sanskrit to Sacred Soap. A Case Study of the Reception of Two Contemporary Televisual Versions'. In *Children's Understanding of Television*, edited by J. Bryant and D. Anderson. New York: Academic Press.

_____. 1995. *Television, Ethnicity and Cultural Change*. London and New York: Routledge.

Gilligan, C. [1982] (1993). *In a Different Voice: Psychological Theory and Women's Development*. Cambridge, Massachusetts and London: Harvard University Press.

Giroux, H. 1986. 'Foreword'. In *Schooling as a Ritual Performance*, edited by P. McLaren. Boston, CT and London: Routledge and Kegan Paul.

Giroux, H. and R. I. Simon. 1989. *Popular Culture, Schooling and Everyday Life*. New York: Bergin and Garvey.

Glaser B.G. and A.L. Strauss. 1967. *The Discovery of Grounded Theory: Strategies for Qualitative Research*. Aldine Transaction New Brunswick USA and London UK.

Goffman, E. 1959. *The Presentation of Self in Everyday Life*. Garden City, NY: Doubleday.

Gordon, T., J. Holland and E. Lahelma. 2000. *Making Spaces*. Basingstoke and London: Macmillan Press Ltd.

Gottschalk, P. 2001. *Beyond Hindu and Muslim*. Delhi: Oxford University Press.

Grossberg, L. 1996. 'Identity and Cultural Studies—Is That all There is?' In *Questions of Cultural Identity*, edited by S. Hall and P. Gay, 87–107. London, Thousand Oaks, CA and New Delhi: SAGE Publications.

Gupta, A. 2006. *Early Childhood Education, Postcolonial Theory and Teaching Practices in India*. New York: Palgrave Macmillan.

Gupta, L. 2008. 'Growing up Hindu and Muslim'. *Economic and Political Weekly*, 43 (6): 35–41.

Hahn, T. 2007. *Sensational Knowledge: Embodying Culture Through Japanese Dance*. Middle Town, CT: Wesleyan Univ. Press.

Hamera, J. 2011. 'Performance Ethnography'. In *The SAGE Handbook of Qualitative Research*, edited by N. K. Denzin and Y. S. Lincoln, 317–30. Thousand Oaks, CA: SAGE Publications.

Hamm, C.M. 1989. 'Interpersonal and Social Issues in Education'. In *Philosophical Issues in Education: An Introduction*, 105. UK: Routledge Falmer.

Hammersley, M. 1980. 'On Interactionist Empiricism'. In *Pupil Strategies*, edited by P. Woods, 198–213. London: Croom Helm.

Hammersley, M. and P. Atkinson. 1995. *Ethnography*. London: Routledge.

Hammersley, M. and G. Turner. 1980. 'Conformist Pupils?' In *Pupil Strategies*, edited by P. Woods, 29–49. London: Croom Helm.

Hargreaves, A. 1980. 'Synthesis and the Study of Strategies'. In *Pupil Strategies*, edited by P. Woods. London: Croom Helm.

James, A. and A. L. James. 2004. *Constructing Childhood: Theory, Policy and Social Practice*. New York: Palgrave Macmillan.

Jeffery, P. 2005. 'Hearts, Minds and Pockets'. In *Educational Regimes in Contemporary India*, edited by P. Jeffery and R. Chopra, 13–61. London, Thousand Oaks, CA and New Delhi: SAGE Publications.

Jeffery, P. and R. Chopra. 2005. *Educational Regimes in Contemporary India*. London, Thousand Oaks, CA and New Delhi: SAGE Publications.

Kaufman, G. D. 1981. *The Theological Imagination: Constructing the Concept of God.* Philadelphia, PA: The Westminster Press.

Kehily, M. J. and A. Nayak. 1997. '"Lads and laughter": Humour and the Production of Heterosexual Hierarchies'. *Gender and Education*, 9 (1): 69–87.

Knoblauch, H. 1999. *Metaphors, Transcendence and Indirect Communication.* Available at: http://www.as.tu-berlin.de/fileadmin/fg225/material_knoblauch/meta.pdf (Accessed on 27 January 2016).

Kolakowski, L. 1989. *The Presence of Myth.* Chicago, IL: The University of Chicago Press.

Kumar, K. [1991] 2005. *Political Agenda of Education: A Study of Colonialist and Nationalist Ideas.* New Delhi: SAGE Publications.

———. 1996. *Learning from Conflict.* Delhi: Orient Longman.

Kumar, N. 2000. *Lessons From Schools: The History Of Education in Banaras.* London, Thousand Oaks, CA and New Delhi: SAGE Publications.

———. 2007. *The Politics of Gender, Community and Modernity.* New Delhi: Oxford University Press.

Lather, P. 1991. *Getting Smart: Feminist Research and Pedagogy Within/In the Postmodern.* New York: Routledge.

Leavy, P. 2010. 'Performance Based Emergent Methods'. In *Handbook of Emergent Methods*, edited by S. N. Hesse-Biber and P. Leavy. New York and London: The Guilford Press.

Lembo, R. 2000. *Thinking through Television.* New York: Cambridge University Press.

Lemish, D. 2010. *Screening Gender on Children's Television.* New York and Abingdon, UK: Taylor and Francis.

Levinson, B. A. and D. C. Holland. 1996. 'The Cultural Production of the Educated Person: An Introduction'. In *The Cultural Production of the Educated Person: Critical Ethnographies*, edited by B. A. Levinson, D. E. Foley and D. C. Holland, 1–57. Albany, NY: State University of New York Press.

Litosseliti, L. 2013. 'Gender and Language in the Foreign Language Classroom'. In *Gender and Language: Theory and Practice*, 82–83. Abingdon Oxon: Routledge.

Liu, F. 2006. 'School Culture and Gender'. In *The SAGE Handbook of Gender and Education*, edited by C. Skelton, B. Francis and L. Smulyan, 425–38. London, Thousand Oaks, CA and New Delhi: SAGE Publications.

Luckmann, T. 1967/1974. *The Invisible Religion: The Problem of Religion in Modern Society.* New York: Macmillan.

Lynch, K. and A. Lodge. 2002. *Equality and Power in Schools.* London: Routledge Publications.

MacNaughton, G. 2006. 'Constructing Gender in Early-years Education'. In *The SAGE Handbook of Gender and Education*, edited by C. Skelton, B. Francis and L. Smulyan, 127–38. London, Thousand Oaks, CA and New Delhi: SAGE Publications.

Madan, A. and Tiwari, G. 2012. *Educational Achievement Through the Lens of Social Inequality: A Study in a Tribal Belt of Madhya Pradesh.* Available at: http://www.eklavya.in/pdfs/reports/social_inequality_and_educational_achievement_spk-2010.pdf (Accessed on 3 February 2015).

Madison, D. S. 2012. *Critical Ethnography: Methods, Ethics and Performance.* SAGE Los Angeles

Manjrekar, N. 2013. Gender, Childhood and Work in Nation: Voices and Encounters in an Indian School. In *Sociology of Education in India: Changing Contours and Emerging Concerns*, edited by G. Nambissan and S. Rao. New Delhi: Oxford University Press.

Marcus, G. E. 1995. *Ethnography Through Thick and Thin.* Princeton, NJ: Princeton University Press.

McGuire, M. B. 2008. *Lived Religion: Faith and Practice in Everyday Life*. New York: Oxford University Press.

McLaren, P. 1986. *Schooling as a Ritual Performance*. Boston, MA and London: Routledge and Kegan Paul.

Mead, G. H. 1934. *Mind, Self and Society*. Chicago: Chicago University Press.

Meyenn, R. J. 1980. 'School Girls' Peer Groups'. In *Pupil Strategies*, edited by P. Woods, 108–42. London: Croom Helm.

Moore, R. 2004. *Education and Society*. Cambridge: Polity Press.

Morrow, D. 1967. 'Discipline and the Social Setting of the School'. In *Discipline in Schools: A Symposium*, edited by L. Stenhouse. Oxford, London and New York: Pergamon Press.

Nambissan, G. 2013. 'Opening up the Black Box? Sociologists and the Study of Schooling in India'. In *Sociology of Education in India: Changing Contours and Emerging Concerns*, edited by G. Nambissan and S. Rao. New Delhi: Oxford University Press.

O'Donnell, M. and S. Sharpe. 2004. 'The Social Construction of Youthful Masculinities'. In *The Routledge Falmer Reader in Sociology of Education* edited by S. J. Ball. London and New York: Routledge Falmer.

Okano, K. 1993. *School to Work Transition in Japan: An Ethnographic Study*. UK: Multilingual Matters Ltd.

Orsi, R. A. 2005. *Between Heaven and Earth*. Canada and USA: Princeton University Press.

Ottaviano, C. 2010. 'Schools and Religions: Experience, Symbols and Practices'. *Italian Journal of Sociology of Education*, 4 (1): 192–207.

Paechter, C. F. 2006. 'Constructing Femininity/Constructing Femininities'. In *The SAGE Handbook of Gender and Education*. London, edited by C. Skelton, B. Francis and L. Smulyan, 365–77. Thousand Oaks, CA and New Delhi: SAGE Publications.

————. 2007. *Being Boys Being Girls: Learning Masculinities and Femininities*. UK: Open University Press.

Pathak, A. 2002. *Social Implications of Schooling: Knowledge, Pedagogy and Consciousness*. New Delhi: Rainbow.

Pollard, A. 2004. 'Towards a Sociology of Learning in Primary Schools'. In *The Routledge Falmer Reader in Sociology of Education*, edited by S. J. Ball, 285–97. London and New York: Routledge Falmer.

Queder, Sarab A. R. 2012. 'Education, Tradition and Modernization: Bedouin Girls in Israel'. In *Learning from the Children: Childhood, Culture and Identity in a Changing World*, edited by J. Waldren and I. M. Kaminski, 35–52. Oxford and New York: Berghahn Books.

Rajagopal, A. 2009. *The Indian Public Sphere*. New Delhi: Oxford University Press.

Rajagopal, S. 2009. 'A Gendered Analysis of Secondary Schooling Process in India'. In *Exploring the Bias: Gender and Stereotyping in Secondary Schools*, edited by E. Page and J. Jha, 169–206. London: Commonwealth Secretariat.

Reay, D. 2003. 'Shifting Class Identities'. In *Social Justice, Education and Identity*, edited by C. Vincent, 51–64. London and New York: Routledge Falmer.

————. 2006. 'Compounding Inequalities: Gender and Class in Education'. In *The SAGE Handbook of Gender and Education*, edited by C. Skelton, B. Francis and L. Smulyan, 339–49. London, Thousand Oaks, CA and New Delhi: SAGE Publications.

————. 2010. 'Sociology, Social Class and Education'. In *The Routledge International Handbook of the Sociology of Education*, edited by M. W. Apple, S. J. Ball and L. A. Gandin, 396–404. London and New York: Routledge.

Reed-Danahay, D. 2005. *Locating Bourdieu*. Bloomington and Indianapolis: Indiana University Press.

Reid, K. 1986. *Disaffection from School*. London New York: Methuen.

Riddell, S. 1992. *Gender and the Politics of the Curriculum*. London: Routledge.

Ridgely, S. B., ed. 2011. *The Study of Children in Religions: A Methods Handbook*. New York and London: New York University Press.

Rist, R.C. 2015. 'On Understanding the Process of Schooling: The Contributions of Labelling Theory'. In *Schools and Society: A Sociological Approach to Education*, edited by J. H. Ballantine and J. Z. Spade, pp. 47–55. Thousand Oaks, California: SAGE Publications.

Ritzer, G. 2011. *Sociological Theory*. 5th ed. New Delhi: Tata McGraw Hill.

Romero, M. 1991. 'Work and Play in the Nursery School'. In *Critical Perspectives on Early Childhood Education*, edited by L. Weis, P. G. Altbach, G. P. Kelly and H. G. Petrie, 119–38. Albany, NY: State University of New York Press.

Sarangpani, P. 2003. *Constructing School Knowledge: An Ethnography of a School*. New Delhi: SAGE Publications.

Scott, J. 1986. *Everyday Forms of Peasant Resistance*. New Haven, CT: Yale University Press.

Sewell, W. H. 2005. *Logics of History: Social Theory and Social Transformation*. Chicago, IL: University of Chicago Press.

Skelton, C. 2006. 'Boys and Girls in the Elementary School'. In *The SAGE Handbook of Gender and Education*, edited by C. Skelton, B. Francis and L. Smulyan, 139–51. London, Thousand Oaks, CA and New Delhi: SAGE Publications.

Smith, S. J. 1997. 'Observing Children on a School Playground: The Pedagogies of Child-watching'. In *Children and Their Curriculum: The Perspectives of Primary and Elementary School Children*, edited by A. Filer, A. Pollard and D. Thiessen, 141–61. London: The Falmer Press.

Srinivas, M. N. 1976. *The Remembered Village*. Delhi: Oxford University Press.

Srivastava, S. 1998. *Constructing Post Colonial India: National Character and the Doon School*. London and New York: Routledge.

Subrahmanian, R. 2005. 'Education Exclusion and the Developmental State'. In *Educational Regimes in Contemporary India*, edited by P. Jeffrey and R. Chopra, 62–82. London, Thousand Oaks, CA and New Delhi: SAGE Publications.

Sundar, N. 2004. 'Teaching to Hate'. *Economic and Political Weekly*, 39 (16): 1604–13.

Thapan, M. 1988. 'Some Aspects of Cultural Reproduction and Pedagogic Communication'. *Economic and Political Weekly*, 23 (13): 592–96.

———. 1991. *Life at School: An Ethnographic Study*. Delhi: Oxford University Press.

———. 2005. 'Cultures of Adolescence: Educationally Disadvantaged Young Women in an Urban Slum'. In *Educational Regimes in Contemporary India*, edited by R. Chopra and P. Jeffery, 216–36. London, Thousand Oaks, CA and New Delhi: SAGE Publications.

———. 2006. '"Docile" Bodies, "Good" Citizens or "Agential" Subjects? Pedagogy and Citizenship in Contemporary Society'. *Economic and Political Weekly*, 41 (39): 4195–203.

Thomas, W. I. 1923. *The Unadjusted Girl*. Boston, MA: Little Brown and Co. Ltd.

Thorne, B. 1993. *Gender Play: Girls and Boys in School*. New Brunswick, NJ: Rutgers University Press.

———. 2002. 'Do Girls and Boys have Different Cultures?' In *Gender: A Sociological Reader*, edited by S. Jackson and S. Scott, 291–302. Abingdon, UK and New York: Routledge.

Tucker, E. 2008. *Children's Folklore: A Handbook*. Westport, CT: Greenwood Publishing Group.

Underwood, M. K. 2008. *Gender and Peer Relations: Are the Two Genders Really All That Different?* Available at: http://www.cds.unc.edu/cchd/s2008/02-25/underwood 1.pdf (Accessed on 26 November 2009).

Valentin, K. 2011. 'Accounting for Agency'. *Children and Society*, 25 (5): 347–59.

Velaskar, P. 2013. 'Sociology of Educational Inequality in India: A Critique and a New Research Agenda'. In *Sociology of Education in India: Changing Contours and Emerging Concerns*, edited by G. Nambissan and S. Rao. New Delhi: Oxford University Press.

Viruru, R. 2001. *Early Childhood Education*. London, Thousand Oaks, CA and New Delhi: SAGE Publications.

Vivenza, G. 1997. 'Classical Roots of Benevolence in Economic Thought'. In *Ancient Economic Thought*, edited by B. B. Price, 185–204. London and New York: Routledge.

Vries, Hent De. 2008. *Religion: Beyond a Concept*. New York: Fordham University Press.

Waldrop, A. 2004. 'The Meaning of the Old School-tie: Private Schools, Admission Procedures and Class Segmentation in New Delhi'. In *Education and Democracy in India*, edited by A. Vaugier-Chatterjee, 203–27. New Delhi: Manohar Publications.

Waller, W. [1932] 1965. *The Sociology of Teaching*. New York: J. Wiley.

Wankhede, G. G. 2013. 'Caste and Social Discrimination: Nature, Forms and Consequences in Education'. In *Sociology of Education in India: Changing Contours and Emerging Concerns*, edited by G. Nambissan and S. Rao. New Delhi: Oxford University Press.

Ward, J. V. and T. L. Robinson-Wood. 2006. 'Room at the Table: Racial and Gendered Realities in the Schooling of Black Children'. In *The SAGE Handbook of Gender and Education*, edited by C. Skelton, B. Francis and L. Smulyan, 325–38. London, Thousand Oaks, CA and New Delhi: SAGE Publications.

Wazir, R. 2000. *The Gender Gap in Basic Education*. India: SAGE Publications.

Weedon, C. 1987. *Feminist Practice and Post-Structuralist Theory*. Oxford: Basil Blackwell.

Willis, P. 1977. *Learning to Labour: How Working Class Kids Get Working Class Jobs*. New York: Columbia University Press.

———. 2000. *The Ethnographic Imagination*. UK: Polity Press.

———. 2011. 'Elements of a Culture'. In *The Structure of Schooling: Readings in the Sociology of Education* edited by R. Arum, I. R. Beattie and K. Ford, 228–42. Thousand Oaks, CA: Pine Forge Press.

Woods, P. 1976. 'Having a Laugh: An Antidote to Schooling'. In *The Process of Schooling*, edited by M. Hammersley and P. Woods. London: Routledge and Kegan Paul.

———. 1979. *The Divided School*. London: Routledge and Kegan Paul.

———. 1983. *Sociology and the School*. London: Routledge and Kegan Paul.

Woods, P., ed. 1980. *Pupil Strategies*. London: Croom Helm.

Woods, P. A. 2009. 'Rationalisation, Disenchantment and Re-enchantment: Engaging with Weber's Sociology of Modernity'. In *The Routledge International Handbook of Sociology of Education*, edited by M. W. Apple, S. J. Ball and L. A. Gandin. London and New York: Routledge.

Youdell, D. 2010. 'Recognizing the Subjects of Education: Engagements with Judith Butler'. In *The Routledge International Handbook of the Sociology of Education*, edited by M. W. Apple, S. J. Ball and L. A. Gandin, 132–42. London and New York: Routledge.

Zondervan, A. 2005. *Sociology and the Sacred: An Introduction to Philip Reiff's Theory of Culture*. Toranto: University of Toronto Press.

Index

About the Author and Series Editor

Author

Anuradha Sharma is Assistant Professor of Sociology, Jesus and Mary College, University of Delhi. She has taught sociology to undergraduate students for the past 14 years at several colleges in the University of Delhi.

Series Editor

Meenakshi Thapan is Professor of Sociology at the Delhi School of Economics and Co-ordinator of the D.S. Kothari Centre for Science, Ethics and Education at the University of Delhi. She was co-ordinator of the European Study Centre Programme, University of Delhi (January 2010–March 2012) and country partner (India) for the EU FP7 Project on EuroBroadMap. She has also published *Life at School* (1991, 2006), *Living the Body* (SAGE 2009) and edited *Ethnographies of Schooling in Contemporary India* (2014) with SAGE. Her most recent publication is edited *Education and Society: Themes, Perspectives, Practices* (*Oxford in India Readings in Sociology and Social Anthropology*) (2015).